MY YOUTH IN VIENNA

Arthur Schnitzler

MY YOUTH IN VIENNA

ᐤᑲᐤᑲᐤᑲᐤᑲᐤᑲᐤᑲᐤᑲᐤᑲᐤᑲᐤᑲᐤᑲᐤᑲᐤᑲᐤᑲ

Foreword by Frederic Morton

TRANSLATED BY CATHERINE HUTTER

HOLT, RINEHART AND WINSTON, INC.

NEW YORK   CHICAGO   SAN FRANCISCO

English translation copyright © 1970 by Holt, Rinehart and Winston, Inc.
Introduction copyright © 1970 by Frederic Morton
Originally published in German by Verlag Fritz Molden as *Jugend in Wien*
Copyright © 1968 by Verlag Fritz Molden, Vienna-Munich-Zurich
Published simultaneously in Canada
by Holt, Rinehart and Winston of Canada, Limited.
Library of Congress Catalog Card Number: 70–117273
First Edition

Published under the editorial guidance of
Theresa Nickl and Heinrich Schnitzler

Designer: Paula Wiener
SBN: 03–083148–2

PRINTED IN THE UNITED STATES OF AMERICA

Contents

APPENDICES

16 pages of photographs appear following page 146.

Prefatory Note

BY THERESA NICKL AND HEINRICH SCHNITZLER

IN THE comprehensive "Instructions for the Disposal of My Literary Estate," dated August 16, 1918, which forms the greater part of Arthur Schnitzler's last will and testament, he stipulates that his autobiography, "as far as it is completed," should be transcribed as soon as possible after his death. Actually he attended to this transcription while still alive. The resulting copy, which he read through himself, and in which he made various corrections, has formed the basis of this publication. We are therefore dealing here with a text authenticated by the author.

The literary estate includes the handwritten original, as well as a copy of the first transcript with numerous additions and corrections in his own handwriting. On a sheet of paper, also in the literary estate, Arthur Schnitzler wrote down the dates which we find on the first draft and on the transcript. From these we may deduce that the autobiography was begun on May 25, 1915, continued during the following years and brought to a conclusion, for the time being, on August 14, 1918. The transcript was begun on October 30, 1918 and finished on January 28, 1920.

The intention to write an autobiography, however, lies further back, as is indicated in his "Autobiographical Notes." These were found in a folder labeled "Miscellaneous Autobiographical Material." The earliest of these notes were jotted down in the year 1901. Another sheet of paper dated July 25, 1915—two months therefore after the transcript was begun—contained an outline

for an autobiography of seven "books," which was to go beyond
the part completed here, namely to the year 1900. However, apart
from a few notes concerned with later years, no initial efforts or
synopses for a continuation of the material included in this publication were ever found.

The autobiography was to be titled *Life and Reminiscences—
Work and Echo.* The handwritten draft and the transcript both
bear this title. However, since the part in existence takes us
only to the year 1890, ending at a time when Arthur Schnitzler
had barely begun to emerge as a writer, one could scarcely speak
of a body of work, much less its echo. Another title had to be
found. Except for the replacement of the original title with a
new one—*My Youth in Vienna*—nothing in the text has been
changed or omitted. The editors did decide to include the dates
given to the various "books." Wrong spelling of names was corrected; names that were conveyed by initials were given in full
whenever they could be identified with certainty, frequently with
the help of other autobiographical notes made by the author,
especially his diaries.

Excerpts from *My Youth in Vienna* were published in the *Neue
Zürcher Zeitung* supplement, "Literature and Art," January 9,
1966; and in the magazine *Literature and Criticism,* No. 12, March
1967, published by Otto Müller, Salzburg. The "Autobiographical
Notes" appeared first in the *Fischer Almanac 80,* published by
S. Fischer, Frankfurt-am-Main, 1966.

The early works mentioned in the text form a part of the literary estate. The few that were published after Arthur Schnitzler's
death are mentioned in the Brief Biography and Main Works
(pp. 274–282), as being included in the S. Fischer *Prose Works*
(two volumes, 1961), in the *Plays* (two volumes, 1962), and in the
Aphorisms and Reflections (1967). The Notes were kept to a minimum. The illustrative material was taken from Heinrich Schnitzler's collection, except for the photographs of the house in which
Arthur Schnitzler was born and of the Thalhof Hotel, both of which
are the property of the Historical Museum of the City of Vienna.

Acknowledgments for invaluable help and various references
must go to Professor Heinrich Benedikt; Dr. Felix Czeike, archivist; Professor Hanns Jäger-Sunstenau, senior archivist; Dr. Erwin
Schmidt; Dr. Heinz Schöny, museum director; and Dr. Ferdinand
Wernigg, senior librarian.

Foreword

BY FREDERIC MORTON

ARTHUR SCHNITZLER's plays and fiction are the definitive genre pictures of fin-de-siècle Vienna. And since many of the best captions to those pictures were supplied by his contemporary, the aphorist Karl Kraus, it's hard to start talking about one without thinking of the other—of one aphorism in particular. "Vienna," said Karl Kraus, "is the laboratory of the apocalypse."

Such labs tend to have lush furnishings. I know because I spent my Austrian childhood, in the thirties, among the chipped monuments left over from the last experiment, the Hapsburg self-destruction via World War I. I also know because I live in New York where right this moment they're building still more cloud-high things that might become the ultimate props for the ultimate Götterdämmerung. And it comes to me that what we have in this book isn't just autobiography. Schnitzler does more than look back on the years of his youth from the 1860's to the 1880's in Vienna. Yes, he evokes a world long gone, where you could pick up a girl in a horse-tramway. But he also suggests how a world goes—it goes not all that gently, into not such a good night—and therefore he breathes a whiff of today's news. His canvas is gorgeously antique, dimly familiar, and it may be, God help us, faintly clairvoyant.

Schnitzler spent his childhood in a great empire a shade past its halcyon days, which means in the prime years of its myth. The good Emperor Franz Joseph had been mounted on his throne for enough decades to become his own statue, yet he had decades to go before he or the throne grew feeble. The monarchy reached from the Swiss Alps through the German-speaking heartlands to Hungary, Bohemia, southern Poland, down to the minarets of the eastern Balkans. It was a cornucopia of races, tongues, costumes and customs, all lavished around Vienna which during the very period of Schnitzler's youth ripened into the sumptuous *Alt Wien* that still exercises the world's nostalgia today.

When Schnitzler was born in 1862 the medieval walls of the capital were being demolished. Throughout his school and university years and the time he served as an intern and as young army doctor, there rose on the site of those walls—rose like a mirage—the masterpiece of Imperial Vienna. Round the city's ancient core the Ringstrasse rose up in festoons of marble munificence: neo-gothic Votive Cathedral, renaissance university, neo-gothic City Hall, renaissance museums, Grecian-columned Parliament, renaissance Opera, all huge jewels set in flower-studded and tree-shaded promenades. It was (and is) a unique five miles of gracefully orchestrated majesty. And even before the Ring was finished, the city burst across it toward the Vienna Woods, unfolding the wine gardens, the inns, the mixture of royalty and *Gemütlichkeit*, the sense of a courtier people delighting and perfecting their pastoral in the foothills of the Alps. Somehow that aura has not yielded to the gas stations built there since.

In Schnitzler's youth Vienna was the earth emporium of culture, comparable to New York in the century to come. Beethoven's body had lain in state not many blocks from where Schnitzler's father was to set up his clinic. Mozart, of course, had long gone to his pauper's grave, but Brahms, Bruckner, Mahler and Hugo Wolf were alive and fertile. And, starting from Vienna, the waltz conquered the world, as shockingly and thoroughly as generations later rock-and-roll would conquer it, starting from New York.

The waltz, like rock, represented a liberation from the linear—in this case from the minuet; like rock it was accused of being a too bald erotic confrontation; like rock it obliterated tame beginning-middle-end steps and swept into the ecstatic infinity and renewability of sheer rhythm. For these among other reasons the Johann Strausses, father and son, became the first global popmusic stars. Composer-conductor-performers, they wielded charismatic violin bows; they ignited riots as well as raptures. In this sense the Beatles are but latter-day Strausses at best, if you consider that the fame of the two Johanns traveled across continents without benefit of media.

Schnitzler's quasi Bar Mitzvah came close on the heels of the première of *Die Fledermaus* by Strauss junior, the operetta par excellence of all time. And the very lives of the Strausses, father and son, personified Schnitzler's obsession with the intertwisting of canker and rose. Johann Strauss senior, "magician of the lilt," was a pitiful, driven neurotic. It was said of him that "he died like a dog and was buried like a king." Johann Strauss junior, even more renowned, a still more glistening and triumphant sower of joy across the world, suffered even more from depression and nervous exhaustion, from recurrent despair. "His biography," writes a Viennese critic, "is a case history."

The Strauss irony was endemic to the glitter of the Hapsburg lands. It afflicted many of Schnitzler's boulevardier figures. In these recollections it's mixed into every bit of local color. Here is the hidden, yet almost axiomatic, prevalence of syphilis in all layers of society, particularly among the dashing and the fashionable; the anti-Semitism among Vienna's best-educated classes which was part of a general racist exasperation; the etiquette— exquisite far beyond the occidental norm—which was designed not to express but to hide the morals underneath. Characteristic is an episode in which young Arthur and his pal, both hand-kissing cavaliers, escort home the lovely mistress of a Hungarian aristocrat—and then with the girl's full acquiescence cast lots as to which of the two would jump into bed with her.

Here are oblique but graphic glimpses of how an empire began to fester just as its image flowered most gaily. No other city even approached Vienna's contrapuntal loveliness—palatial core balanced against the bucolic idyl of the vines. Yet the nexus between the two consisted of long stretches of new slum. It was the bill the city had to pay for industrialization which in turn paid for the myth's spectacular staging.

Franz Joseph's realm was like a pageant of ambivalences, exemplified by the literal duality of the crown. The Emperor of Austria doubled as King of Hungary. This made Hungary an autonomous domain and was hailed as a model of intra-national accommoda-

tion. In practice, their autonomy let the Hungarian nobles exploit
their peasants; it allowed them to oppress the huge Slav minorities
within their lands and to provide a vicious example for their
counterparts in other ethnic regions. The vitality of the Austro-Hungarian
idea withered even as its splendors and ceremonies flourished. It
was a fairyland with a squalid underbelly and all its roads led—
at least metaphorically—to Mayerling.

In the popular fancy and therefore in the movies, Crown Prince
Rudolph died together with Mary Vetsera for the sake of their
impossible great love. Actually Franz Joseph's son—talented,
drug-ridden, alcoholic, demoralized, a veritable prince of aliena-
tion—asked Vetsera to join him in suicide only after some chorus
girls had turned down the honor. His motive was agony; hers the
ultimate in social climbing. She crashed history as the leading
lady of the Archduke's despair. That macabre tryst took place on
January 30, 1889. A few weeks later there was born, a few express
stops away in Upper Austria, a baby boy named Adolf Hitler.

No, the center wouldn't hold. With surprising speed, radiance
turned to phosphorescence. As usual, the forces of the future attacked just where the present century made its most spectacular
stand. (Again imperial Austria seems to prefigure imperial
America.) Since nothing energizes the arts like change, the Vienna
of young Schnitzler vibrated with esthetic insurgencies. Arnold
Schoenberg and Alban Berg broke the great molds of Beethoven
and Brahms. And as they composed atonal music so Adolf Loos
created a-traditional, anti-ornamental, anti-Ringstrasse architec-
ture. His work, no less than Berg's and Schoenberg's, touched off
demonstrations. In painting, the new Austrian impressionists
ostentatiously marked their mutiny against the academics and the
romantics by terming their movement (and their joint gallery)
"The Secession." But the ultimate subversive intellectual enterprise took place in the study of the man who called Schnitzler
"my *Doppelgänger*—Sigmund Freud.

Of course Freud and Schnitzler were contemporaries, fellow
Jews, fellow students in the same university, fellow physicians,
fellow devotees of hypnotism in their early careers, and fellow

explorers of the erotic in their lifeworks. But their *Doppelgänger-dom* rests most significantly on the fact that both focused on the tension between man's inner motives and the choreography of his adjustments, between the instinctual core and the acquired façade. In 1893 Freud published his first important paper with psycho-analytic implications ("On the Psychical Mechanisms of Hysteri-cal Phenomena"). The same year Schnitzler had his first première, the production of *Farewell Supper* at the Stadttheater in Bad Ischl. And when Freud brought out his *Psychopathology of Everyday Life* in 1904, the book version of Schnitzler's *La Ronde* had just been banned in Germany, almost by way of illustrating Freud's title.

It's obvious from these dates that most of the important Schnitz-ler canon came into being after the 1880's; that is, after this auto-biography ends. Yet the Schnitzlerian leitmotif is foreshadowed here by his fascination with his own love affairs. Already he dis-plays a cool, alert astonishment at his most headlong emotions, the kind of astonishment which is the writer's greatest engine and which later powered Schnitzler's investigations into the drama-turgy of sex, from the blush of infatuation to post-coital politesse.

In the seven one-acters of the Anatol cycle we have seven epi-sodes from a philanderer's life, showing that all his deceptions are matched in smoothness by his self-deceptions. In *La Ronde*, Schnitzler's other cyclical masterpiece (are these structures sar-donic echoes of the Ringstrasse?), ten affairs succeed each other. Their participants, from very different walks of life, keep chang-ing partners until the male of the last scene makes love to the woman of the first. By the time the circle is closed, Schnitzler has paraded past us a whole spectrum of decent lies dressing up sex as if in a fashion show of straitjackets. And strangely, hauntingly, the pose that insists on decorating lust with love accomplishes in the end not decoration but debasement. "Oh, *Alt Wien!*"

Civilization is a lie the brain forces on the flesh: that theme also informs Schnitzler's prose. In *Lieutenant Gustl* a gutsy young officer of the Imperial Army finds himself pressed to the edge of suicide because a common baker has insulted him. In *Fräulein Else* a young girl must expose herself naked to a lecher who other-wise won't save her father from bankruptcy. Both novellas, done in virtuoso stream-of-consciousness style, wring fresh, evergreen anguish out of rotogravure plights. Both Gustl and Else suffer in order not to betray a life style, when in fact the life style is betraying them.

But the most memorable Schnitzler character is *das süsse Mädel*, the Sweet Girl, who in one guise or another appears not only in these reminiscences but in *Anatol*, in *Liebelei*, and other plays frequently revived today. The Sweet Girl's secret lies in her very vulnerability. Because of it she is no sooner bedded than betrayed. But because of it she also fascinates her betrayers—and us. In her willingness to be victimized there is an innocence and an odd strength, a dumb sensuous faith which none of her seducers can tap no matter how furiously they thrust themselves through her. For they, the smoothies, swingers before their time, are really the empties; they have given up on the world, while for the Sweet Girl the world continues sweetly—at least for a while. Such faith scrapes the jadedness off our nerve ends, it even attunes us, perversely, to the possibility of renewal. At his best Schnitzler talked not just about old Vienna but about the aging of any culture; about the late, the very late, the maybe too late hour in search of dawn. Which may be our time of night right now.

NEW YORK CITY   FREDERIC MORTON
APRIL, 1970

Jottings for an Autobiography

IDEA OF WRITING *an autobiography vivid in my mind for first time in 1901, in Vahrn,* during stay there with Olga and Liesl. At the time I was working on* Living Hours.

At eighteen I planned to write a book on natural philosophy when I reached the age of fifty. I soon gave up the idea as all theorizing beyond the aphoristic aspect of things became less and less important to me. I was concerned more with the formulation of things; I always wished I had come closer to this goal than I succeeded in doing.

Not only the wish, but the profound necessity to be truthful in these pages.
Difficulties. Above all, lapses of memory.
The deception of memory.
Stylistic reasons.
Whether a thing happened on the first of March or on the fifteenth of August can be a matter of complete indifference under certain circumstances. Absolute chronological accuracy has to be sacrificed for clarity of presentation.
Truth in the highest sense does not require the reporting of all secondary matter, especially not purely physical information,

---

* For explanation, see Notes beginning on p. 287.

yet there are cases when to conceal it would actually be falsification.

I shall put down some of my friends' experiences, not only when they influenced my development, but also when they serve to characterize those with whom I had more or less friendly intercourse; sometimes also when their stories seem to me to be of interest per se, or interested me at certain periods of my life, which in turn contributes to my own characterization.

It is of course my intention to write my memoirs absolutely truthfully, as far as truthfulness of memory is ours to attain. I don't know if the inclination to be truthful toward myself was a part of me from the beginning. One thing is certain—in the course of years it has increased, in fact today the tendency seems to me to be my liveliest and most steadfast impulse.

Within the confessions one makes amid that which one deems memorable, there are two ways of being honest. One: to express what one has to say precisely and utterly unreservedly; the other: to tell everything one can possibly recall. I doubt if the latter is even possible. Furthermore, is it useful? And finally, isn't such unreserved honesty, in the end, evidence of yet another form of vanity? Certainly it takes no exceptional courage to write down all the ugly emotions or evil deeds one has knowingly committed, if one knows that before the death of the writer no one is going to have access to these records. I also ask myself if the necessity to be truthful does not perhaps arise, in part, from a characteristic that may be rooted in a pathological feeling of compulsion, in the tendency on the surface toward a pedantry which may have developed more and more decisively in the course of the years as a corrective influence over one's inner negligence? In times or hours of my own extreme confusion, I occasionally relieved the tensions within me by jotting down as schematically as possible the actual, or only surmised, reasons for the temper of my soul. In a similar fashion, the ordering of letters, writings, clippings, etc., when I didn't feel in the mood to do anything else, frequently gave me a convenient illusion of action, which, among other things, lacked all aspects of responsibility. When I see that I destroyed certain diaries from my Gymnasium days for no better reason than that the format of the pages didn't happen to fit the size of the paper I chose to use for my notes later at a certain time, I realize that even such apparently harmless activity can develop into a sickness.

And yet, however these memoirs should happen to develop further, whether I choose to report on every infamy of which I can accuse myself or only on those which I can gloss over in one way or another, I do not intend consciously to record anything untrue.

It is difficult to say whether any conscious untruths may be found in my diaries. One thing is fact: up to a certain period in my life I often strove to present myself in a stylized fashion. The circumstance that I spent my childhood and adolescence in an atmosphere that was determined by the so-called liberalism of the 1860's and 1870's, did not leave me unscathed. The basic error of this world viewpoint seems to me to have been the fact that certain idealized values were taken for granted from the start as fixed and incontestable; that a false belief was aroused in young people, who were supposed to strive on a prescribed way toward clearly defined goals, and then forthwith be able to build their house and their world on a stable foundation. In those days we thought we knew what was true, good and beautiful; and all life lay ahead of us in grandiose simplicity. Thus the thought was far from my mind that every one of us was, so to speak, living in a new world at every moment; and that, just as God had made the world, every man had to build his house anew each day.

But what purpose could all individual experience have if everyone were to come to the same conclusion? In no way does experience enrich us by giving us the ability to pronounce an aprioristic verdict. Experience does only one thing for us—it intensifies our judgment for a later day.

1901

*I am aware of the fact that I am not an artist of the highest
caliber. If in spite of this I occasionally elaborate on early, im-
mature works of mine in relatively too much detail, this practice
does not imply a false evaluation of these efforts, nor of my creative ability in general. But my works happen to be the intrinsic
element of my existence; therefore, even if the story relating to
some of them may not belong to literary history, it certainly does
belong in the story of my life, and that is what we are concerned
with here.*

*Friends are only too ready to make the arguments of the enemy
their own.*

*Even if they knew I was right, they seemed to like to withdraw,
or at least leave me in the lurch for a while.*

*The most startling example of such a friend, startling because
he was the cleverest and truest one is this: As I was telling about
my summons to appear before a court of honor in connection with
my novella,* Lieutenant Gustl, *I said that as I had forgotten to
resign my commission, it was evidently my duty to appear. This
friend let out a superior, almost malicious "You see?" as if it were
my fault, as if he had warned me.*

*The upbringing characteristic for a liberal regime: Good will,
a tendency to affectation, sentimentality directed toward oneself,
respect for all superficial values, no actual feeling for the truth,
no actual comprehension of discretion. Mediocre qualities are
described as virtues.*

On Snobbery.

*Right into my university years I adopted a rather nonchalant
manner which was to some extent studied: Rembrandt hat, fluttering cravat, long hair. A slight contempt for everything conventionally termed elegant. This aversion originated in various impressions of my youth (Fräulein Lehmann).*

*A change during my year in the army. The snob in me is aroused
and develops in the most ridiculous fashion. I find it pleasant to*

drive in a fiacre *and be seen in one. Friendship with Richard Tausenau and other influential people. I change my tailor, no longer wear floppy hats. Change over to stand-up collars. Suddenly I can't fathom how anyone could want to drive in a one-horse carriage; am astonished one day to see Dr. Schiff driving by in one. My ambition: to become truly elegant, but am in general satisfied to be indolently elegant.*

Until Derby Day I wore a top hat. The race track plays an important role in my life. Strangely, just during this period, and because of our mutual interest in the races, on more intimate terms with my brother.

Started off in the "gulden" seats, then in the paddock. Gambled. Lost.

For a while was lucky in guessing hurdle and steeplechase winners.

Sociability. A gunner from the artillery, a fat Jew called Eissler, was often with us. Louis Mandl, Petschek, and in the lead role— Tausenau, who with his adventurous and gambling nature felt most at home in this setting. Always elegant, and with an absolute minimum of expense, always well dressed. His luck with women.

The unattainable ideal image: Henry Baltazzy, whom I met later at B.'s, and who became the prototype of the count in Reigen. *In the Prater, Henry Baltazzy, with a few friends at a nearby table, looking summery in a gray hat.*

Not impossible that my artistic ambitions had to take a back seat in the face of all this modishness, until my common sense and powers of self-recognition showed me the right way.

Actually the duke in Beatrice *is a powerful expression of snobbery, in this case with overtones of grandeur; and in discontented Filippo's yearning to be a man like Bentivoglio there surely glows a little of my childlike, envious admiration of the Henry Baltazzys of this world.*

My snobbery was completely cured by the snobs with whom I came in contact in the course of time.

If one may call snobbery, in general, the longing to be counted as one of a species of humans who possess some attribute or other in a more highly developed capacity than we, and who therefore cannot look upon us as equals, then I had occasion to recognize this emotion in myself in another circumstance, namely at the wedding of one of my cousins to a certain Herr K., a totally inferior individual. I functioned as witness at the Votivkirche. In spite of the fact that I had to shudder over my own stupidity, I was not able to suppress completely a feeling of satisfaction as I signed the document in the heavily incensed sacristy.

Human beings, especially women, sometimes remain frozen in one's memory in certain attitudes which they adopted under strange, specific circumstances; or in a pose which is somehow the arithmetic mean between all actual or even possible poses in which they have been or might have been observed.

Thus I can see M. G. suddenly letting her umbrella fall, standing there with her mouth half open, as she did in the porte-cochère *when I spoke about D.*

Sometimes, too, like a marionette on loose wires.

M. R., with the script of Reigen *on her lap, her pencil touching her lips, mildly critical, in our little room on the Rue Maubeuge.*

M. E., hungrily eating her supper one summer evening in a garden restaurant, in spite of the fact that there was a possibility that I might have been murdered a half-hour before.

1912 (?)

In these pages a lot will be said about Judaism and anti-Semitism, more than may at times seem in good taste, or necessary, or just. But when these pages may be read, it will perhaps no longer be possible to gain a correct impression (at least I hope so), of the importance, spiritually almost more than politically and socially, that was assigned to the so-called Jewish question when these lines were written. It was not possible, especially not for a Jew in public life, to ignore the fact that he was a Jew; nobody else was doing so, not the Gentiles and even less the Jews. You had the choice of being counted as insensitive, obtrusive and fresh; or of being oversensitive, shy and suffering from feelings of persecution. And even if you managed somehow to conduct yourself so that nothing showed, it was impossible to remain completely untouched; as for instance a person may not remain unconcerned whose skin has been anesthetized but who has to watch, with his eyes open, how it is scratched by an unclean knife, even cut into until the blood flows.

On Anti-Semitism.

During my Gymnasium years, scarcely felt. The first who was considered an anti-Semite, or, since the word didn't exist in those days, a Judenfresser (Jew devourer), was a certain Deperis, who wouldn't speak to a Jew, but was also considered ridiculous by his Gentile colleagues. He was very elegant, didn't have to pay for his tuition, was stupid and today enjoys the title of Privy Councillor. Among the professors—Professor Blume, still relatively harmless. A moderately gifted man, Wagnerian, very German-national, pronounces all Jewish names with derision but is not unfair in his behavior toward his Jewish pupils. Marries a Jewess.

At the university—the beginning. In the committee of the Subsidies for Medical Students Association. Agitation against the Hungarian Jews. One of the chief instigators: young Bamberger, later killed in an accident. Spokesman for the anti-Semitic group: Karl August Herzfeld, who at the time hadn't even been baptized yet. Later dissolution of the association.

The German-national dueling corps expel all Jews (Herzl).

War flashes.

England's declaration of war posted at the hotel in Celerina.

The closed bank in Pontresina.

The cadet in Hellbrunn with his family, having his picture taken.

The house on the Solenweg. The lonely peasant woman with her child, that had never seen its father.

The station in Innsbruck.

Book One

✧✦✧✦✧✦✧✦✧✦✧

May 1862 to May 1875

I WAS BORN on the fifteenth of May 1862, in Vienna, on the Prater-strasse—in those days it was called the Jägerzeile—on the third floor of a house adjacent to the Hotel de l'Europe. A few hours later, as my father liked to tell so often, I lay for a while on his writing desk. I don't know whether this rather unusual spot to deposit an infant was the midwife's idea or my father's, but the incident gave rise to many a facetious prophecy concerning my career as a writer, a prediction my father was to see fulfilled only in its modest beginnings and not with undivided joy.

My father's family came from Gross-Kanizsa, a medium-sized Hungarian town. Originally the family name was Zimmermann; it was my grandfather who changed it to Schnitzler, or was given that name by the local authorities. My grandmother, Rosalie, was the daughter of a certain David Klein from Puszta Kovacsi in the Lake Balaton district, and his wife Marie, *née* Rechnitz; and that is as much as I know of my father's side of the family.

My grandfather, a carpenter like his forefathers, spent his entire life in poor, one might almost say needy, circumstances. At the end of a letter, which my father wrote to him a few days after my birth, he expressed the hope that "this grandson may bring the good fortune which has always so mercilessly turned its back on you."

My grandfather could neither read nor write but was considered a master in his craft. I don't remember whether it was he or my father who, while still a boy, went from house to house distributing leaflets for itinerant troupes of actors, but something that my father, in childlike respect, kept from me, was the fact that my grandfather was a periodic drinker, which happens rarely in Jewish families and may well be traced back to the chronically ruined state of his finances. I found this out only long after his death. He died in 1864 of pneumonia, still in the prime of life and a few hours after lamenting, "Am I really to die without ever having seen my grandson?"

After his death my bereaved grandmother would visit us occasionally and stay a few days or weeks—a gaunt, ugly woman, dressed in glossy sateen. Her pathological miserliness led to quite a few disrespectful remarks after her departure. Once she presented me with a silver watch, paid for of course by my father. On the morning, a few years after the death of her husband, when the news arrived that she too had departed this life, I saw my father, sitting at his desk, his head in his hands, weeping, which impressed me as strange because I had never seen him cry before, but failed actually to touch me.

Of my father's two sisters, the oldest, Charlotte, died young, like her husband, of a lung ailment. Her four daughters, all married but not impartially favored by providence, live in Budapest, as does my father's younger sister, Johanna, the widow of an unfortunate merchant whom it was possible to save several times from the courts but not, in the end, from bankruptcy. If today she is able to enjoy a comfortable old age it is due in some measure to her blithe egoism, but mainly because of her efficient and practical son's devotion.

I visited my father's home town just once—I was five or six at the time—and spent a few days there. A farmyard, a few hens, a wooden fence, the railroad nearby, trains passing, the whistle of a locomotive fading into the distance are all that remain with me of that experience. I don't know when my ancestors settled in Gross-Kanizsa, or for that matter in Hungary, where they may have wandered before that or settled down after having left their original home in Palestine two thousand years before. The only thing I am sure of is that neither longing nor homesickness ever tempted me to return to Gross-Kanizsa; and if fate had chosen to direct me to this town in which my grandparents once lived and my father was born, I would have felt like a stranger, perhaps even an exile. Thus I am tempted to come to grips at this point with the curious view that a person, born in a certain country, raised and active there, is supposed to recognize as his homeland another country, not the one in which his parents and grandparents lived decades ago but the one his ancestors called their native land thousands of years before, and this not solely for political, sociological or economic reasons—which would bear discussion—but also *emotionally*. However, it seems premature to pause here and deal with a problem which may have occupied the minds of quite a few people in that liberal or liberalizing era, yet has failed until now to have much practical meaning.

A more rewarding and lively relationship developed quite naturally with my mother's relatives who lived in Vienna. Her father, Philip Markbreiter, son or grandson of a Viennese court jeweler, doctor of medicine and philosophy, had been a popular physician in his day and in his leisure hours an excellent pianist. With his education and talents he could certainly have gone further in every respect, or at least have achieved a *niveau* worthy of him, if he hadn't fallen victim, incurably as the years went by, to the vice of gambling. Already early in life he began to squander everything he owned or earned in lotteries and stock speculations. He was always in financial straits or on the lookout for new ways to invest the little money he had and did not hesitate to get whatever sums he needed through less than the customary channels. For instance, with the wedding scarcely over, he borrowed his oldest daughter's dowry (which he had just presented to her husband), to settle a pressing debt and was never able to repay this relatively small sum of six thousand gulden. Well into his seventies, and in a state of health that fluctuated constantly, he liked to visit Monte Carlo in the winter; and just as regularly it became necessary to send him money for the return journey, often more than once, since he invariably lost everything he had at the roulette table. At home he liked to play games of chance with his wife and daughters and other relatives for small stakes. Twenty-one was his favorite game, later also poker. Childishly he would try to better his luck by hiding cards under the table, on his knees or up his sleeve. In this respect he was treated with indulgence, especially when a disease that affected his wrists prevented him from practicing such clandestine maneuvers skillfully. He would get up, furious, when his ridiculous little deception had failed, only to sit down again a few minutes later as if nothing had happened. All in all I remember him as a restless, peevish, but not insignificant or undignified old man. On his good days he would display a certain man-of-the-world charm and a surprisingly keen and facile mind. In his old age, for instance, he could still recite from the Greek and Roman classics.

One thing I didn't like about him was the surly way he treated his only living sister in a manner that was incomprehensible to me. She was without means, hard of hearing and almost blind; and with his foul moods he seemed to be punishing the wretched woman for her undeserved infirmities and spinsterhood, which she bore with dignity and patience, as if they had been wrongs done him. But her nieces and nephews, to whom she gave piano lessons and taught foreign languages, adored "Aunt Marie," and their gratitude toward her was heartfelt. The next generation also developed an affection for the kind, serene creature. As children we frequently visited her in the summer, with our mother, more often than not in Mödling. She finally retired to that little town, and we could be sure of finding her in her modest but well cared for home, with her canary, sitting by the window, bent over a book from the library, her cataract spectacles on her nose. It was in her house that we sometimes met two other old maids, also members of the family. One was long and lean, the other short and deformed. We dubbed them "the cousins," and since one never appeared without the other, I didn't even try to imagine them as separate entities.

My grandmother, born not far from the Lower-Austrian border, in the German-Hungarian town of Güns, was a member of the eminent Schey family whose ancestry can be traced back to a descendant called Israel, whose son Lipmann died in 1776. Lipmann's great-grandson Markus, married to Sossel Strauss, was my great-grandfather, and I can recall him clearly—a hoary old man, crippled, in a wheel chair and no longer able to talk. He died in 1869. His brother, Joseph, predeceased him in 1849; the youngest, Philip, the first Schey to become a baronet, lived until 1880. I can see him too—a tall, upright, corpulent man with a mocking smile, smooth-shaven and dressed with old-world refinement, standing in the spacious, almost sumptuous drawing room of his Praterstrasse apartment, the windows of which came down to the ground and were protected by gilded railings from the balcony type projections outside. I still find it difficult to keep his imposing and rather intimidating appearance separate in my mind from that of the elderly privy councillor, Goethe.

The prosperity of the Schey family may be traced far back. At the beginning of the nineteenth century it developed into actual wealth, thanks to highly astute financial transactions with debt-ridden Hungarian aristocrats. Some members moved to the big cities; the family branched out and intermarried, often advantageously. Bankers, officers, scholars and farmers may be counted among them; and the family tree shows no lack of eccentrics in whom the Jewish patriarch and the aristocrat, the entrepreneur and the cavalier are curiously intermingled. Some of the youngest members differ from the older aristocracy only by a little more wit and the racial idiosyncrasy of an irony directed against oneself. Among the women and girls, beside those who because of their appearance and mannerisms can't deny their origin or don't want to, we find some who indulge in sport and fashion, and it is self-explanatory that snobbery—the world ailment of our times—found exceptionally favorable conditions for development during the epoch I touch upon fleetingly here.

My grandmother, Amalia Markbreiter, came from a more serene and less problematic era. Raised in a bourgeois milieu and blessed with a simple wisdom, she was a capable housekeeper, a devoted and long-suffering wife to her difficult husband and a loving and beloved mother to her numerous children. I can scarcely recall an evening of my childhood when my mother, and her sisters who married later, also frequently sons, sons- and daughters-in-law, did not pay her a short or lengthy visit. While the grown-ups came and went, chatted and played harmless games of chance, we children amused ourselves by reading and playing games. These evenings in my grandmother's house flow together in my mind, but a few occasions stand out more clearly and festively, as for instance once every year when the Day of Atonement was coming to an end and we could look longingly for the glitter of the evening star on the horizon which would herald the end of fasting. In the center of the room the table was set with delicious pastries, all prepared according to ritual—sweet buns and spiced pretzels, poppy-seed and nut cakes, which could be enjoyed also by those who hadn't fasted for twenty-four hours, that is to say by the children and free-thinking male members of the family. It was an occasion on which one could really begin to have one's doubts about divine justice, for just those members could feast to their hearts' content without the discretion recommended to those who had fasted religiously. I believe though that the most devout member of our family, perhaps the only truly pious one, was our good grandmother who had probably spent most of the day in temple, praying. Her children and grandchildren, as long as they continued to celebrate the Day of Atonement, did so mainly for her sake, and after her death solely out of a feeling of reverence for her. Yet even for my grandmother this fasting on the Day of Atonement, as well as the eating of unleavened bread on Passover (which incidentally is delicious when crumbled in coffee), was the only tradition to which she adhered strictly, strictly, however, only in so far as she was concerned. The Feast of Tabernacles, even the Sabbath, were not celebrated in my grandparents's house; and the generation which followed, in spite of all stubborn emphasis on racial solidarity, tended to display indifference to the spirit of Jewish religion, and opposition, sometimes even a sarcastic attitude, to its formalities.

In the 1860's my grandparents were living in the Carltheater building; if only for this reason my first contact with the theater can be dated back to an exceptionally early age. However, the first event I have to relate may be called a theatrical experience only conditionally—it consists of the simple fact that at the age of two or three I threw an opera glass out of the window of my grandparents' apartment; yet this incident was interpreted so often as being symbolic, or at least prophetic, that I was soon quite illogically close to considering it so myself.

My first personal recollection of the theater is of an actor in an old-Vienna costume, whom I could see as I looked out of the courtyard window of my grandparents' apartment onto the glass roof below, coming from the dressing rooms, a basket on his back, on his way to the stage. The sight of him merges in my mind with that of another figure, similarly dressed, which is painted on the curtain of the Theater an der Wien. It is supposed

to represent the famous comedian Scholz, whose prototype may
have crossed spectrally past my childish eyes, walking along this
passageway from dressing room to stage. It was probably also
in the Carltheater that I saw my first stage performance, and one
of the first, if not *the* first, was the Offenbach operetta, *Orpheus
in the Underworld*. This happy yet almost extinguished memory
is connected closely with another, rather embarrassing one which
is therefore perhaps all the more clear—the memory of my first
definite failure. The famous comedian Knaack had played Styx
in the Offenbach performance, and among early signs of an affinity for the stage I was in the habit of imitating his voice and
gestures and was usually highly successful when performing for
my family or friends. Thus encouraged, I decided one day, with
the undisciplined fervor of my sixth or seventh year, to render
the song, "When I was still Prince of Arcady," in the Knaack manner and manipulating a broom, for a lady, a total stranger to me,
who was visiting my mother. To this day I can remember the look
with which she mustered me from top to toe when my little act
was over—unmoved, cold, annihilating. Of all merited and unmerited failures experienced since then, this first rebuff made the
strongest impression on me.

In those days the Leopoldstadt was still a fashionable and distinguished district, and the main thoroughfare, on which the Carltheater stood, managed to preserve some of its festiveness even
during the quieter hours when an elegant and carefree world
came tearing back from the races or flower shows in their equipages and *fiacres*. During my childhood I often enjoyed this exciting sight from the windows of my grandparents' apartment; later,
too, after they had moved from the Carltheater building to a
house on the Circusgasse, the windows of which also looked down
on the Praterstrasse. Most of my relatives lived nearby; in the
same district; only my parents soon left their apartment on the
Praterstrasse and moved into one on the Schottenbastei, which
wasn't "a bastion" even in those days, but a simple street like any
other.

From this time, my fourth or fifth year, I can recall my first
playmate, little Count Kalman, whose father was one of my
father's patients. I certainly would have forgotten the games we
played if I did not remember, probably because of its absurd-

ity, a rather quaint question which I asked my governess. We had placed our wooden soldiers in battle array on our little white table when it suddenly occurred to me to ask her who was the enemy—those with the green revers or those with the red? My governess passed on the question with the same seriousness to the Kalman *bonne*, who categorically declared the reds to be the enemy, whereupon, mollified, I decided to go into battle, I can't remember if as friend or foe.

The park nearest the Schottenbastei was the so-called Paradeisgartel which in my memory appears less as a real garden than as a faded *aquarelle*. I can see a green lawn, flower beds, fragile tables and chairs in front of a low white building with long windows. At the feet of a female figure sitting on the right side of a bench, a child in a light dress is playing, and somewhere a red parasol provides a highlight of color. Am I the child? Is the female my *bonne*? Or my mother? Do memories of things experienced or of things told us or of a painting seen at some time or other flow together, as happens so often, to form one picture? I don't know. Actually the Paradeisgartel disappeared from the face of the earth toward the end of the 1860's, as did the Löwenbastei on which it had flowered for many a year. On practically the same spot stands today's Burgtheater.

About 1868 we moved to No. 11 Giselastrasse, into the same house, and if I am not mistaken, into the very rooms a few of which I was to occupy as a young doctor at the beginning of the 1890's. This was the apartment in which, every morning, I would pull out two footstools for me and my brother to slide on and race each other; the apartment from which I saw flames bursting out of the nearby Musikvereinsgebäude; where, neatly combed and properly dressed, I was allowed sometimes to converse with my father's patients in the waiting room. Of my playmates during this time I recall the two sons of the exiled Rumanian Prince Couza, who was my father's patient; and it seems to me that this was also when I met Milan Obrenovic, who was later to become King of Serbia. At the time he was living with his mother on the Döblinger Hauptstrasse, in a villa opposite Prince Couza. Once, in the afternoon, as I sat reading—something I liked to do until late in the evening, to the displeasure and pride of my parents—a carriage drove up to our house filled with the most magnificent toys for me and my younger brother, a princely Couza present, to be greeted in just as princely a fashion, since it wasn't Christmas or Easter or anybody's birthday. The prettiest thing was a Lilliputian garden with brown tree trunks, green paper leaves, colorful flower beds and grass; yet once my curiosity was appeased, I didn't play with it, nor with the contents of any of the other boxes. I couldn't muster any great interest in toys, not even in those early years. Of course there was a puppet theater in our nursery, yet in spite of occasional efforts I don't believe I distinguished myself as poet, actor, or puppet manipulator, or through any specific puppet-show inventiveness. I was much more fascinated by the acting itself, which we indulged in enthusiastically and always *ex tempore*, sometimes with members of the family; or outside the family circle with friends my own age, above all with the children of the famous actor, Sonnenthal, and those of a dealer in fancy goods, Von Rosenberg. It was usually I who provided the plot from which the dialogue flowed in whichever direction the spirit of the moment happened to inspire the actors. We rarely found a serious or enduring audience; the joy of playing and our mutual approbation sufficed. We weren't old enough yet for the flirtations and jealousies that tend to thrive in such an atmosphere, but I do recall one evening on which, after saying goodbye to my male actor colleagues with childishly friendly embraces, a little girl rushed to the door of the apartment after me and spoke the hesitant words, "Please give me a kiss too," a request with which I complied, not without gratification, my cheeks still red from the excitement of the performance. We preferred to act out stories of a magical fairy tale or adventurously Red Indian nature rather than those with classical or romantic themes, in spite of the fact that just in those days not only my literary efforts but also a more general trend toward a loftier literary culture were quite clearly emerging.

About this time I have a new governess to thank for more decisive inspiration. She came to us around 1870. Now there were three of us to look after—I, my brother Julius, born in 1865, and my sister Gisela, born in 1867. A boy, Emil, born a year after me, died a few months later. This young governess from North Germany, Bertha Lehmann, pale, slender, fair-haired, good-natured but without any specific charm, was the one who persuaded me to spend most of my pocket money on the little buff-colored books of the Reclam Library, a publishing house founded recently. My father wasn't too pleased to discover his nine-year-old son reading *The Robbers* and *Fiesko*, but his disapproval was mitigated by a pride he could scarcely conceal. I must confess that I don't know whether these classical masterpieces, soon augmented by *The Maid of Orleans, The Bride of Messina, Emilia Galotti*, and many others, also Shakespeare's plays, made the deep impression on me which I imagine having experienced at the time, or whether my childish delight wasn't kindled far more by my governess's enthusiasm. Even if the latter was not entirely spontaneous, it is fact that my participation in literature and the theater benefited not only from the personal influence of Fräulein Bertha Lehmann but also by my introduction to her family, where for the first time I saw an interest in the arts and artistic endeavor being actually practiced. Fräulein Lehmann's parents, who had moved to Vienna from Berlin years before, were simple people—I don't know what her father's profession was—and they lived with their three grown children in fairly poor circumstances in the Freihaus in the Wieden district. I remember most vividly old Lehmann's North German accent, his resemblance to Heinrich Laube, and the ironic smile that played about his mouth when I replied to his asking me who was the greatest doctor next to Oppolzer, with the answer I had been taught jokingly at home—my father. His youngest daughter played ingenue parts at the Burgtheater; the oldest brother was employed there also, as an extra.

The strangest member of the family though was the youngest son. Here I not only made the acquaintance of an actual poet but also had an opportunity to see him at work when he settled down in the kitchen to write a play on a sheet of ledger paper resting on a noodle board. He wrote the most delicate script and started off by listing the cast, among whom there was a Countess whose name he underlined meticulously with a ruler. I don't know whether I was still in need of such inspiration or if I hadn't embarked on my first playwriting efforts before this; all I do know is that although five acts and a prologue were planned, he never got beyond the latter and the cast of characters. My play was to have the title *Aristocrat and Democrat*, and the cast consisted of "The Prince," "The Princess," "The Count," "The Countess," "The Baron," "The

Baroness," as well as a plain "Youth," called simply, Robert. It was his duty to bring the prologue to an effective conclusion with a fulminating revolutionary speech, whereas all the aristocrats were given very shabby roles, in the spirit of the Lehmann family, whose views influenced me for a long time. I had written my prologue in a small, red leather notebook, not that the color had anything to do with its tendencies, but I liked to buy myself little notebooks like this in various colors. I always walked into the stationery store with a terse preamble concerning my financial status, such as, "I have twenty kreuzer on me," and it never occurred to me that one could possibly leave the shop with a penny left over. The completion of my first play may well have been delayed by the limitation of my means, because only much later did it occur to me to buy cheaper paper rather than these expensive notebooks.

Not only was my interest in classical literature and social problems stimulated and developed by Fräulein Bertha Lehmann, but she also introduced me, quite by chance, to the much more mysterious regions of affairs of the human heart. I am thinking specifically of a blond young man who lived or worked in our house with whom I had some brief and lengthy conversations when we happened to meet on the staircase, what the Viennese call *Standerln*, or "little standing talks," and of a letter from this gentleman which Fräulein Lehmann, when she thought we were asleep, read aloud, deeply moved and proudly, to our seamstress. The well-chosen words, "Please do not take my words too literally," did did not fail to make an impression on my burgeoning feeling for style; it didn't however prevent me from embarrassing my governess on the following morning by mischievously quoting them.

A more serious and momentous relationship developed between Fräulein Lehmann and a lieutenant in the infantry. I can see him now, slender and young, his shirt half open, no tie, receiving us at the door of his apartment; behind him, in a room darkened by the curtains that were drawn in the summer, his mother, leaning against a chest of drawers, greeting her son's sweetheart and her little pupil with a friendly smile. In this modest apartment house on the main street of Hernals, the aura of Vienna's suburbs, one might say, the ambiance of Viennese folk drama, touched me for the first time, and, without my being aware of it, captured me. Unfortunately the tender love story, of which my boyish vision had

caught the opening lines, was to run its course in a very unpoetical
bourgeois fashion and end most realistically and deplorably. Fräulein Bertha married the lieutenant who soon gave up his army
career but was unable to prosper in civilian life. Poverty, quarrels,
drink, misery and early widowhood, and again—misery, alcohol
and toil, these were the trivial content of the remaining chapters
which came to my knowledge only much later. For many years I
lost sight of the unfortunate woman who, in spite of all misery,
was able to maintain an indestructible optimism, but then she began to turn up, sadly reduced in circumstances and smelling a
little of wine, as needlewoman, or begging modestly for alms.
Later she found support in the home of a nephew, an actor who
played bit parts at the Burgtheater, the son of a sister who had
died young. Today (1916) an old woman, she keeps up the connection with me, probably also with others who have survived
those better days, by occasional visits or the present of some needlework she has made, or by letters, the cultured and at times exaggerated style of which bear testimony to the influence of
classicism in her past and to her astonishingly grateful heart.

Similarly the more childish than childlike conversation which
took place on a beautiful summer's day at the Thalhof Hotel near
Reichenau, between me and Felix Sonnenthal, oldest son of the
famous actor who was friend and patient of my father, may be
termed an impromptu comedy, like the play-acting already mentioned. While the grown-ups were imbibing black coffee in the
dining room, we two boys—seven or eight years old at the time
—were seated in the garden letting the beauty of the landscape
affect us. Gradually we worked ourselves up into such a state of
delight that we decided, in unison, to conquer the world, the whole
big beautiful world, literally, and to begin with Reichenau—undoubtedly the most magnificent spot on earth. It was my brilliant
idea that to carry out this rather far-fetched scheme, devil masks
should suffice. When the two of us would appear so gruesomely
costumed, then, I declared categorically, "the old superstitions of
man would be awakened" and the victory would be ours. I didn't
bother my head over any further aspects of the enterprise, nor
about what we would do with the world, once conquered, because I was fully aware as I spoke these grandiose words, of their
bombast, and of the absurdity of our plan for world conquest. But

it was here, in Reichenau, at the foot of the Schneeberg and Rax Mountains, that a loftier mountain panorama than I was accustomed to seeing in the distance from the environs of Vienna manifested itself to me for the first time, and the mystery of great heights and distances overwhelmed me; all of which probably sufficed to bring on a mild euphoria. I don't really think it is necesssary to burden this episode with the prevision that decades later the Thalhof and its surroundings were to mean so much to me, a grown young man, as a magical framework for an adored beloved.

My predilection, consciously or subconsciously, for acting, any kind of acting, was encouraged most of all by going to the theater often, and this was made possible by my father's many professional and friendly connections with the theater. One of my first, strange and most enduring impressions is connected with a performance of Gounod's *Marguerite*, in the old Kärntnerthortheater, in which Gustave Walter played Faust and Dr. Schmid sang Mephistopheles. How could I help but be surprised when in the garden scene, after Faust and Mephistopheles had withdrawn behind some bushes during a pause in the singing, they waved and bowed up to the box in which we were sitting, after which they re-entered the scene to sing and act with Marguerite and Martha? Yet in spite of my astonishment, I did not have the feeling of being torn painfully out of an illusory world; in fact I don't doubt that even then, although probably not as consciously as today, the world of the theater did not mean to me one of deception, in which any unexpected intrusion of reality had to have the effect of an affront or leave me startled out of a lovely dream; it was more as if a stimulating world, a world transformed, a world of merry and sad entertainment had been revealed to me, in short—a world of play, and anyone with any common sense couldn't be deceived for a moment by its unreality, even when faced with the most artistic performance and however deeply moved. In fact, this trivial incident may have played a part in developing within me that basic motif of life as a constant intermingling of seriousness and play, of reality and farce, of truth and mendacity, which has absorbed me always beyond the stage and play-acting, yes, even beyond all the arts.

A few years later a similar event took place in the Wiedner

Theater when the tenor, Szika, came to see us in our box during the intermission of a Strauss operetta, dressed in the magnificent uniform of his part. He too could recall this meeting a quarter of a century later when we met on the stage of the Frankfurt theater where he was playing the part of the musician Weiring in my play *Liebelei*, the first actor to play the part outside Vienna.

That my father's patients consisted for the most part of theater people was due to the branch of medicine in which he specialized —laryngology. He had begun his secondary school education in his home town and completed it in Budapest, where he also subsequently completed his first year at the university. The impetus for leaving Budapest before completing his medical studies was provided not only by the desire to go to a more prestigious school of higher learning and one where German was spoken, but was influenced also by an affair of the heart. He was tutor at the time in the home of a well-known book dealer who, beside the sons my father taught, had two beautiful but rather frivolous daughters. My father fell in love with the younger one and she did not object to the adoration of an impecunious student without, however, taking him seriously. He wooed her with due formality but she kept him dangling without ever completely discouraging him. Then, at one of the dances which she attended, sometimes clandestinely, she met a lieutenant and soon became his mistress. The affair could not be kept from her father, who did not turn her out of the house as had been his first intention, but from then on refused to speak to her. My father, once he began to see clearly what was going on, never visited them again, but the city had lost its charm for him and in a four days' journey on a rack-wagon—as he often told me later, but without giving me the reason for his departure—he traveled to Vienna. His faithless beloved was soon abandoned by her lieutenant and found solace with other men. After a rather unstable youth she married a clockmaker, in her opinion beneath her, at any rate below the standards she had hopefully set for herself. Their honeymoon took the couple to Vienna. During a walk through the city streets, the young wife had to retire to the entryway of a house to retie a shoelace. As she raised her head she caught sight of a sign which read: DR. JOHANN SCHNITZLER. DISEASES OF THE NOSE AND LARYNX. OFFICE HOURS FROM 2 TO 4.

That the story might have had a sequel if the clockmaker husband had not been walking up and down in front of the house is unlikely, since my father was already happily married at the time, more happily probably than the clockmaker. My father never mentioned this shattered dream and error of his youth to me; he consistently chose to remain silent about the human, all too human, episodes of his life. I was told the story many years after his death, during a walk in Dornbacher Park, by a friend whose mother had known the book dealer's family. She had occasionally spent the night in their home, in the daughters' room, and could recall how, when everyone else in the house was asleep, they had put on their ball gowns and stolen away only to return when the day was dawning.

So my father completed his studies in Vienna. He earned the money necessary for this and for his living and the support of his dependents, as he had done in Gross-Kanizsa and Budapest, by tutoring in well-to-do houses. Soon after getting his degree he was made assistant in Professor Oppolzer's clinic and in a few years had a quite sizable practice of his own, in the course of which his natural amiability and worldliness, beside his considerable practical knowledge, stood him in good stead. The only thing he lacked was a deeper understanding of human nature. He devoted himself with special fervor to laryngology, which in those days was a fairly new field, and was soon considered, beside Leopold Schrötter and Karl Stoerck, one of Ludwig von Turck's most outstanding pupils.

During his *Gymnasium* years he had written a few plays, in German and Hungarian, and one of his teachers in Gross-Kanizsa —so he liked to tell—had prophesied that "the little Jew boy" would one day be Hungary's Shakespeare. I once held one of his manuscripts in my hands and, I believe with his permission, was allowed to keep it for a while. It was the first act of a drama entitled *Bar Kochba*, was written in German and later lost. However, after reading Hyrtl's *Anatomy*, which he was inspired to do during his vacation between *Gymnasium* and university, he gave up any plans for a literary future and decided enthusiastically to make a career of medicine. To the end of his days though, he used to declare with conviction, not only to me, that as far as his talents were concerned he could have harbored the same literary aspirations as I did. It is of course impossible to ascertain today how right he was in this belief in a poetic vocation, but his gift for writing and journalism remains undisputed. Before long he was given the opportunity to prove it in medical and sociological fields.

As a student he had worked in the editorial offices of the journal *Medizinal-Halle*, later called *Medizinische Presse*, which had been founded by my grandfather. Shortly after his marriage, my father was made editor-in-chief; twenty years later, when he was eased out by the professional jealousy of others, he decided to found a new publication, which he edited until his death. Since he was constantly in the thick of medical politics, he needed a publication in which to air his views. This was especially important and advantageous to him and his colleagues during the struggle between the professors of the College of Medicine and the general practitioners over the Polyclinic my father and several other young doctors had founded.

The writing of articles, the proofreading and the time spent in editorial offices and printing plants fulfilled a need in him which was just as strong as the need to lecture for medical societies, at naturalists' meetings and medical conventions and to have lively intercourse with colleagues and friends. The artistic element in his nature found expression in his interest in people related to the arts, especially the stage; in his somewhat naive sympathy for their apparently gayer and brighter way of life; in his admiration of famous people and celebrities—which here was not limited to the stage—more therefore in a tendency toward show and superficiality than in a deeper relationship to the intrinsic aspects of art as represented by work, dedication and destiny. On the other hand he did not lack judgment or taste, but he was easily influenced by personal sympathies and antipathies, and by outside opinion. As a physician appointed to the Concordia, he could naturally count among his patients numerous members of this writers' and journalists' professional organization. Of the poets of that day, I can recall having seen only Mosenthal at our house; he was a stout, red-bearded, friendly gentleman whom I have to thank for the first autographed book in my library, his play *Deborah*, in a pretty gray binding. His revolutionary drama *Lambertine*, gilt-

edged and bound in red, lay on a table in our drawing room for
everyone to see, in spite of the fact that nobody thought very
much of it.

With all his far-flung activities, my father found little time for
reading *belles-lettres,* and his views conformed on the whole with
those of a compact majority who in those days were represented
by the *Neue Freie Presse,* and who were not always wrong. He
went often to the theater, if for no other reason than to please his
patients, whom he liked to visit in their dressing rooms and treat,
if they needed it. He did not go to many concerts, although he
loved music, without however being musically educated or taking
a very lively interest in it. Here too it was more the social aspects
which he enjoyed. True musicality, a deeper appreciation of the
art and something which might be called a gift for it, came to our
family from my mother's side. But my father, and with him therefore, for a long time, our entire household, had no understanding
whatsoever for the fine arts. He liked to scoff at those travelers
who rush through galleries in the cities they visit, religiously con-
sulting their Baedekers, a scoffing in which we joined, as if they
were really ridiculous creatures doing something because it was
the thing to do, not—which after all must occasionally have been
the case—out of a true feeling for the arts and a serious cultural
incentive. Since I and my brother and sister lacked any talent at
all in this respect, my father's rejection sufficed for a long time to
prevent any idea from forming in our minds that here a vast realm
of cultural delight lay in store for us. Not until I was a young man
did some interest, and later I suppose also a measure of understanding, develop in me; at first for the plastic arts and after that
for the graphic arts and painting, an appreciation which grew
steadily until—above all when faced with Rembrandt—at last I
was able to enjoy the reverence I had felt for Goethe and Beethoven at a much earlier date. I firmly believe that where there is
an innate relationship to any science, art or other sphere of life,
the influences of upbringing and environment play a secondary
role; in fact, a definite talent usually likes to triumph over discouraging influences; but receptivity and pleasure in those things
which lie outside one's specific talents and interests are influenced
strongly by the impressions of childhood. On the other hand, it
may frequently be observed that an innate talent, which at home

has been tactlessly furthered or subjected to undesirable pressures, may be destroyed, sometimes even transformed into rejection, or at best be doomed to languish until the young creature has matured to a state of self-recognition and independence.

This is what happened to me, to a certain extent, in my relationship to nature. In spite of my willingness to absorb its charms and delight in them, I was again and again estranged by the fact that the enjoyment of a beautiful scene and the good fresh air were forced on me for reasons other than pleasure. Their practical advantages and wonders, which I am sure I would have recognized more unquestioningly and unconditionally under more favorable circumstances, were pointed out to me all too programmatically.

On pleasant spring and summer evenings my father would take his family with him when he visited his patients in the environs of Vienna. Often we waited for hours, reading most of the time, in Schönbrunn, Hietzing, Dornbach, Kaltenleutgeben, and elsewhere, seated in a carriage in front of a villa or on a bench in a park until he came back to us, usually in a much more stimulated mood than the one in which we, bored and impatient, greeted him at last. In Hietding it was usually Count O'Sullivan and his wife, the famous tragedienne, Charlotte Wolters, who liked to detain him and by whom he liked to be detained. In Dornbach he would visit a family called Strache, in whose garden I for the first time saw a tricycle, a clumsy precursor of the bicycle. In Pötzleinsdorf my father, and sometimes we with him, called on the dentist, Rabatz; in Kaltenleutgeben we visited Dr. Winternitz's springs, and after a consultation at the bedside or wheelchair of some patient or other, the doctor would serve coffee, graham bread and honey. Then we would rumble back to town in our *fiacre*, and we children had usually dozed off by the time we reached the city line, where a toll of eight kreuzer had to be paid. If we hadn't already had supper in the country, we would dine in a suburban garden restaurant such as the Golden Cross in Mariahilf or the Victoria Hotel in the Wieden district, which brought our outing to a close. Later these drives into the country irked me, even if they were frequently quite merry affairs, especially when, because of them, and sometimes with my father's knowledge, I was having to deny myself a harmless but precious walk with an adored blonde beauty in the Rathaus or Volksgarten.

Beside these excursions, and the rare but all the more welcome outings on holidays, which took us farther away from the city, to the Rote Stadl or the Brühl, we found recreation in the country during short trips to the mountains and at vacation resorts. The first place I can recall visiting for a few holiday weeks and frequently later was Vöslau, in the tepid spring waters of which spa I learned to swim. In the year 1870 or 1871 I first breathed Salzkammergut air. It was there, one evening in Alt-Aussee, as I looked down onto the dark waters from the terrace of the Seewirt Hotel, waters which seemed to merge endlessly with the night, that for the first time I felt something I like to call Nature-horror. Forever associated with the place where I experienced it, it had a more lasting effect on me than that first Nature-delight, felt in the Thalhof garden in Reichenau. Generally speaking though, I tended for a long time to absorb a panorama only in its overall aspects; details, unless made irresistible by some outstanding peculiarity, failed to impress me. A few fleeting visions from the animal and plant world, however, remain indelibly stamped on my mind. I shall never forget the first wild anemones I picked in the Vienna woods, the twigs from a hazel nut tree, the red convolvulus and the deadly nightshade bushes in Vöslau, the whirring stag beetles in our summer garden, and especially a glittering gold ground beetle which ran across the road at my feet somewhere between Hütteldorf and Neuwaldegg. These are impressions which rise up in me more as symbols than as memories of what nature meant to me as a child. My father had a special preference for the leaves of nut trees which he liked to rub between his fingers; apart from that he advised us to breathe deep when we were outdoors, and walked on ahead of us, setting a good example, with his cane pressed horizontally against his back between his outstretched arms.

In the year 1872 our parents undertook a trip to Switzerland with us two boys—my sister was too small to join us. In less than two weeks we passed through Munich, Zürich, Lucerne and Geneva, and returned home again. This tempo, which was an expression of my parents' excessive mobility and impatience, of their curiosity and superficiality, was requisite and a way of life with them, and in the portrayal of a married couple called Makarius and Genevieve Restless, who chase episodically through a comedy entitled *Before the World* (*Vor der Welt*), I tried, as a frivolous youth of sixteen, to derive a caricaturizing effect from this idiosyncrasy. At the time I must already have realized that the restlessness, which in my mother's later years became almost pathological, was to be transferred to me, possibly more because of the example they set than by the laws of heredity. Although quite a few things experienced on this first Swiss tour impressed me—the sunrise on the Rigi Kulm; the sight of the early risers, shivering in the cold morning air, their colorful plaids slung about their shoulders; the boat trip on the Lake of Geneva; the bears in a pit in Bern; to say nothing of the delicious breakfasts in the Swiss hotels, with tea, butter and honey, so different from our breakfasts at home because of the festive atmosphere—what I remember most clearly is a performance of Moser's farce, *Founder's Day* (*Das Stiftungsfest*), at the Munich Residenztheater, probably because the plop of a watering can, which the sleepily comic father in the play had to hold, wakened not only him, as the play dictated, but also me, out of the deep sleep which had overpowered me after my first all-night journey on a train.

An important change in my young life had taken place before this first long trip. In the autumn of the year 1871, shortly after we had moved to No. 1 Burgring, into a very nice apartment opposite the so-called Kaisergarten, in which we lived and gradually took up more and more room until my father's death in 1893, I became a first-year pupil in the *Akademische Gymnasium*, a secondary or high school. As I write this, I can suddenly recall a day that lies much further back, on which Mama lifted me out of my little bed with the green railing, put a white dress on me and sat me down on a chair at my table, where my first tutor, a Herr Fränkel, was waiting to give me my first lesson. I can see his finger pointing to the open primer and hear his kindly voice saying, "See? That is an A." I must have been five years old at the time, but I cannot recall a single lesson after that until my entry into the *Gymnasium*, as if this first lesson had been the only one I had ever had.

Tutor Fränkel was soon followed by a Herr Maximilian Lang, who was studying to be a doctor but never managed to get his degree. He was basically a good and capable man, slightly unctuous and painfully pedantic when it came to speaking nicely; even more so in writing beautifully, to which the letters bear witness which he still writes to me and members of my family on festive occasions or at any times that seem appropriate to him, from the small Hungarian town where he lives—over seventy years old now—in poverty and retirement, reading the classics and the Bible.

It was Herr Lang who one day took me to the *Akademische Gymnasium* to inquire when the school year began and what the requirements were for registration. Old Professor Windisch gave him the necessary information in the conference room, and I suppose I stood before him, on my best behavior, clutching my straw hat which was fastened by a narrow ribbon to a button on my jacket, my head bowed a little, with a half-hearted feeling of submissiveness and humility of which I was slightly ashamed; and it was the living memory of this moment which prompted me, eight years later, in a romantic tragedy, to put the following words into the mouth of a monk:

> For sometimes one may find within the human heart
> The seed of such a will to servitude.

However, after having thus for the first time passed judgment on myself in the Ibsen manner, I was never again able to catch myself trapped in sentiments of a similar nature; in fact the contrariness—a basic trait of my character—which developed more and more decisively out of such childish beginnings may have had its origin in this first inner rebellion against an emotion which I considered shameful.

Nevertheless I behaved myself, especially during the first school years, and with some coaching proved sufficiently diligent and could count myself among the best pupils, in fact among those who enjoyed certain prerogatives. I was also considered, from the first day and not altogether unjustly "a mother's boy," a reputation I couldn't shake off, possibly because of the following incident: After my first singing lesson, which was held late in the afternoon, our teacher, Professor Machanek, kept us late. Due to a misunderstanding he had waited in vain for us the time before and now wanted to make up the hour missed. Suddenly my tutor, Herr Lang, strode into the classroom and insisted on taking me home because my mother was upset over my unscheduled absence. I was permitted to leave and really did find my mother in tears and wringing her hands, and she threw her arms around me as if I had escaped from dreadful danger. For several years after that I was fetched regularly from school, in broad daylight, although we lived only ten minutes walk away.

The move up from the first to the second class meant more to me—at least in anticipation—than any earlier or later advancement of my life. I can still remember the awesome shiver that ran through me when once, in the summer and while still a freshman, I passed the open door of the second-year classroom. A pupil was standing on the rostrum and the professor was putting questions to him. Inconceivable that I should ever attain such heights. But a year later I not only did so, but was a classmate of the boy whom I had admired and who had been left back. That time, on the rostrum, he had looked like a giant; but he developed into one of the most obstreperous boys in the school and once, out of mischief and to my profound annoyance, tore up a list I was keeping pedantically of the examination marks I felt should have been given to my classmates. Soon he seemed to stop growing entirely and became more and more dwarflike; later, a violinist on the concert stage, he looked like a wicked gnome.

In spite of my good behavior, which though not altogether simulated was pretty superficial, I felt drawn from the start to some of the poorer pupils, and in my second year a boy at the bottom of the class called Thomas became one of my best friends. Unlike me the only thing he could do well was draw. But I steered clear of the bad boys, of whom naturally there was no lack; and they instinctively paid no attention to me. I therefore remained innocent for a relatively long time and the inevitable enlightenment took place one evening in the Vöslau park, on a bench in front of the Rademacher villa where we were spending the summer. I was eleven or twelve at the time, and my instructor was my schoolmate and second cousin, Ludwig Mandl, who strangely enough was to play a quite important role in my life later, as gynecologist.

It may have been during the same summer that I was granted a glimpse of the life of the actors in that small spa. One morning, in the park, I saw a young couple approaching the theater and could hear them converse, using the intimate "Du." The evening before I had seen them play the lovers in Friedrich Kaiser's drama

Monk and Soldier, and naturally didn't doubt for a moment that a
tender relationship existed between them in real life as well. Curious and strangely moved, I watched them disappear through the
stage door. It so happened that I was to be permitted to follow the
lives of these two for a long time after that summer during which
their theatrical careers may have just begun. The pretty girl never
married and today plays comic and character roles at one of our
finest Vienna theaters. I ran across her partner of those Vöslau
days in Salzburg, during the winter of 1890 to 1891, and his standing at the theater then was of greatest interest to me for personal
reasons. The indisputable fact that his wife, at home, was receiving her lovers while he, drunkard and ham actor, was singing and
playing secondary roles, fitted well, in its grotesque triviality, into
the overall picture of provincial theater as I was gradually to experience it.

Until now the psychological and physiological enlightenment
acquired by me had had no emotional or physical consequences.
On the whole I was even spared the puppy-love affairs which are
so prevalent during this period. I can recall only once, during my
eleventh or twelfth year, experiencing a jealousy which manifested
itself in the sound beating I administered to my brother when I
noticed that one of our little cousins seemed to favor him. I did so,
however, not from any inner necessity but more out of a sense of
duty, as if I had to prove to myself the existence of a passion in
which I really didn't believe. Altogether it seems to me that the
tendency to play a part, not so much in front of others as for
myself, regardless of whether I happened to enjoy the role or not,
was much stronger in me in those childhood years than at any
later time. For instance, once I lost my way while walking in the
woods in Vöslau. When I finally got my bearings again, I began
to embellish the trivial incident in my mind, and while hurrying
back in the shade of the trees, my overcoat slung across my shoulders, I composed a monologue, aloud, which it was my intention
to repeat before an assembled audience when I got home. I studied
the part assiduously until I noticed an old gentleman, sitting on a
bench I happened to be passing, looking at me with wry astonishment, whereupon, ashamed, I promptly shut up. I can also recall
how a small relative annoyed me once with a certain arrogant
twitching of the lips and nose, which I began to imitate, if for no

better reason than to demonstrate to her that I had no intention of letting it pass unnoticed, and I kept up the mannerism for quite some time. I therefore have every reason to ask myself if the desire to act the poet, and the childish urge to imitate, and finally the encouraging applause on which I could always count in those days, weren't just as responsible for my first poetic efforts as any innate urge to write, although I naturally dare not doubt that such an urge existed, even if the most forbearing critic could discover in my first literary efforts at best some signs of precocity but scarcely a valid talent.

An experience inspired me to write my first poem, the content of which emerges quite clearly in the verse itself. I would like to insert it here as chronicler therefore, since it is my first poem, not, as the reader will soon note, out of vanity. It runs as follows:

> Figaro's wedding has passed by,
> But you can still hear Arthur cry.
> This is because he's lost his hat;
> Mother's beside herself over that.
> But he finds it at last,
> And falls asleep fast.

I recited this poem, and another, more serious one entitled *Sardanapalus*, to my Israelite friends while the Catholic students were having religious instruction. It is understandable that my success left much to be desired, and I was to experience a writer's envy for the first time when, right after me, one of my schoolmates met with considerably greater approval on reciting his amusing verses. Soon I was able to compensate for my failure, before the same audience, by reading aloud a few satirical verses, some of which were directed against my schoolmates. One quite lengthy poem was aimed at Professor Windisch, our class professor. I don't know if I recited it; the only thing I do remember is that one night, after I had gone to bed, my father discovered it in one of my note-books, and with it a little book of Egyptian dream interpretations, as well as a manual of geomancy, both of which peculiar volumes I had acquired, for purposes unknown, on the advice of my friend, Thomas. Now I had to recite the poem to my father who, I could see clearly, was suppressing his laughter; in spite of which he visited my school on the following day and came back with a serious admonition from my professor, not because of the poem, which I imagine my father hadn't mentioned, but because of the dream and geomancy books, and his special concern over my incomprehensible friendship with the poorest scholar in the class.

Professor Windisch, a secular priest, who in our first year taught us Latin and Greek, was a capable pedagogue and at the same time a good-natured human being, a combination that was to be found in very few of his colleagues, at any rate according to my experience. Our mathematics professor, Woldrich, was a feeble teacher and a thoroughly insufferable fellow who took obvious pleasure in tormenting and frightening his young charges. One of his more harmless caprices was to make his pupils change their seats frequently, for no reason, or to let them stand in the corner for an hour. Our drawing and calligraphy teacher, Fallenböck, is another repulsive memory, a dandy with a red moustache. I shall never forget the malicious, annihilating look with which he turned once to glare at me when I absent-mindedly laid my arm across his shoulders while he was correcting my paper, as I was accustomed to do with my tutor. In that look of his I was faced for the first time with the incomprehensible enmity, born only of the hatred of man for man, which one meets up with so often in this world and against which one finds oneself increasingly better armed as the years go by. Still, far be it from me to excuse or try to seriously establish the fact that my miserable handwriting is the unhappy result of this ridiculous teacher's behavior, especially since calligraphy was taught only in the first year. As for drawing, it was not a compulsory subject, and with my utter lack of talent I gave it up voluntarily after the first year. Our Greek professor, Ambrosius Lissau, was not without merit, although he was strict and bad-tempered, and his biased rancor against pupils from well-to-do houses was only too evident. I have this basic attitude of his to thank for the fact that once, on passing the corner where I was seated, he grasped my propped-up arm and without saying a word, in fact without disturbing the rhythm of his pacing, knocked it against the sharp edge of my desk. He ended, as was to be expected, as director and superintendent of the school.

I intend to report later on those professors who accompanied us through the years to come, or to whom we were assigned at a later date; but here I would like to mention assistant director Rutte, a foppish simpleton, constantly twirling his moustache, who taught us German in the third year. For a while he went in and out of our house as tutor, since I and my brother—who needed it more—were coached throughout our *Gymnasium* years, to a greater or lesser degree and with greater or lesser benefit. Our admirable Maximilian Lang was followed, as tutor, by his cousin, also a medical student, an awkward, untalented fellow of whom we liked to make fun. He didn't last long with us but remained in occasional touch. To acquire the means to finish his studies and take his oral examinations, he married a *passée* Hungarian actress from the provinces, much to everyone's merciless amusement. At some time or other he probably introduced her to us, but I really don't know if I ever actually saw her or whether I have preserved a memory of her from hearsay as no longer youthful, ridiculously rouged and startlingly overdressed.

The Professors Strassmann and Holzinger managed to arouse a little more respect than Neuhaus and Rutte, yet I can scarcely tell them apart in my mind as far as their appearance is concerned and consequently find it difficult to fit them in chronologically. One of them, I recall, took pride in the fact that, as a reserve artillery officer he had never missed a performance of *Lohengrin* in the standing room section of the opera house. None of the gentlemen mentioned were permitted to enjoy a term of any appreciable length in our home; but a poor, unprepossessing little Jewish boy, who took it upon himself to tutor us while still a sixth-year student at the *Akademische Gymnasium*, and at the time two or three years ahead of me, was able to hold the position to everyone's complete satisfaction until after my graduation. Serious, ironical, clever, conscientious and indefatigable, he was not only an excellent instructor but managed imperturbably and with ever increasing success to keep up his own study of law. He soon entered the civil service and today is considered one of the best authorities on constitutional and international law. He officiates in the civil court as Hofrat Tezner, a position he could scarcely have achieved, even with equal merit, under his original name of Tänzerles. That, unlike my brother, I was an easy-going, unambitious and rather superficial student even under his capable tutelage is something of which he reminded me humorously only a few years ago, during one of our rare but as far as I am concerned always welcome meetings.

I took piano lessons. I was encouraged to learn how to play at an early age and did so with mild enthusiasm. I was taught the rudiments by an extremely short man called Basch, who had given music lessons in the house of my grandparents and whose secondary or perhaps main profession was that of marriage broker. In this dual role he turns up episodically in one of my uncompleted plays, *Albine*, under the name of Tüpfel.

His successor—as music teacher, of course—was a certain Peschke, who bore an astonishing resemblance to Napoleon III and was soon relieved by a coach from the Vienna opera, Hermann Riedel, a blond, pleasant but irascible young man, who as the composer of the music for Scheffel's *Trumpeter of Säckingen* (*Trompeter von Säckingen*) enjoyed loud acclaim which was silenced all too soon. His opera, *Accolade* (*Der Ritterschlag*), was performed at the Imperial Opera House, without success. Still in his youth and shortly after his marriage, he was appointed court musical director in Braunschweig, and after fulfilling his duties there for decades in a highly praiseworthy fashion but without ever composing another work, he died in the year 1914. He moves, pale and fleetingly, through the pages of my novel, *The Way Out into the Open* (*Der Weg ins Freie*).

I didn't like to practice and was therefore never able to acquire a technique, but thanks to an interest in music that was furthered by my frequent attendance at operas and concerts, I was able to achieve a certain dexterity, especially in playing duets, on which occasions my partner was usually my mother, with whom Hermann Riedel also liked to play when our lesson was over. My brother gave up the piano for the violin and outdid me in music, as he did in school and later, in the study of medicine, thanks to his tenacity and conscientiousness, but also because he was more talented and his powers of comprehension were greater. Unlike me he had been what is termed, without signifying much, a bad boy. While still a youth, however, this changed, again to my disadvantage; but we got along very well, also with my little sister, even if we did occasionally conspire to tease her. All in all our relationship at the time and in later years may be termed affectionate rather than intimate, which applies also to the basic mood in our home. My father, despite all the tenderness lavished on us and the pains taken with our instruction—far more than with our upbringing in a broader sense—was absorbed in himself. This may be attributed to his natural tendencies, his profession and ambitions. The latter, in spite of his tireless medical, scientific and journalistic activities, were directed mainly toward the obvious success and visible honors (yet not at all toward material gain). One could almost say he was dependent on himself; and my mother, with all her proficiency and diligence as a housekeeper, had attuned herself utterly and to the extent of self-denial to his personality and interests. Neither of them was therefore in a position to participate to any great extent in the development of their children, and were able to offer much less real and productive understanding than they would ever have admitted. We were just as barely conscious of this lack during our boyhood years as they were. The parental love offered us was in its outer manifestations so warm and rich that I am sure my expressions of filial gratitude even then lagged considerably behind what they should have been.

Just the same, the atmosphere of a house in which recognition counted more than achievement, in spite of all beneficial activities practiced for their own sake; and in which world opinion was valued above self-recognition, was bound to influence my development, especially that of my basic talent (great or small as it may have been is here beside the point). When I look today at the copy book in which I wrote my first poems in my awkward childish handwriting, and in a plea for indulgence described them as "First Efforts," I realize that I was not always affected by an innate poetic drive but more frequently grasped any occasion that offered itself to again demonstrate to my parents or any other audience, and to myself, that I was a poet. "Rome in Flames" was the title of the first poem which I evidently considered worthy of inclusion in this collection. I wrote it in June 1873, in Vöslau, and it was greeted by my good grandmother with the outcry, "A second Schiller!" It is followed by "The Happy Shepherd," "Ulysses and Achilles," "Hector's Death," "The Last Words of Achilles," "Andromache's Grief," "The Homesickness of a German Fugitive," "Memnon" and "Penthesilea," with which I brought

this first collection to a close. It is followed at the end of 1875 by
a second set of poems of a similarly mixed character in which the
historic and mythological material gradually becomes less prominent and an intellectual lyricism begins to emerge boldly beside
verses of a more emotional character, as for instance a poem in
which the Four Temperaments may be heard in turn, speaking on
the problem of fame.

In our close family circle these trifling efforts were evaluated as
proof of my talent, and more often than was to my liking my
father would reproach me, at a time when I considered my lyrical
period closed, with the question, "Isn't it a long time since you
wrote a poem?" He was also concerned with the improvement
of my prose when he induced me to write compositions on our
journeys in the summers of 1874 and 1875, for which I received
a reward of ten or twenty kreuzer, depending on my success, after
concluding a chapter or the description of a day of travel. On such
journeys there was naturally no lack of episodes which could be
treated humorously, and I put a lot of effort and verve into the
description of an encounter with a good country doctor in the
vicinity of Heiligenblut, who in the course of our conversation at
the inn turned out to be a subscriber to my father's medical journal. My father, however, in a sort of Kaiser Joseph mood, didn't
choose to reveal the fact that he was the highly respected editor
and professor from Vienna until just as our carriage was taking off.

My future in the field of the theater, which becomes much
more clearly evident when compared with my somewhat forced
lyrical efforts, was heralded in a more decisive and spontaneous
fashion, and again I feel I may ignore any question of talent
because with what I am writing here I do not presume to be
describing the development of a poetic genius but of a human
soul in which artistic, dilettantish and quite a few other elements
interacted, disturbed and furthered each other. Unlike my poems,
my efforts as dramatist remained my private affair for a long time.
I felt no urge to share them, especially not with my parents. I
wrote my plays in secret, and if my father or anyone else happened to enter the room, I would let them disappear between the
pages of my homework. In this manner I produced, while still
at the *Gymnasium* and up to the year 1875, the following works,
the titles of which I list here because of their curiosity: *The*

Lorelei (Die Loreley), a tragedy in five acts with a prologue;
The Chinese Prince (Der Chinesische Prinz), in four scenes;
The Lorelei (again), in two parts; *Gold and Honesty (Gold und
Ehrlichkeit)*, a four-act play in free verse; *Queen Heavenly-Blue
(Königin Himmelblau)*, a fairy tale in four acts; *Cornelius Ombra*,
a dramatic fairy tale; *The Burnt Cat (Die verbrannte Katze)*,
a one-act play; *The Big Crash (Der grosse Krach)*, in five acts;
The Magic Violin (Die Wundergeige); *The Guardian Spirits (Die
Schutzgeister)*; *A Fairy Tale in Three Acts*; *Tea Party (Thee
gesellschaft)*, a one-act comedy; *Prince Ernest and Werner von
Kyburg*, a historical tragedy with a prologue and six acts; *The
Treasure Hunter (Der Schatzgräber)*, a fairy tale in five acts;
Hunter in the Alps (Der Alpenjäger), a tragedy in two acts;
Higgledy-Piggledy (Kraut und Rüben), a comedy in two acts;
and finally the third part of a trilogy, *Tarquinius Superbus*, the first
part of which I began to write years later. Of all the plays mentioned here, only *Gold and Honesty* and *Tarquinius Superbus*
remain; of the rest I would remember little if I hadn't kept the
list. But I do recall that *The Burnt Cat* dealt with a not entirely
clarified event which had taken place in school; and *Hunter in
the Alps*, the plot of which I have forgotten, was inspired by the
view from the terrace of a hotel on Lake Wolfgang in the evening,
and by the storm lanterns alight on a set table.

In the same time span, a tragedy, *The Brothers (Die Brüder)*,
remained incomplete; also something akin to a folk-drama called
The Turks at Vienna's Gates (Die Türken vor Wien); a fairy tale,
Cinderella (Aschenbrödel); *The Actors (Die Schauspieler)*; and
—this one has survived—a satirical comedy, *Teutschlingen*, in
which I tried, with little wit and slight unease, to satirize our
professors, especially Zitkovsky, with his exaggerated reverence
for all things German. I probably picked on Zitkovsky because it
seemed important to me to get even with the first person who
had consciously disapproved of me in literary matters. For when
he had taken us over in the fourth year, he had asked the best
scholar in the class who wrote the finest German compositions
and had been told that I did. When my first efforts didn't come up
to his expectations, he remarked in an offhand manner that he
couldn't see anything so exceptional about them, a judgment
with which I must not only concur, as I leaf through the school

notebooks I have preserved, but with which I had to agree at the time. For although I was jokingly called "the poet laureate" in school, and a rumor had been started that I and my friends Wechsel and Obendorf, who were equally devoted to literature, had formed a club for "the improvement of the classics," I was not at all proud of my compositions or other literary efforts, and had no desire to display them in close or wider circles. I found complete satisfaction in the indefatigable but aimless writing down of scenes and plays. I seldom spoke to anyone about my work and only on rare occasions discussed it with my best friends (beside Wechsel and Obendorf, a certain Otto Singer), to whom I once read *Tarquinius Superbus* aloud, not however without letting the manuscript disappear under the sofa when my father came into the room. Briefly the plan for a school poetry paper was brought up once in a conversation between me and a certain Conrad Willner, which was to appear once under his name, the next time under mine, but nothing came of the idea if for no other reason than that my co-editor soon left school.

All I can say in summing up is that nothing I wrote during this period would have led anyone to believe that they were in the presence of a great literary talent unless one wants to let the unrestrainable urge to write, at least in the field of drama, count as evidence of such a gift. I would even like to see the word "precocious" which was used casually in connection with me during my childhood, replaced more aptly by the word "precultured." I have the feeling that just by this tireless, somehow mechanical, literary production I was able to preserve a certain lack of self-consciousness, a childishness and immaturity, for a longer time than is usually the case under different circumstances. For the little life which happened to come my way was at once grasped by the productive element in my nature, worked up and done with, without my even trying to come to grips with it as an individual.

I was interested in very little beside what transpired at home, at school, in the theater, in what I was reading and in that which I liked to call writing. Whatever was going on in city or country, or in the big outside world, found little echo in my heart. Of the Franco-Prussian War, which broke out when I was nine, I can recall only the tall headlines in the newspapers and that in the beginning my sympathies, like those of every Austrian, were on the side of the French. I was touched more closely by the economic catastrophe that took place two years later and which is still known today as the Big Crash, in which my father, like so many innocent victims, lost all his savings, and which inspired me, as can be seen on the list of plays mentioned, to write a five-act, probably humorous play. On the first of May 1873, a few days before Black Friday, which is the name under which the day lives on in Vienna's local history, the Vienna World's Fair opened and I can see myself sitting opposite my parents in a carriage which is slowly approaching the Rotunda, rain splashing against the windows. Until now any hint of political and social events had been remote, as was the case with most of the boys in my circles; just as world history scarcely affected me directly but served rather as an inspiration for my lyrical and especially my dramatic efforts.

However, with all my poetizing, I was by no means a dreamy or eccentric boy, but rather, in spite of occasional absent-mindedness, quite alert and sociable. My schoolmates came to the house, I visited them, there must have been some with whom I had more serious and confidential conversations, but without this resulting in any intimate or rapturous friendships, as are not rare at this age. I would have forgotten completely how we passed the time if one evening were not so clear in my mind, on which I read a novel by Zschokke or Hackländer aloud to a school friend and his sister, at their house, and can recall, on arriving at a slightly erotic passage, turning a deep red. I still have a postcard from this friend, Leo Arnstein, written at a much later date, in which he asks me— without success, by the way—to join him on a holiday trip, with the explicit injunction that any crazy mountaineering stunts were out. As fate would have it, during the summer following this invitation he fell from a rocky mountain ledge while picking flowers and died instantly.

At this point I would like to mention a few other school friends of whom I saw more for a semester or two or whom I remember more vividly for some reason or other; for instance, Ernst Radnitzky, son of the famous etcher and during our first year head of the class, a gifted boy with a rather peculiar way of behaving. During recess he liked to walk up and down the Gothic archways of our building, alone, his overcoat slung across his shoulders. In the upper classes, after losing his rating as top student, he became a little more sociable and so intimate with some of his schoolmates, including me, that a correspondence started between us, in school from bench to bench and during the holidays between Vienna and a spa near Graz where he was staying. He seems also to have indulged in some poetic efforts of his own, judging by the sonnet he gave me to read in which he demanded that, "like me, a hopeless striver," I give up poetizing. I didn't take offense over this or any other derisive remarks of his, but our friendship wasn't strong enough to survive our graduation, and whenever I happened to meet him again, on the street, as university student, or later as government official, always with his coat slung over his shoulders, neither of us felt inclined to enter into a lengthy conversation, and as time went by, as if in silent agreement, we even ceased to greet each other.

A boy called Katzer had been top student of the A-class from the first year and kept his rank even after our B-class was joined with his two years before graduation. He was a studious, friendly, modest but rather limited fellow who, probably in consideration of his family's needs, had to go to work at an early age and took an insignificant civil service job in the post office. However, even in this not very demanding position he failed, as far as I know, to go far.

A certain Lubowienski was second in our class, an alert, gifted boy who in later years tried to play a political role in Salzburg as lawyer and member of the German National Party. He changed his name—which would have been a handicap to his career—for one that sounded more German. Once the entire class had their picture taken—I can't remember for what purpose— and Herr Kilcher-Lubowienski, who kept the picture, let it circulate among his friends with the melancholy observation, "Just take a look, what a lot of Jews I had to go to school with," and I don't doubt that his political friends commiserated with him duly over his sad fate.

In the lower classes, Marcel Barasch was one of my closest friends, but he soon lost out with me because of his affectations, and I was definitely through with him when, after the death of some relative or other who had been only fifteen years old, he cried out, "If only it were our turn!" Alfred Rie was a more normal fellow, not particularly stimulating but sympathetic and clever, and the only one of those mentioned whose home I visited. In the summer he lived with his family in Hütteldorf, and I can recall an afternoon coffee hour in their garden, in the course of which Alfred's mother asked me, after we had eaten a lot of fruit, whether I would like coffee or beer. I answered very sensibly, "I think coffee goes best with red currants," a reply which amused old and young alike and was quoted for years by my colleagues.

Also unforgettable is Samuel Spitzer, a gifted philologist and enthusiast for all things pertaining to antiquity. I met him again years later, now a *Gymnasium* teacher of ancient languages in Bisenz, as enthusiastic as ever and just as modest as when I had known him as a boy. All in all, scarcely any of my schoolmates —in so far as I was able to keep track of them—developed in a direction different from the one indicated in his youth, and one begins to realize what a difficult, in a sense almost insoluble, problem the education of a child is when one considers with what a pre-shaped, yes, in spite of all immaturity, with what a finished product parents and teachers are faced.

Increasingly frequent gatherings with cousins, male and female, among whom I was the oldest, took place quite naturally because of the liveliness of our family intercourse, with the home of my grandparents remaining the focal point. In conventional intervals and one after the other, all my mother's sisters had married. Emma, the one next to her in age, had espoused a Hungarian land-owner, Leo Fried, and had gone to live with him on an estate not far from Debreczin. A few years later she returned to her native land, an inconsolable widow, with two children—Gustave and Gisela. Her clear, keen mind did not prevent her from resenting the providence that had ordained a happier fate for her sisters and other totally uninvolved persons, and the severity of her nature gradually took possession of her total personality with the result that it became increasingly less pleasant to be with her.

Irene, guileless and good-natured, married a grain merchant named Ludwig Mandl, who was also experienced in stock exchange dealings and was soon the wealthiest member of the family without ever really showing it. He was a sloppy fellow, one could almost say he was shabby. He insisted on traveling third-class on the train and was delighted when he was occasionally able to do the railroad out of a few kreuzer on a commutation ticket, in the course of which the small sum involved played no part—he was accustomed to losing a hundred, a thousand times more at cards or through his gifts to charity; the only thing that mattered to him was the fact that he had outsmarted somebody.

His trips never covered much more ground than lay between Vienna and Vöslau, where he later bought the Rademacher villa, which we sometimes rented for the summer. Four of Irene's children died young, two of diphtheria within a few days of each other. These deaths caused their mother to sink into the deep depression that tends to develop, even after such tragic experiences, only in a spirit already darkened; which under more favorable circumstances might never have been stricken or even anticipated such misfortune. Olga, Alfred and Grete, who were born later, survived.

Unlike her sisters, Pauline, my youngest aunt, pert, clever and gay, did not look at all Jewish, nor were her mannerisms or speech in any way Semitic. She was very young, just seventeen, when she fell in love with the son of the operetta composer Suppé, an impecunious savings bank employee and amateur singer who looked like a Sunday photographer. My grandmother was against the match, mainly for religious reasons; but my mother, with sisterly affection, encouraged the love affair, and the marriage finally did take place and resulted in numerous children but otherwise not much good fortune. At first Uncle Peter, blond and blithe, knew how to ingratiate himself with the family, and with botany box and butterfly net sometimes took us young people with him on outings; but as the years went by he drew away from his wife's family, undoubtedly for racial reasons, gradually also from her, and soon had to support not only his wife and legitimate children but also the maid, with whom he kept up a sort of common-law marriage until his early death, a union which also resulted in children. Of his legitimate daughters, two predeceased him; in the personalities and fates of the other three, the decline of the family continued its logical course. The only son, his mother's hope and joy, and to all appearances without a care in the world, died quite unexpectedly while still a young man. His mother, as a result of too much tragic excitement, had fallen victim at an earlier stage to a nervous condition, most markedly claustrophobia; and it

seems miraculous that with all her troubles which included financial worries—even though these were alleviated to some extent
by her sisters—she never entirely lost the sense of humor of her
younger years.

My mother's oldest brother, Edmund, married an ugly, not very
bright or well-to-do girl from Lemberg, and among the toys she
brought back from her honeymoon I can recall a miniature game
of nine pins, which was for me. Since during some periods of my
life I was closer to them physically and in spirit than to the rest of
my family, I shall come back later to Uncle Edmund, his rise, his
fame, his mistakes and downfall, and to his children—Otto, Else
and Raoul, who also, in their own way, are living examples of the
inexorable effects of heredity.

Irene's twin brother, Carl, was an ordinary fellow with a gruff
personality, above all a business and stock exchange man. In his
youth he was considered a man-of-the-world. At the age of fifteen
I met him once in an obscure spot in the Prater where some wild
women of obvious disrepute were riding around on rather tame
horses in a dimly lighted arena. After this encounter, which neither
of us was too happy about, my friend Richard Horn, one of my
companions on outings like this, and I, dubbed Carl "the Hippo-
drome Uncle." Among the Markbreiter grandchildren, his two
sons by his marriage to Rebecca Lakenbacher would stand at the
end of the line if one were to arrange them according to aptitude.

Felix, my mother's youngest brother and her favorite, was only
seven years older than I and was, so to speak, middleman between the older and younger generation which gave him a rather
special position in both categories. Once, on a walk with me, we
stopped for a snack and he not only enjoyed a glass of raspberry
juice with soda water but also struck up a gallant conversation
with the girl who was serving us, probably not the first flirtation of
his life, and my vanity was flattered when he begged me not to
report this *risqué* little adventure to my grandfather. Felix was
quite bright, passably cultured, very talented in business, painfully
proper and possessed of a nervous restlessness which was superficial rather than basic. He soon found a position in a prominent
Paris banking house where he advanced rapidly and refused the
hand of his employer's beautiful daughter to marry an almost completely destitute but good and clever relative of his from Vienna.

With her he moved to London where he was at first employed in
a branch of the Paris house but soon made himself independent.
We shall meet him and his family frequently in the years that lie
ahead. I would like, however, to mention here his musical efforts,
which in those early days had their influence on my relationship
to the art. I shared his enthusiasm for Wagner, especially for *Die
Meistersinger,* an opera that was not so generally loved and admired then as it was later; and I liked to listen to him extemporiz-
ing on the piano or playing little pieces he had composed, among
which the theme of a Hero and Leander overture remained longer
in my memory than in his.

I just said he was my mother's youngest brother; however, there
was another, born after him—Julius, who at the age of seventeen,
while in Schachendorf, shot himself, allegedly out of homesickness. By a curious coincidence not only my grandmother but two
other daughters of Markus Schey each lost a child by a shot. In
the year 1848, in Pressburg, Iritzer, the husband of the oldest girl,
threw a pistol he had found into the oven; it went off and shot his
daughter fatally. The second girl, Nanette Rosenberg, had a son
who served in the Italian Foreign Legion. He was shot in his
barracks by a careless comrade. My Uncle Julius, whom I can't
remember at all, was the last one to suffer this seemingly fore-
ordained fate and at the same time the first one of the Markbreiter
progeny to manifest, in tragic simplicity, an inherited mental
frailty.

Beside his three daughters, my great-grandfather Markus Schey
had a son, Anton, who liked to maintain a close relationship with
the family children. On Sundays he would invite them to dinner.
His sisters didn't think too highly of him, nor therefore did my
grandmother, because of the machinations by which he had
managed to acquire the greater share of his father's fortune, which
the injured parties, probably not unjustly, liked to describe as
"legacy hunting." Still, the family did not break with him completely because, although he had married, he was childless, and
they could therefore hope that he would one day compensate his
sister's children for what he had done to their mother, a hope only
partially fulfilled later on. He liked to affect a patriarchal-tyranni-
cal air, had a brusque sense of humor and took special pleasure in
giving certain female relatives derisive pet names such as *Lintscherl*

Plattschnas for Cousin Caroline Jellinek. In other cases he
would be satisfied to express his scorn by a peculiar form of questioning, asking in an offhand manner, "You haven't seen the Lakenbacher creature for a while, have you?" a reference to the wife
of his favorite nephew, Carl Markbreiter, who was not unlike him;
at the same time implying that as far as he was concerned a marriage he hadn't sanctioned could never be considered valid, a fact
which he expressed in his will in an even less endearing fashion.
He was in the habit of repeating other remarks and snide questions such as this until one became weary of them, above all with
those concerning his cuisine. Again and again we had to assure
him that no one knew how to prepare a salad as well as he did—
something he always attended to himself, at the table, in front of
his assembled guests; and that nowhere could one be served such
delicious beef as in his home. Sometimes we were joined by the
two children of a poor Jewish tailor, and rumor had it that they
were actually the children of our cordial host. His wife was small,
plain, miserly and false, but not stupid; anyway, she accepted fact
or rumor with equanimity. In turn there was talk to the effect that
she still dreamed of a love of her youth, an Italian tutor whose
name was always greeted with meaningful smiles and was mentioned frequently by other family members, not that anyone had
ever even caught a glimpse of him.

As soon as we had left the table, my uncle would start up a
music box which stood against a dimly lighted wall and looked
like a coffin. Among other pieces it played Rossini's "William Tell
Overture" with a thumping rhythm of the drums. As I hear its
echoes now, the semilighted room with its old-fashioned furniture,
filled with smoke from the men's pipes, rises before my eyes out
of the depths of the past. The question, "Have you had a look at
my pipes?" was unfailingly the next item on the agenda. The
choice collection was set up on a mahogany stand in a corner of
the salon and had to be duly admired every time. In later years
our uncle would read his East-West travel diaries aloud to us. He
was very proud of them in spite of the fact that they contained
nothing but dry reports of the sights worth seeing and all sorts of
railway and mailing dates, rather as in a Baedeker, but without
the compactness and precision of that useful book which his
diaries were doubtlessly supposed to imitate. After the second or

third time the readings became exceedingly boring. On these travels, which had taken him as far as Constantinople and Asia Minor, his favorite nephew Carl had often accompanied him, naturally before he had married "the Lakenbacher creature," and it was bruited that on these journeys—and not only in the Far East —things had taken place which for good reason could not be included in diaries that were to be read by his wife and other family members. But it would be unfair if one were to let the hospitality which my Uncle Toni extended to his sisters' grandchildren (although not always in equal measure) pass as nothing more than a down payment or even a modest substitute for the share of the family fortune which was hopefully expected but never received. For he wasn't really a hard man; sometimes he was even quite helpful, as for instance when he came to the assistance of my Uncle Edmund, whose honor and freedom were endangered by his financial calamities, with amounts that in the course of years reached a quarter of a million gulden, but in the end, unhappily, did not spell salvation. This has to be recognized as a noble gesture, even if he never let an opportunity pass for displaying his cash ledger to relatives and acquaintances, in which one could read, inscribed under certain dates, the words, *Gave that good-for-nothing E. M., for the last time, two-hundred-thousand gulden, with the stipulation that he never dare to show his face again,* an edict that was meant to include his wife and children, and with which their eventual rights to any share of his estate were abrogated.

I would like to go back for a moment to the aforementioned Caroline Jellinek, or *Lintscherl Plattschnas,* niece of my grandmother and Uncle Toni, not so much for her sake but because of her daughters. The oldest, Matilda, showed a friendly interest in my early poetic efforts since she herself was not without literary ambitions. Once she read aloud to me, out of a household ledger, the opening of a novel which I imagine never advanced beyond the first chapter, of which I recall the figure of a cook, standing with arms akimbo, not because this effort at characterization seemed a sign to me of exceptional talent but because the author saw it that way. As an expression of my gratitude I dedicated a poem to her which glorified the Wildenstein ruin near Ischl, and with that our literary relationship ended. She soon married her uncle, Sandor Rosenberg, a thin, jolly man who bore a slight resemblance to Heinrich Heine. He was supposed to be suffering from a heart condition and everyone prophesied that he didn't have long to live. He took his young bride to Paris where he opened an antique shop which soon made him wealthy and in due course rich.

In his earlier years he had already displayed a harmless inclination to boasting and had liked to play Maecenas, and I have this to thank for my first encounter with the most renowned painter of the day, Hans Makart. Uncle Sandor, in Paris, asked his brother-in-law, Felix (my favorite uncle), to commission a painting from Makart, with the explicit injunction that the subject be left entirely to the discretion of the painter, and that price was to play no part. Uncle Felix took me with him to see Makart. After we had given our names, we had to wait for a while in a beautifully furnished but rather gloomy anteroom until Hans Makart appeared on the stairs that led down from his studio, wearing a brown velvet suit with baggy trousers, a lighted cigar in his hand, looking pale and Spanish. Without coming any closer he asked us why we had come. Uncle Felix said what he had to say in carefully chosen words, a little self-consciously but with dignity. There was a short silence, then Makart shook his head and answered coolly that it wasn't his custom to paint pictures to order and dismissed us with a farewell that could barely be termed friendly. Uncle Felix, who liked to hear himself praised, asked on the way home what impression his little speech had made on me, and I wasn't chary with my appreciation. He explained that he had rather expected Makart to refuse, and after thinking it over for a while added, "And that wasn't a bad cigar he was smoking." At the time I had little understanding for such things, but since then the memory of Hans Makart is implicitly joined in my mind with the vision and aroma of a lighted Havana cigar. Our Parisian Maecenas was not offended either over the rejection of his commission, decided to order his paintings elsewhere, and lived as happy husband and father of four children to the ripe old age of seventy, in spite of his heart condition.

I am sure I would have forgotten long ago that at the age of thirteen, on a beautiful summer's day, I stayed to have lunch, without permission, at the Jellinek home—the father, a doctor, had died a long time ago—if on this occasion I hadn't received from Matilda's younger sister, Julie, who was my own age, a heart-felt kiss on the mouth in front of everybody and with no warning whatsoever. It was to be our last kiss, but it helped me to cope with my parents' reproaches because I had stayed for lunch without their permission. It was Julie whom my Uncle Felix brought home to London, ten years later, as his good, wise wife. Altogether I remember her as one of the best and cleverest women I have ever known. My heart tells me that our mutual sympathy, which never flagged whether we were separated or close, and which was of advantage to me later when I established my meager literary connections with England, was born of that innocent kiss in the days of our youth, which I am sure she promptly forgot, and I credit my heart with at least as much understanding and a much better memory than my head.

My thirteenth birthday was celebrated without any elaborate ritual but with exceptionally numerous and handsome presents from parents, grandparents and other relatives—the classics, handsomely bound, a gold watch, a few ducats—and knowing very well what I owed to my career as a writer, I didn't fail to express my gratitude by a humorous epic poem in hexameter that was supposed to have ten verses, entitled "Barmizvah"; a gratitude that must have been sincere since I didn't let my benefactors know anything about the few verses I actually composed.

At this time, between lower and upper classes of *Gymnasium*, and on the threshold of adolescence, which in more mature boys may be called the first years of manhood, I have to reflect on an unforgettable and significant hour which may lie somewhat further back chronologically, in which for the first time I became aware of the concept—death. It was a night on which, either suddenly awakened or not yet fallen asleep, I began to weep aloud in a horror that rose out of the depths of my soul at the thought that I would have to die. It rose to my consciousness for the first time in its total inescapability, and I cried because I wanted to awaken my parents who slept in the next room. Before very long my father was at my bedside, asking me worriedly what was wrong. He sat down beside me and gently stroked my forehead and hair. I sobbed on for a while without however betraying by a word what had shaken me so violently; and when my father left, after saying a few comforting words, I fell asleep again, pacified. I never experienced anything like this again, but at about the same time something happened in which again the subconscious elements within me seemed touched by the enigmatic. In the middle of the night I found myself, half-asleep, standing beside my bed, and I walked through my parents' bedroom, into the dining room, where it seemed to me that I could see my brother, in his nightgown, sitting at the table. When my father, who had followed me, wakened me fully, I realized that it was the rays of the moon falling to the floor across table and chair that had lured me to this far-off room. Although as far as I know nothing like this ever happened again, I flattered myself for quite some time with the idea that I was moonstruck.

Book Two

❁❁❁❁❁❁❁❁❁❁

May 1875 to July 1879

IMAGINE FOR A MOMENT a person who finds himself unexpectedly in an establishment where fancy dress is rented. All around him, along the walls, in open closets, on racks, hang costumes with limp sleeves and coats with no content. Paper masks stare at him out of hollow eyes; holes yawn between red lips—a colorful, fantastic, but dead world. Then slowly a sleeve here and there, which at first seemed to hold nothing but air, begins to move; fingered hands stretch out toward him; a coat balloons as if a living breast were swelling inside it; something seems to look fleetingly out of the empty eye sockets of a mask; lips begin to smile, to grin, and what until now had seemed hollow attire or painted cardboard turns out suddenly to be breathing, seeing, moving. It would be the craziest adventure, yet it may be compared to what a boy experiences, sensitively and acquiescently, when the true meaning begins to shine through words he has heard a hundred times, has read, spoken, written, and thought he had understood. All of a sudden he no longer moves between masks and costumes; the glitter of life itself crowds in on him, and even where it has not yet manifested itself, he is aware that at any moment he may expect a miraculous surprise.

I have already mentioned how during a sleepless night the word death came to life for me out of the petrifaction of its five letters; not much later the same thing was to happen to me with the word love.

In the year 1875, directly opposite us and only one floor higher up, on the other side of the Eschenbergergasse which runs between the Opera and Burgrings, a merchant, or perhaps he was a stock broker, lived with his wife, four or five sons and one daughter. We were therefore not strangers when the formal introduction took place one early summer day in the Volksgarten where Fännchen and her youngest brother, three-year-old Fritz, liked to stroll and where I, with our *Fräulein*, brother and sister, or with some of my school friends, also liked to enjoy the fresh air. Already during our first conversation we discovered that both of us had just celebrated our thirteenth birthdays a few days before, on the same day, the fifteenth of May; and in obedience to this fateful sign we promptly decided to fall in love. Walks on the green malls of the Volksgarten, mutual assurances of affection, a pressure of the hand, a look, and other ways of making ourselves understood from window to window, some of them incredibly naive—once I stood on a chair to show my beloved my first pair of long trousers—these were the innocent expressions of our love; but in spite of the harmless beginnings and progress of our relationship, our parents were indignant. Once I walked into the room just as my father and mother were discussing the necessity of coming to some sort of understanding with Fännchen's parents, so that at least our scandalous window telegraphy might cease. This we had developed to perfection with the help of window cushions and lighted candles. But such measures proved to be unnecessary because that autumn Fännchen's family moved, and since neither my beloved nor I enjoyed much freedom, there was nothing for me to do but wander around after school in the vicinity of their new apartment in the Wieden district and hope by some happy chance to catch a glimpse of her. But this was not to be until spring came around again. Then I began to meet her fairly regularly in the Volksgarten on evenings when the weather was good or when I didn't have to participate in the rides out into the country with my father, which now made me feel increasingly desperate. Fännchen and I exchanged letters, we assured each other of our love, we had our little differences, and since our friends—male and female—our confidants and those who didn't approve of us, had to play their parts, there was no lack of talebearing and petty jealousies with the subsequent reconciliations. In short it was a typical adolescent love affair such as a fourteen-year-old *Gymnasium* student and especially a poet feels he owes himself. Unfortunately, however, the best ingredient was missing, to which a bittersweet poem written at the time bears rather humiliating witness. It opens with the words, "And not a single little kiss yet from her rosy lips. . . ."

Nearly all the young ladies and gentlemen who belonged to our circle, singly or in pairs, have been not very artfully but quite faithfully described in outlines and fragments written in those days —in a comic epic, *Meyeriad,* and in a humorous novel, *Academic Hearts (Akademische Herzen).* In the former I seem to be following in the footsteps of Kortum, poet of the Jobsiad, whereas in the novel, influences of the charming and inventive writer Hackländer, and of Winterfeld who was so much more banal, are quite obvious. In some passages, whenever I was wise enough to adhere to realistic reporting, I think I achieved a quite passable description of the fun we had; and the parts that take place in school or in the Volksgarten betray a self-irony not often found at my age, an irony however which more often than not was considerably mitigated by my sympathy for myself. But wherever I daringly tried to introduce university students or older men, ballet dancers or demonic baronesses, in a satirical-sentimental or frivolous vein, the wit is dulled and the contrivance foolish.

In other efforts dating back to these years, that fascinating couple, Arthur-Fännchen, turns up beside other figures from our familiar circle, with nothing but their real names to remind one of their actuality. An absurd farce, *Carnival Night Tales (Fastnachtsgeschichten);* another, not much more sensible one entitled *Oh, what joy to travel! (O, welche Lust, zu reisen!),* and a three-act comedy, *The Inimical Hoteliers (Die feindlichen Hoteliers)* (1878), in which I occasionally imitated Kotzebue's style quite cleverly, may count as examples of this highly naive form of writing with living characters.

Most of my Volksgarten friends, even Fännchen, portrayed in perhaps an even more lively fashion in these writings than in my memory, especially in the novel fragment, disappeared from my life during the inclement seasons, to turn up again with the burgeoning of nature and the renewed possibilities of walks in the park. Only one remained with me also during the winter months, Jacques Pichler, who appears in the *Meyeriad* and *Academic*

Hearts (Akademische Herzen) as "Steile," a good-natured, harm-less fellow with a typically Viennese elegance, who never let his studies worry him. For a while he was my companion at billiards but later, after having become superfluous as a confidant, he was dropped not only by me but also by my closer friends. He finally reached the university level, belatedly; it took him even longer to get his degree in medicine. His first practice was with an army unit; finally he ended up in civilian life as a dentist.

I want to mention a few other figures, fleetingly; above all two who stand out not only because of their luck with ladies of all categories, with young girls as well as the coarser type of female, but also because of their urge to talk about their successes. I have in mind Emil Weichsel, a jovial, superficial business-school stu-dent, and Krisar, a more seriously inclined polytechnic scholar, and a third whom we called "the carnation beast" behind his back. He had the boutonnière he always wore to thank for the first part of his name and had earned the second, less gentle designation, because he dared to pay court to my beloved. He was not my only, and by no means my most dangerous, rival. Joseph Kranz, later lawyer and financier, expressed his admiration of my Fännchen in poems which seemed to me much better than mine, and who knows—perhaps they were. A few decades later, when we spoke once of these bygone times, he expressed his regret, not only for me but also for himself, that "in those days" we hadn't been more mature and adroit.

There were two schoolmates with whom I was on more intimate terms than with those just mentioned. Both were a few years older than I and were forced to leave school before graduating because of their lack of enthusiasm for learning, their general instability and a few circumstances that were not their fault. One of them, Moritz Wechsel, came from a poor Jewish family who had emi-grated from America; he was therefore able to take it upon him-self to teach my brother and me the rudiments of the English lan-guage. My father, in benevolent commiseration for this poor schoolmate of mine, gave his permission for the lessons. They soon turned out to be fruitless and were discontinued, but not our friendship, which I had no intention of giving up since Moritz sympathized not only with my love affair but more seriously than anyone else ever had with my literary aspirations. He dealt with them like a full-fledged critic and in an unfavorable review of *Tarquinius Superbus,* Part Three, turned out to be a born journalist if only by the fact that he called me, sarcastically, "Herr Sch." Later, when he brought a report on my drama, *The Rape of the Sabine Women* (*Der Raub der Sabinerinnen*), to a close with the words, "My hat off to a poet who shows promise," one could fairly sense the ominous smell of printer's ink. If only they still existed, it would be possible to trace the difference between our world viewpoints from a series of compositions in which we debated with each other. He was the stoic; I was the hedonist, as is quite evident by the title I gave to the entire series: *Fruere Vita* (*Enjoy Life*). I think I may safely say that my outlook was more sincerely expressed and his more skillfully formulated.

He was a short, pale, bushy-headed boy, poorly groomed and dispirited. The aura of a dismal ghetto atmosphere hung over him, an ambiance that emanated even more palpably from the apartment in the Leopoldstadt district where he lived. He stuck to me all the more closely since there were not many others who wanted to have anything to do with him; but our friendship also waned after he left school, and when he set out on the career for which he was best fitted, I lost track of him completely. All I knew was that he was political correspondent for one of our leading Viennese newspapers. Our subsequent meetings were brief, and years later, in the summer of 1915, on the occasion of our first lengthy conversation in the lobby of a hotel in Ischl, all I could see, instead of the squat, gray-haired old man in a loden suit, editor of the *Neues Wiener Journal,* was the pale Jewish boy, who when we were still school boys, and long before the advent of Maximilian Harden and other stern critics, had disparagingly called me "Herr Schnitzler."

My father's objections to my friendship with Moritz Wechsel were of a pedagogic nature, but a schoolmate of mine, Adolf Weizmann, who could scarcely have been classified as a better student and who anyway counted Moritz as a friend, tried to supplant him as my confidant. Weizmann's family lived in Moravia, also in poor circumstances, while he resided with relatives in Vienna. Unlike Moritz he was a tall, handsome boy, less inhibited and more forward. He was not only a more lyrical type than Moritz but because of his powerful, albeit rather dry, voice, of which he was inordinately proud, was filled with oratorical and theatrical aspirations. In 1876, on a school outing which took place every year on the first of May and was chaperoned by one of our professors, he revealed to Moritz and me, with rather mysterious overtones but with the inclusion of some most convincing details, that he had a platonic relationship with a cousin, whereupon I could think of nothing better to do than reveal my affair of the heart to him. Shortly after that he admitted, with a superior smile, that he had invented his little story in order to get mine— which he had suspected for some time—out of me. I wasn't offended, and from then on divided my favors equally between him and Moritz, not without some teasing, jealousies and injured feelings between all parties concerned. Adolf also soon became indispensable to me as literary adviser and critic, and I have saved the version of *Tarquinius Superbus,* Part One, in which he inscribed some quite clever remarks with examples from the classics. His letters too were filled with such commentary. In this way he soon became my best friend and maintained the position for quite some time after leaving school during the sixth or seventh year. We would walk the streets for hours, he declaiming *Faust* and *Uriel Acosta;* we would sit, without permission, in coffeehouse corners or small sweet-shops, conversing on serious topics, above all on poetry and the theater; sometimes though we just chatted aimlessly. One of the many hundreds of hours spent together stands out in my mind with exceptional clarity—the cool, windy, early spring day on which we strolled through the Prater amusement area between booths which were still closed, munching bread and cheese.

The theater was not only his main interest—once I felt impelled to pawn my watch so that he might buy a ticket for a performance of *Götz* in the Burgtheater—but to go on the stage was also his personal dream for the future. In fact, with a recommendation from my father he once had the famous elocution professor Alexander Strakosch test him for his suitability as an actor. Strakosch explained to him that he would ruin his voice, which was still not fully developed, if he took elocution lessons at that point; so Adolf temporarily gave up his plan for a theatrical career, also for more material reasons. After a short interval as tutor, with the obligatory falling in love with the rich and beautiful daughter of a millionaire whose son he was coaching, he resumed the profession of traveling salesman, which had been interrupted by his years of military service, and for which he was better suited than he would ever have cared to admit. Our ties loosened, not only because we were separated physically but because I had never had any illusions about his obsequious and not wholly sincere character, a conclusion that did not require any great understanding of human nature. But this was not to remain the only case in which such recognition failed to influence my feelings of sympathy as long as I thought I could profit intellectually or at least find some modest inspiration in the continuation of a friendship. Naturally I learned later how to take better care of my soul than in those days of my youth; even if not always of my heart, especially where women were concerned. I was scarcely ever the one to make the first overtures, which may be traced back simply but not entirely to a combination of a certain coolness in my nature and a self-absorption which was later frequently characterized as reserve and preoccupation, and sometimes, all too harshly, as egoism. But it is certainly true that I preferred to let people come to me rather than go to them. However, once a relationship was established, no one could accuse me of a lack of sincerity or warmth.

Even in those young years I am sure it was frequently not my personality as such that won me friends. Without wishing to cast any doubt on the spontaneity of the emotions of which I was the happy recipient, the desire to gain a materially better or socially somewhat higher position by befriending the doctor's or professor's son must have played a part, consciously or subconsciously, with some of my comrades, with Moritz and Adolf, for instance, whom I have already mentioned. With others a more natural relationship was possible because of our social equality, and was easily enhanced by mutual spheres of interest outside school, for as long as these happened to last.

The first boy I must mention in this category is Richard Horn, in whose family circle I felt very much at home long after any great friendship still existed between us. We met above all in our love of the romantic. Among the poets, E. T. A. Hoffmann was our favorite; after him came Tieck and Immermann. Their influence showed up in quite a few of my outlines and efforts of those days, most clearly perhaps in a childish, somewhat mawkish piece, *The Story of the Poet Amadeus* (*Geschichte von Amadeus, dem Poeten*), which in the end I botched completely. My favorite of E. T. A. Hoffmann's works was *Murr, the Cat* (*Kater Murr*). Tieck came next with *Sternbald's Wanderings* (*Sternbalds Wanderungen*) and *William Lovell*. Immermann enchanted me, not only with his *Münchhausen*, but with a much weaker work—*The Epigones*. My idea of striking up a correspondence with an unknown person, who in a newspaper advertisement was looking for female companionship, was less romantic than mischievous. I signed with the name of a character from *The Epigones*—*Flämmchen*, or Little Flame. Since I soon tired of the lark, something that happened to me frequently, also in the case of more sensible behavior, my last letter was seemingly too transparent. My partner, realizing that he had been fopped, didn't reply.

A correspondence with Richard Horn had a more genuinely romantic aspect. It includes extra leaflets in the Jean Paul manner—not that I, for my part, would ever have read beyond *Katzenberger's Resort Trip* (*Katzenbergers Badereise*) and *Quintus Fixlein*—and pedantic chancery councillors and demonic archivists, in the genre of E. T. A. Hoffmann, haunt the pages. The main content though remains the idle babble of school boys and reports of piquant events experienced, or at any rate observed, which Richard seems to have enjoyed in the primitive bath house of a Salzkammergut lake. I still have his letters; he destroyed mine later because, so he wrote, his feelings were hurt over the fact that at a certain time I had given up all my friends from an earlier, pre-literary epoch, which generally speaking wasn't true. A character trait that still makes its presence felt, even after thirty—which was when Richard destroyed my letters—and after fifty—which was when he told me about it—has to be recognized, in fact must be deeply rooted and pre-shaped from birth; and actually over-sensitivity and a tendency toward maudlinism was strongly developed in Richard even in those boyhood years. Otherwise he was an ambitious fellow, but not very perceptive and with a leaning toward irony and arrogance. His rapturous sentiments for a talented, charming boy his own age repeatedly aroused my impatience and scorn. The fellow was as pretty as a girl—one boy went so far as to proclaim him the Savior!—and there was a certain amount of rivalry to win favor with him, entirely without his encouragement—he seemed unmoved by it—but the whole thing struck me as ridiculous and slightly repulsive. Those involved were totally unconscious of the fact that homosexual feelings might be playing a part in their adoration. So was I, since none of us had any idea of the existence, much less of the important role being allotted to such drives in the human soul, which today, in my opinion, is overestimated. Like me, Richard experimented not only in the field of *belles-lettres* but also composed short pieces for the piano, in the Schumann tradition, some of which met with the approval of his uncle, Ignaz Brüll. Yet he soon abandoned his creative efforts in both arts, and rightly so, and he was satisfied to enjoy and understand them in a somewhat limited and complacent fashion, although where music was concerned his appreciation was lively and genuine. We were agreed above all in our love of Schumann. My interest in music had in the meantime progressed considerably. I went to many concerts and with fair regularity to the Philharmonic and the Hellmesberger Quartet. A new piano teacher, Anton Rückauf, young, gentle, with blond curly hair, seemed to consider me quite talented. I got along with him better than with my former teachers, and he declared that if I had been willing to apply myself more I could have gone further than Moritz Rosenthal, whom, by the way, he detested.

I continued to play duets with Rückauf or my mother, and liked to improvise on the piano, in the course of which I was sometimes lucky enough to hit on a melodic passage or a pleasing harmony. But when my teacher asked me once to elaborate on a theme he had given me, I failed utterly, and just barely managed to extricate myself by going over into a Bach-type fugue, something that came easiest to me. I was spared then and later, even in my most inspired moments, the danger of imagining I had a creative gift for music, because I was always to remain aware of the fundamental difference between artistry and dilettantism, if for no other reason than that I had been granted true understanding and talent in another field (I am not referring here to its measure). This basic difference does not preclude the fact that the dilettante with taste may occasionally succeed, by a coincidence of favorable circumstances, in creating something of artistic value on a small scale; nor that even the most serious and dedicated artist, in a weak moment, or under the pressures of opposition, may not at some time or other produce something vapid, with a dilettantish effect. Faced with the work of a cultured person, of someone with taste, the thing to do, if doubts have to be assuaged, is to proceed from the singular accomplishment to the roots of the personality, which doesn't happen to be every man's inclination; and even the professional critic has been known to justify his verdict emotionally rather than reasonably. However, faced with the production of a lifetime, such judgments are not so difficult, but I doubt very much if it would have been possible to find in what I produced poetically up to my seventeenth year—thoroughly unoriginal and for the most part childish stuff—any trace of individuality or anything that might have proclaimed the developing artist. I don't even know if I felt thus blessed; whether even I took seriously my occasional efforts to appeal to the judgment of those in my immediate surroundings or to the public at large. Wasn't I half-consciously playing a part for my own benefit and for that of others, in this case the aspiring poet? It still did not seem advisable to show my father the results of my efforts to write novels and plays, much less my love poems. I did not reveal *Tarquinius Superbus* to him until my sixteenth birthday and then without expecting him to read it. Yet he had previously shown poems of mine—not at my request—to friends of his, for their judgment; for instance to an editor of the *Neue Freie Presse*, the kindly humorist J. Oppenheim, as I can see from a letter written by my father, which must have accompanied my poems and somehow come back to him. He also seems to have shown some of my writings to the novelist and "Concordia" president, Johannes Nordmann, who according to an entry in my diary found my poems "charming," possibly only because the author was the son of the "Concordia" doctor to whom Nordmann felt obligated. I don't recall how—again according to an entry in my diary—the novelist and traveler to the Orient, Vincenti, happened to get the idea that I had "a talent for epic writing," nor what he had read of my works, nor how he got hold of them. Moritz Wechsel had permitted a Frau Schaff, whom I didn't know personally, to take a look at the fragment of a novel. She had declared that for a fifteen-year-old boy I was too frivolous and had gone on to say that according to my precocity and handwriting I must be small, deformed and un-

stable. In July 1887, I sent a few poems to someone called Sieg-
mey, the editor of some weekly or other, and received an encouraging reply which never led to anything. I submitted a few verses
to the Viennese *Salonblatt,* under the romantic pseudonym of
Richard Bleich, (Pallid), without however being considered
worthy of a reply. The same thing happened to the poems I addressed to Robert Hamerling in Graz, even after I had been so
bold as to appeal—I admit, in rather poor taste—to the possibly
not forgotten dreams of his own sixteen-year-old poetic aspirations.
A light article entitled "Twenty Million Worlds," was written with
a Monday weekly in mind, in which I had found a fascinating
astronomical-cosmic piece written in popular style, dealing with
the manifold aspects of the solar system; but the editor, less fascinated than I, rejected the piece with an ironic reference to my
youthful spirit. A harmless, foolish little poem, "Omnibus Dreams,"
was turned down politely by a colleague of mine called Ostersetzer, who was editing a school paper, because its content was
"unsuitable for class officers." I can't remember how another
humorous poem, "Oh my, how did that happen?" was received by
my classmates, to whom I read it aloud during a recess period;
but I took my failures just as lightly as my occasional small successes. I valued not only Joseph Kranz's poems considerably
higher than mine, but also those by Adolf Weizmann. Meanwhile
I had struck up a friendship with another school and poetry
friend, a Tyrolese called Engelbert Obendorf, with whom I liked
to correspond in doggerel during class. I used to visit him occasionally in his student quarters in the Lerchenfelderstrasse, opposite the old church which was to assume such importance to me in
later years. Once I left a play with him, of which two acts were
completed. It was called *The Wandering Jew (Der Ewige Jude),*
and meant more to me than anything else I had ever written because I felt that in it the essential aspects of my style, which I liked
to call "modern romanticism," found their most decisive expression. In spite of repeated dunning, I was never able to get it back
until at last, in a humble, anguished letter, he confessed that the
maid had accidentally burned it. Since I was never able to recon-
struct the beginning nor make up my mind to pick up the theme
again, it was easy to tell myself that with this fragment the best
and most promising thing I had ever written had been lost.

Beside the above-mentioned works and a number of poems, a few of which I copied into a notebook more precisely and clearly than was my wont, and dedicated to "My Fännchen," under the heading of "Dreams," I also embarked on innumerable themes in prose or dramatic form, among them a romantic play in doggerel, *The Comedians (Die Komödianten)*. However, since I invariably started off without a plan and let my pen run on at will, I usually paused when encountering the first serious obstacle and put the thing aside, never to take it up again. Although I was understandably not without vanity, I don't think I was overly ambitious; certainly I did not suffer from any great resoluteness or drive, and the idea of some day becoming a professional writer was far from my mind then, and for a long time to come; in a sense, perhaps, always. Through my father's example and ideal image I seemed destined inexorably and hopefully for a medical career. However, I showed no signs of a serious interest in the natural sciences which may have been due more to a mistake in upbringing than to a lack of ability. Altogether this was an era in which we were not directed sufficiently to see and watch, and the school curriculum —which in the meantime has surely been improved—did not put enough stress on the observation and study of nature; added to which we were badly off in so far as the professors instructing us in these categories were concerned. A Professor Mik was supposed to teach us natural history, something he attended to in a dry, sulky manner; and it was crystallography which gave me the greatest difficulty because of my poor grasp of geometry. Professor Dvorak instructed us in physics and mathematics. Not only did he know nothing, but he was also an unjust and venal man who treated some of his pupils—those who he knew came from wealthy families—badly, until the expected success of his maneuvers materialized in the form of money or presents. You could buy him off with relatively small sums; the safest thing though was to ask him to come to the house to give private lessons, which is how we got around it. Sometimes he was wrong in his evaluation of a pupil's financial standing, as for instance in the case of my friend Adolf, who was in no position to change his probably well-earned bad marks for better ones by producing a few ducats, which would probably have helped him to graduate. Soon after leaving the *Gymnasium,* the new Minister of Education, Gautsch, pen-

sioned Dvorak, without the customary honors, and another professor called Schenk, who could also be bribed but at least never
resorted to blackmail, and was moreover quite a good teacher of
his subject. Professor Dvorak's daughter, whom we had admired
shyly because of her beauty and bad reputation, became a popular actress, and as Josefa in Anzengruber's *The Fourth Commandment* gave one of her finest performances. I didn't get to know
her personally until a few years before her death, for which she
had alcoholism to thank.

For a while Zitkovsky remained with us as teacher of German
and history of literature. He and I never learned to like each
other, and this may have been the main reason, and not my quite
healthily developed argumentativeness nor my sense of justice,
why I raised my hand one day when Zitkovsky spoke somewhat
derogatively of Anastasius Grün. To his irritated question as to
what I wanted, I replied with the simple statement that, after all,
Anastasius Grün was a poet of stature. For a long time this was
quoted in class, more to make fun of me than of the professor.

In time Ludwig Blume, who had taught us German during our
first year, took over our German class. Contrary to most of his colleagues, he was well-to-do and was of interest to us boys not only
for this reason but also because he had the reputation of being a
man-of-the-world, whom one could meet frequently on the streets
of the inner city in the company of women of doubtful repute. But
a pretty girl, who appeared with conspicuous frequency in the
main hall of our school always, strangely enough, asking Blume
how her brother was getting along, succeeded in guiding this
risqué professor onto safer paths; and we were soon able to greet
him as a good husband and brother-in-law of our worst pupil. The
latter was advised, in spite of this new relationship, to try his luck
at some other seat of learning. Formerly we had attributed the
fact that Blume would fall asleep at his desk to his wild life, but
we soon discovered that the serener joys of marriage did nothing
to change the ease with which he tired. He would still start up
out of a deep sleep when a pupil had finished his oral examination
and try to read on the faces of those who had been listening,
whether the student had said the right thing, whereupon he
would send him back to his seat either with the words, "Well,
all right," or, "It could have been better." He also had his brighter

moments during which he would hold forth with verve and humor, especially when launched on a familiar subject or one with which he was in sympathy. He was a staunch nationalist, and his favorite question in history class was, "Who can list the German kaisers?" With skill it was possible to be called on to answer this question several times in the course of the semester. In this way I was able to improve my originally poor history marks and during the last two years achieve the desirable exemption from the history finals. We were probably correct in attributing Blume's enthusiasm for Wagner, whom he considered not only Germany's greatest musician but also its most renowned poet, to his political rather than to his aesthetic leanings. Similarly his antipathy to all things Jewish was rooted more in conviction than in emotion. For even if it amused him to pronounce the names of his pupils with a certain tendentious emphasis, this did not prevent him from writing the "excellent" he deserved into Spitzer, Samuel's report card; and Kohn, Isidor got what he deserved when, unlike diligent Kohn, Richard or Löwy, Ernst, he failed.

In those days—the late-blossoming period of liberalism—anti-Semitism existed, as it had always done, as an emotion in the numerous hearts so inclined and an idea with great possibilities of development, but it did not play an important role politically or socially. The word hadn't even been invented; and one was satisfied to call those who were particularly inimical toward Jews, almost contemptuously, *Judenfresser,* or "Jew devourers." A certain separation of Gentiles and Jews into groups which were not kept strictly apart (nor was there any idea of such a division into "parties") could be felt always and everywhere, also therefore in school; but only one member of our class could have been termed a *Judenfresser,* and that was a certain youth called Deperis. He was unpopular and considered a ridiculous fellow not only because of this characteristic, but also because he was a dandy and a snob. It was furthermore taken amiss that although he was always exceedingly well-dressed and quite evidently from a good family, he did not have to pay for his tuition and was moreover one of the densest pupils. He is supposed to have retained this reputation later, in the civil service, where he was finally able to achieve the position of departmental head. Only one other pupil could contest his reputation as class dullard, a good, decent boy called Karl Leth. Forty years were to go by before this worthy civil servant managed to become minister.

In the classical languages our old Windisch was followed by Professor Hauler who was efficient, strict and fair. In the fifth year, Jacob Meister, a devout but quite malicious man, taught us Greek, and we were in the habit of making fun of him because of the peculiar way he pronounced every "k" like a "ch," and for his boring and unctuous way of talking. Once, when he started one of his castigating lectures with the words, "Well, now, whoever is at fault is going to have to . . ." the whole class finished in unison, "pay the piper!" whereupon Professor Meister cast his eyes to the heavens, with which he seemed to stand on very good terms, and went on with the business at hand. The boredom with which he and the majority of his philological colleagues introduced us to the classics gave me the idea for a farce in which Homer, in the Underworld, is suffering from stomach pains, and comes to the conclusion, after visiting this earth in the guise of a Swedish school inspector, that his pains could be blamed on the foul treatment being dealt out to him by *Gymnasium* professors. Thirty years later two Viennese writers did something similar in a much more successful playlet, in which Goethe is shown as the despairing victim of his interpreters.

Johann Auer, a secular priest, taught us Latin for a year or two. He was popular not only because of his benevolence but also because of his matter-of-fact and sagacious utterances which were frequently given a burlesque touch by some absent-minded twist or other. Many of his priceless sayings, and naturally some we made up, were published at the time in a slender volume entitled *Aueriana.* I also made a collection of things I had heard with my own ears; unfortunately I lost it and can recall only one saying which went, "Fragrancy is something with which the ancient Greeks were already familiar."

Auer was a gaunt, rangy old man whose figure blends in my mind with that of the aged Grillparzer. He was a truly beneficent personality and in his subject, philology, a scholar of stature. Rarely did he lose his temper, and once I was the cause of such an explosion when I threw a paper ball at the rostrum, the sort of nonsense I didn't usually go in for. For the first and only time my name was inscribed in the demerit book, and this by a teacher who hardly ever asserted his authority with such measures. He did so with the humiliating words, "Arthur Schnitzler behaves like a ragamuffin." I was so upset about it that when my father and I happened to pass the school that evening in our carriage, I was suddenly attacked by violent nausea. On a later occasion, however, Auer gave me an example of his esteem which touched me all the more because, after his former attitude, I was in no way prepared for anything like it. After one of his questions, I raised my hand, whereupon a sniggering could be heard in the classroom. I can't recall whether my schoolmates expected something comic or impertinent, or if the suppressed laughter arose after my answer, which may not have been generally comprehensible; anyway, with a threatening look at his pupils, Auer cried, "Don't laugh! Schnitzler is a genius!"

I also recall a discussion in which he declared that the ancient Romans had committed suicide by holding their breath, whereupon I took it upon myself to explain that such a form of suicide was impossible. With the beginning of a loss of consciousness, breathing would automatically have to recommence. Once, after he had moved into a summer apartment in Weidlingau to convalesce from a serious illness, I visited him in the company of a schoolmate, Richard Tausenau, about whom there will be more to tell when his turn comes. At the time we had got together mainly in the mischievous hope of bringing home a few juicy "Auerisms." But the estimable old man delivered nothing of the sort. He conversed with us amiably and wisely, pointed gaily from the veranda, where we were sitting, into the room where numerous small white boxes stood in neat rows on a table. He remarked with a smile that these were not intended as presents for lady visitors, which was what they looked like, but were file boxes for his study of the interrelationship of languages, on which he was still working. He proceeded to give us a few examples, thanked us warmly for our visit, and we parted from him, touched and not a little ashamed, with the unfortunately correct feeling that we had seen him for the last time.

And finally, a good memory—of Professor Konvalina, who beside teaching us the classical languages also gave us preparatory instruction in philosophy, in logic, therefore, and psychology. Considering the chicanery that was generally practiced by mem-

bers of the faculty, I appreciated it highly and counted it as a
sign of his more liberal thinking when, in spite of the occasionally
poor marks he had had to give me in the course of the semester,
he marked me "excellent" in my finals.

During my first *Gymnasium* years we had no instruction in the
Jewish religion. At the end of every semester we were given an
examination by a state-approved teacher, the results of which
were nearly always "excellent" and were inscribed in our school
reports. Later, however, study of the Bible and religion became
part of the school curriculum; Hebrew though was discontinued
and resumed only after I had finished school.

Rabbi Schmiedl was the first teacher of the Jewish religion to
appear at our school, a good-natured little man who made life
easy for us, a practice we did not repay in kind. If there
was too much chatter and restlessness, he would jump up and
down on the rostrum in despair, whimpering over and over again,
"But this isn't a school!" while we went on talking unconcernedly.
After him, Dr. David Weiss took the reins into his hands. He was
a scholarly, irascible and spiteful man, who with shrieking severity
tried to enforce the respect that was perhaps unjustly denied him.
He had a special aversion to me which during the last semester
put me into a vexing, in fact for a time almost precarious, position.
We were reading and interpreting the *Book of Job,* and when we
got to the verse—I can't recall the exact words, only the meaning
—in which Job curses the day he was born, Professor Weiss asked
why this, contrary to all logic, was not to be considered blasphemy. I raised my hand with no bad intentions but solely out
of my rationalistic, atheistic world viewpoint to which I felt in
duty bound at the time, and said that I thought I could clarify
the contradiction by the fact that after all, God wasn't responsible for Job's birth. Weiss worked himself into a fine rage and
threatened to denounce me to the director for my blasphemous
impertinence, and I had every reason to fear that he would demand my expulsion. But I got there ahead of him. Directly after
the fateful lesson I went to the director, who was also our Greek
professor, and explained exactly what had happened, with the
result that Dr. Weiss didn't get very far with his denunciation,
and the matter ended without any further consequences for me.

And so I was able to hold my own in the upper classes, not

as one of the first but always among the better students. My diligence evidently sufficed, the outside coaching I received was more than adequate, and there was no lack of time for things which, according to school concepts and in other respects as well could only be called killing time. The theater, concerts, reading, long walks and lengthy talks with friends, my poetizing—all of it could be fitted easily into the day, and when the clement seasons came around again, to say nothing of vacations which, except for a few weeks of travel were spent in the city, I would really have had more time for my blonde Fännchen than I assigned to her in the end, for practical and emotional reasons.

After two years had gone by during which we had seen very little of each other, our friendship seemed to begin all over again on a beautiful September day in the year 1878. This came about through the selfless intervention of a young man I had never seen before, who came up to me while I was strolling along one of the paths of the Volksgarten and handed me a rose. He said he had been instructed to do so by "a pretty trio." I accepted the flower, with my thanks; he said, "I envy you," and vanished. His name was Jaspisstein and I never saw or heard of him again. "The pretty trio" consisted of Fännchen and two friends her age who had been watching the scene from a bench, like school girls, highly amused. Shortly after that they kept passing me with allusive remarks, but not until a few days later, while I was sitting on one of the benches in the Volksgarten, working on *Tarquinius Superbus,* and Fännchen sent her little brother, Fritz, over to ask me for the rose I was wearing in my buttonhole, did I feel impelled to approach her. From then on we simply picked up where we had left off two summers before. Since we had meanwhile reached the threshold of young man- and womanhood, our relationship, although innocent enough, took a more tender and turbulent direction. We no longer needed the excuse of a game of tag or forfeits to find ourselves embracing and kissing on the dusky paths of the Rathaus or Volksgarten. But even more vividly than these evening trysts, I recall the walks we took in the deserted summer streets of the city, the wonderful coolness that was wafted down to us from the high stone walls of the Minoritenkirche and the old palaces surrounding it. Fännchen was frequently in the company of friends who encouraged or disrupted any games

we happened to be playing, also our more serious moments. There
was a charming red-headed girl with whom I fell a little bit in
love, and a plain, pale, all too clever one who fell in love with
me. A thin girl with freckles, who was constantly ill-humored,
harbored a positively inimical attitude toward our young love and
I took my revenge, poetically, in a satirical comedy, *Morality*, in
which the disappearance from the face of the earth of that ethical
quality was due to the fact that chaste Fräulein Lena had mo-
nopolized all of it.

It may seem strange that until now I have had little more to
say about Fännchen's personality than that she was blonde. Am
I so chary with my description of her because so many decades
have passed since then, and could I have explained better at the
time, to others and to myself, why I loved her and no other girl?
I don't think so. She was quite pretty, moderately bright and
possessed of as much education as was considered necessary at
the time for the daughter from a middle-class Jewish family.
I never saw her as an outstanding personality, nor did I feel that
there was anything exceptional about the emotions that united us.
Even while experiencing it, I was fully aware of the typicalness
of our "love affair," and felt no less elation or pain than any
more naive spirit would have done in my place. For even then
I did not have what people like to call illusions, a state of mind
which one hears praised so frequently as enviable but for which
I have never felt the slightest desire. In spite of this I have experienced as much good luck and misfortune as the next person,
and the fact that I have never tried to deceive myself about the
nature of my feelings nor the quality of those humans to whom
I felt close, has not saved me from suffering injustices nor from
inflicting them.

My relationship to this golden-haired love of my youth remained
within the limits customarily prescribed in circles such as ours,
due, I suppose, to unpropitious circumstances, but mainly because
of our inexperience, shyness and so-called upbringing; probably
also because of a lack of true passion. Still, the magic of femininity
had begun to affect me in a more general way. Although a sense
of propriety, or at least a feeling for discretion, were so strong in
me that I once considered it necessary to rebuke our French *bonne*
who—perhaps not altogether unintentionally—had changed her

blouse in my presence, the rouged and suggestively winking ladies whom we passed on our expeditions in the inner city interested me all the more because most of my friends had already begun collecting personal experiences from these sources. I can still recall how Adolf, after his first love adventure for cash, in exaggerated caution immediately set about regaining the vigor of youth which he thought he had lost, by consuming a meal consisting of two portions of roast beef in the Gasthaus zur Linde. However, due to the meagerness of his budget and the increasing number of such adventures, he was soon forced to abandon these costly substitute measures.

We gave the more startling of these females in the Kärntner-strasse the names of Greek goddesses, and it was Venus, Hebe and Juno who inflamed our imaginations most. Despite my well-grounded fear of any too intimate relationship with these charmers, my curiosity found an excuse for my first outing into this questionable quarter of the city. Freely copying my friend Adolf, who after bestowing his favors on such a lady would follow it up by reproaching her, with unctuous lectures, for her profligate way of life and advising her to choose one more virtuous, I decided to restrict myself to a solely disciplinarian approach. Thus, on a beautiful summer's day, with honorable but not entirely sincere intentions, I followed my tow-headed Venus to her quarters on the Stock-im-Eisen Platz. While the pretty young thing reclined naked on the divan, I leaned against the window frame, still fully dressed in my boyishly cut suit, my straw hat and cane in my hands, and appealed to the conscience of my beauty, who was bored and amused at the same time, and had certainly expected better entertainment from her sixteen-year-old customer, who was urging her to find a more decent and promising profession than the one she had chosen. I tried to emphasize what I had to say by reading some appropriate passages aloud from a book I had brought along for the purpose—unfortunately I can't remember its name. Without succeeding in convincing her, or she me, which she tried to do in a much cleverer fashion than could be said of my approach, I left her with two gulden, for which I had my mother to thank. She had given them to me after I had declared that I simply had to have the new Gindeley *Outline of World History*. After that, "the new Gindeley" was given a piquant double meaning among us depraved youths. In the following months I followed up my visits to Venus with ones that included some of the other goddesses. The disciplinary aspect of these outings was gradually reduced to a minimum, still I managed for a long time to preserve myself from the ultimate fall of man in the Biblical sense.

For some time now I had been keeping a diary in which I included, beside school events, all sorts of highly personal experiences, such as the ones just recounted, in disconnected notes; still they would have been comprehensible to someone reading it even if he were not one of my bosom friends. To the last diary, from the winter of 1878 to 1879 I had confided my burgeoning interest in our dentist's youngest daughter; yet Fännchen, who in spite of all other entanglements somehow managed to hold her incontestable, one might almost say academic, place as the love of my youth, was scarcely mentioned. It also gave intimations of my visits to a certain Emilie, who after I had finished off the Greek goddesses, had been the next in line. I remember dimly that she was beginning to truly imperil me, not only physically but also spiritually, since I believed seriously that I was in love with her.

My report for the first semester of my eighth school year was middling, and not to the satisfaction of my parents; and the rather oppressive atmosphere at home, which had been brewing for some time now and which was not helped by my obvious neglect of my studies, my social life with friends to whom my father liked to refer disparagingly, nor by a certain unruliness in my behavior, now became increasingly oppressive and gloomy. One morning, just as I was leaving for school, my father, with a deep frown, asked me to get something or other for him from his study; I believe it was a pencil. I feared the worst and was right. When I got back to my parents' bedroom my father was waiting for me with a severe expression on his face, my little red diary in his hand; I was told that a few days ago he had opened the drawer of my desk with a key (which I certainly hadn't given him), had read my diary and put it back again—evidently I had interrupted my last entry at an especially suspenseful passage— and today had finished reading what crimes I had recorded in the meantime. To deny any such irrefutable evidence was futile. Silently I had to let a censorious lecture pass over me and in the end scarcely dared, with a few timid words, express my consternation over his breach of confidence, which to me didn't seem sufficiently justified by any patriarchal relationship between father and son. In the end he took me into his study and told me to leaf through three huge yellow Kaposi atlases on syphilis and diseases of the skin, so that I might learn from its illustrations the possible consequences of a sinful life. The sight of them had a lasting effect on me and I may have this experience to thank for the fact that for quite some time I avoided such indiscretions and decided that it would be advisable to discontinue my visits to Emilie and other women like her. Although my father had undoubtedly been moved by the best intentions, and even if it was impossible to deny him the desired success of his action, I couldn't forget for a long time the treacherous method he had used; and if we were never able to establish a completely open relationship, the ineradicable memory of this betrayal of trust surely played its part.

The atmosphere at home brightened. I pulled myself together, at least to all appearances, and was able to look forward to my finals with a reduced sense of worry because I could rely with a fair amount of certainty on being relieved of two subjects—history, thanks to the fluency with which I could rattle off the names of the German kaisers; and physics, thanks to Professor Dvorak's coaching. I had enough time therefore to work on several serious dramas, and to play billiards, a game I had been indulging in enthusiastically for some time now (although once I had to endure days of anxiety when a patient of my father's caught me at it and I feared that he would betray me, with the ensuing furore at home—fortunately nothing came of it), and also, as the benign seasons returned, to resume my usual walks in the Volksgarten with Fännchen. Our friendship became closer and we began to feel increasingly impatient with the accidental and deliberate disruptions to which our still oh, so innocent meetings were subjected. On the evening of the commencement of my written examinations, she pressed a note into my hand which read, "Don't you love me any more?" Since we scarcely ever had an opportunity to exchange expressions of love, this was followed by a tender correspondence, so to speak, from hand to hand.

The affairs of my heart occupied me to a far greater extent than the questions on my examination papers, and I was never to learn whether I had answered them correctly or not because, on the last morning, while we were translating from the Greek into German, the school director suddenly appeared in the classroom —he was also our Greek professor—and announced that all those who had left the room that morning for a few minutes, with the customary excuse, were to be searched. I was one of those faced with this humiliating procedure, together with a dozen others, among them the director's son, who incidentally was one of the worst students; and they found on us what they would have found on every member of the class—dictionaries and ponies, the use of which was of course strictly forbidden during an examination. But I also had to show the director a small notebook which, for very good reasons, I had not left at home, however little it could possibly have helped me with Greek translation, namely a new diary, just begun. Overcome with shame, I had to stand there while the director read what I had written the evening before, for my eyes alone—my confession that I was in love, that I was in fact love *sick*, and other things that were not much brighter and had just as little to do with Greek. Silently he gave the notebook back to me, but he didn't mention a word about it to my father who insisted on coming to school the following day to hear more about what had transpired. Together with those found guilty with me, I had to repeat all my written examinations. The punishment didn't mean so much to me, but the fact that I had been caught and punished, and above all the circumstance that an unauthorized person had gained insight into my diary, was so humiliating that I told one of my schoolmates—it happened to be Richard Horn's best friend, Otto—in a house entry on the Ringstrasse immediately after the discovery, that I couldn't see any way out but to shoot myself, a mood that didn't last very long. I also tried to relieve myself, with moderate success, by writing a few bad verses on the subject.

I think I did just as well in the new examinations, without any forbidden props, as in the first series, which had been declared invalid. I also got through my orals, on July 8, 1879, so well that I passed with honors. But I had no reason to be especially proud of this. I had been relieved of history and physics, Dvorak had worked on the mathematic problems with me, all that was left therefore were German and the classical languages, which I was good at anyway. Later I found out that at the final faculty meeting, my mishap during the first written examinations had been overlooked; and although subsequently the suggestion was made that my honors be withdrawn, it was decided in the end to let things stand. What is more, I began to notice that Director Schmidt, who until then had struck me as a pedantic fellow, displayed a certain sympathy for me which I could date back to his reading of my diary. Thus I may have a nostalgic reminder of my director's youth, and, in a humorous association, my love for my blonde Fännchen, to thank for a distinction that was not entirely merited.

Book Three

✣)✦)✦)✦)✦)✦)✦)

September 1879 to July 1882

IT HAD ALWAYS been my dream, even as a small boy, to be a doctor, like Papa. Not only would this have meant that I could drive around all day long in a carriage, but I could have the coachman stop at every sweet shop, if I felt like it, and buy the most delicious pastries, much better than anything Frau Walz brought to our house on the first and fifteenth of every month, when she came to collect the rental money for the *fiacre* we leased by the month. But in a more serious vein—the example set by my father, and perhaps even more, the whole atmosphere at home, naturally had their effect on me from earliest childhood; and since no other profession had even been broached throughout my *Gymnasium* years, it transpired as a matter of course that in the autumn of the year 1879 I was enrolled in the faculty of medicine at the University of Vienna. Until now I had shown no signs of any specific endowment or even a noticeable interest in the natural sciences, but then, neither the *Gymnasium* curriculum nor the personalities of our professors had been conducive to inspiring me in such a direction. Moreover, our upbringing and teaching at home—and in other, similarly conditioned households—was rarely directed toward the palpable thing, nor to learning how to see and watch. For a long time therefore my attitude toward nature was a vaguely poetic-sentimental one rather than naively observing, and my thirst for knowledge was directed toward idealistic subject matter—history and psychology—rather than to

the appearance, presence and form of things. The lectures in elocution and language, which my father gave yearly at the Conservatory of Music, many of which I attended while still in the
Gymnasium, were also hardly inspirational from a medical viewpoint. Actually they were popular talks with which my father
liked to entertain his patients from the aristocratic and artistic
worlds, whom he was delighted to see in the audience, rather than
enlighten the elocution students of the Conservatory.

I had never even glanced at any medical books except for the
two atlases on diseases of the skin which my father had told me
to leaf through the spring before, for pedagogic reasons. After
passing my final examinations, he presented me as a matter of
course with Hyrtl's *Topographic Anatomy,* inscribed with a fond
dedication; but it remained unopened for the time being. With
perhaps a similar reticence, I turned away once in sudden dread
from the door of the anatomical dissecting room to which a young
medical student had offered to show me the way only a few
moments before. But another door was opened for me through
which I was able to walk from my boyish *Gymnasium* existence
into medical life. During the first weeks of September, a medical
convention was being held in Amsterdam, and I was permitted
to join my father, who had taken his entire family along on this
expedition to Holland, as prospective *studiosus medicinae* and
modest observer. I attended the usual open sessions and festive
occasions, and can best recall a steamboat excursion on the Zuider
Zee during which I saw the famous eye specialist, Professor Don-
ders, who was president of the convention, walking up and down
the deck, wearing a cape; on his arm a beautiful, tall young lady
who was his hostess at the convention.

Practical considerations also played their part when I decided
so unhesitatingly for a medical career. Certainly it never occurred
to me to protest against any of the sensible reasons put forth by
my father; but I did find it very depressing to be told right from
the start, repeatedly and with varying degrees of frankness, and
most frequently by my father himself, that it was going to be so
much easier for me than for most of my colleagues, since as the
son of a doctor and professor, my career was not only clearly
indicated but would also be made smoother for me. Soon the
material for a novella began to take shape in my mind, probably

in presentiment of the inhibitions which were bound to result from such obvious facilitation. Entitled *The Son of a Famous Man* (*Der Sohn des Berühmten*), and with the family of an artist as background, it was to reflect romantically enhanced possibilities of my own fate. I only wrote a few pages; the problem itself, however, was to remain with me for a long time, since the mood out of which it had been born was being fed constantly by the tactless and snide remarks I had to let pass as a medical student, and even later, as physician. Actually they were excusable, since my true nature and the proper direction of my talents were to reveal themselves to most people—in a sense even to myself—only very gradually. The medical elements which were undoubtedly present at the same time, developed within me later, paradoxically with increasing decisiveness the more I was permitted to withdraw from the field of medical duties and responsibilities.

The lectures began in October. I took anatomy with Langer; physiology with Brücke; chemistry with Ludwig; physics with Lang; but after a few weeks I stopped attending classes regularly, without giving a thought to making up for such criminal negligence by some sort of study at home. I wasn't much more industrious when it came to practical work in the dissecting room or in the physiological and chemistry laboratories. For the so-called preliminary examinations—mineralogy with Schrauf, zoology with Claus, botany with Wiesner—I at least prepared myself sufficiently so that I was able to complete all of them during my first year, and had not only my luck but probably also the benevolence of my examiners to thank for the fact that I passed the first two with honors.

It never occurred to me to join one of the student *"couleurs."* Altogether I never felt any desire to attach myself to a group with fixed duties and regulations. I did join one club—the German-Austrian Reading Society—albeit not because of its monarchic tendencies but rather because of certain advantages that went with its membership, for instance cheaper tickets at various theaters. Another leading student society at the University of Vienna —the Academic Reading Group—was German-nationalist in its political leanings, a trend which in those days and, justly or not, for a long time to come, was considered unpatriotic, if not treasonable, by the "good" Austrians, especially those ardent supporters of the monarchy. As a result there was friction between the two clubs which, if I am not mistaken, ended with the dissolution of the German-national one.

On the way home from one of the large student gatherings, which took place frequently on all sorts of occasions and at which political differences had been voiced in quite a few violent speeches, I entered into a lively discussion with a philosophy student, the brother of my former schoolmate, Fritz Wahle. I was defending the German-Austrian viewpoint, for reasons I don't recall; but I do remember that I was less concerned with proving my political point than with my dazzling dialectical prowess and my success with the young ladies who were walking home with us, one of whom was a charming cousin of my blonde Fännchen. I don't remember having been particularly interested in the problems up for discussion, except in so far as they included the anti-Semitism which had just begun to develop and which filled me with anxiety and bitterness. My reaction was not rooted solely in the fact that I was Jewish, nor was it the result of any personal experiences. These I was not to suffer in full measure until later. Actually neither the political nor the social aspects of the Jewish question aroused these early reactions in me. In accordance with my whole nature it was predominantly the psychological viewpoint that absorbed me. The religious factor played little or no part. I was repulsed by all dogma, from whichever pulpit it was preached or at whatever school it was taught. I found the subject in the true sense of the word, undiscussable. I had as little relationship to the so-called beliefs of my fathers—to that which was *truly* belief and not merely memory, tradition and atmosphere— as to any other religion. Yet the problem of religion in its widest sense occupied me more between the years of eighteen and twenty than ever before, perhaps even than at any later period of my life. According to my mental processes it had to flow together with the basic questions of philosophy. I am quite ready to admit that in all these disciplines—in so far as they were disciplines—I was a dilettante and remained one all my life. I lacked the patience, attentiveness, possibly also the acumen needed to reach the point where it would have been worth the effort to start studying them systematically, and I consoled myself with a thought that was probably heretical and certainly impudent, that whatever I needed

in the way of religion or philosophy I would do best to find out
or invent for myself, if it was to be of any use to me.

During my first two university years I sometimes felt the need
of coming to grips, in my own way, with the so-called eternal
truths. I jotted down various notes, all of them concerned with
"the thing in itself," from which I can see that I must have leafed
through a history of philosophy or even some of Kant's writings.
I read for the most part in the Imperial Library—*The Life of
Jesus,* by Renan, the *Gospels*—and in my diary dealt rationalisti-
cally with the legendary belief in miracles, maliciously with Pope
and clergy, and ended aphoristically with a statement which I
would let stand today, namely that in the course of centuries
Christianity had become *con*fused rather than *dif*fused. In my
fashion and unburdened by any scientific knowledge I tried to
elaborate on the cell theory, and considered myself a materialist
and atheist and was probably both just as little then as I am today.
For I was not sufficiently mature at the time to recognize that
there can be no such thing as materialist or atheist in the true
sense of the words; and that beyond the confines in which the
thinking man—according to temperament or mood—has felt or
expressed the conviction that "we shall never know," with indifference, with melancholy, lamenting or bitter, we find only idle
talk, quackery, humbug or insanity. At the same time, not as the
result of any profound thought but more as the expression of a
basic mood, I wrote the sentence, *If there is a God, then the way
he is honored by his believers may be considered blasphemy,* and
another: *It is nonsense to say, "As God wills." We will, God has
to.* Yet I probably sensed at the time, as is so frequently true of
sentences such as these, that the opposite might be just as true.

In my distaste for all zealotry and the clergy, I occasionally displayed a tactlessness which, in such early years, is excusable. It was
during the holidays between *Gymnasium* and university, perhaps
the summer before, that I listened to a sermon in the church,
Maria am Gestade. I happened to be facing the priest as he ex-
pounded things which I considered exceptional nonsense, and I
stared at him with deliberate scorn, whereupon he looked straight
back at me, his eyes filled with a fury that couldn't help but attract
the attention of those around me. A few old women turned and
saw me and soon realized that, in my fashionable suit, my cane

in my hand, lounging irreverently against one of the columns, I hadn't any business being in this sacred spot. I thought I could hear a murmuring and sense a threatening attitude—possibly nothing but the result of my guilty conscience—anyway, I deemed it advisable to find the exit, nonchalantly but as speedily as possible, which may be interpreted as a sign that not every revolutionary is born to be a martyr.

At about this time I came upon a certain book of Catholic religious instruction as used in the elementary schools. I read it with increasing bitterness and in the end felt impelled to compose a critique to which I gave the title, How THE WORLD EDUCATES ITS YOUNG TO BE STUPID. I finished it off a few pages later with the childish but sincere outburst, *I simply can't go on—fury smothers my words.* Thus I found out in good time that I wasn't cut out to be an essayist either.

In my last year at the *Gymnasium*, quite some time therefore before my efforts to cope theoretically with God and the world, I had begun to write a drama about a monk, entitled *Aegidius.* It was my intention to include in it all sorts of philosophical and religious ideas that had passed through my mind, especially those concerned with dogma and freedom, free will and fate, eternity and immortality. It is the first and only written effort of mine from this period in which a few indications of a poetic and dramatic talent are unmistakably present in spite of its immaturity. The story of a monk, hungry for life, who is made a fool of by a demonic woman and finds solace with the daughter of an astronomer, with whom the abbot then falls in love, is undoubtedly naively plotted; moreover, toward the end the writing becomes hazy and increasingly confused, since I began it, as I did most of the things I wrote, without any plan. But in some episodes, for instance in a church scene between "two geniuses," and also here and there in the way the verse is handled, artistic potentialities may be discerned which should really have developed more swiftly than they did. Another comedy in five acts, which I wrote at the same time and titled *Before the World (Vor der Welt),* is weak when compared with *Aegidius.* It is written in prose, in a romantic-modern style. Convent, salon and masquerade elements intermingle without resulting in any truly striking effects, and certain frailties may be detected in this effort of my youth which turn up again and again in some of my weaker works of later years, for instance a tiresome tendency to put things in contrast. Nearly all the characters are supposed to illustrate the theme proclaimed in the title, and more out of mood than necessity, every character plays a part "before the world" that is alien, even contrary to his specific nature. A lack of economy fails to result in richness of content, and finally there is a theatricality which might be designated, facetiously, as a Hofburg theatricality, for I liked, then and later, to cast the main roles in my plays with actors from that theater, and to inscribe their names in the manuscript. In this comedy I tried, with little success, to assemble on stage a group of people with no material cares, ensnared only in the machinations of their own souls.

In other fragments and outlines of these first university years, an element of social criticism is noticeable which is evident also in my diary and notes. I jotted down all sorts of ideas for an article that was to deal with nothing less than "The Problem of Universal Happiness," in which I declared, according to the democratic principles in which I had been so well grounded during my childhood, that "original hatred between nations was non-existent," was indignant about "the illiberality of compulsory military service," and considered it a rewarding project—for which my knowledge and perseverance would scarcely have sufficed—"to prove the spuriousness of every war ever fought." A romantic socialist-anarchist drama with rather sensational content, entitled *Lazarus Knorr,* was good for only a few hasty notes, although it was very much alive in my mind; but I managed to put down on paper at least the opening acts or scenes of numerous other plays. In *The Old Students* (*Die alten Schüler*) it was my intention to employ the same schematic method as in *Before the World,* and assemble a group of people on stage who discover their true profession or the meaning of their lives too late. In *Count Unheim* (*Grafen Unheim*) my socialistic tendencies were again more strongly expressed but evidently doomed to be treated skeptically because the "Club of World Reformers," which was the focal point of the play, developed in the course of the action, into a "Club of World Forgetters." A *Carnival Tragedy* (*Faschingstragödie*) seemed destined to be more fanciful but never progressed beyond half an act, in spite of which I cast some of our finest actors in the leading roles. Prince Julian, the hero—a little of Egmont and a little of Prince Hal—was to be played by Ernst Hartmann; Sonnenthal seemed good enough to play his father, and in a small episodic role, that of the student Borromäus Quemberlin, I engaged the young comedian, Alexander Girardi, straight from the Wiedner theater to the Hoftheater, figuratively and approximately forty years before a Burgtheater director was to have the same idea. A drama set in the time of the errant anatomists was more sensibly plotted than those just mentioned and was developed with more assurance, at least as far as it went: An adept in the new science, which in those days was still frowned on by church and superstition, is accused of having murdered his friend who has taken his own life over an unhappy love affair, in order to obtain the body for purposes of dissection. Simultaneously, but this time using the same characters in modern dress, I tried a similar theme, robbed of its cultural-historical basic motif. Both efforts—*Sebaldus* and *The Whims of Imagination (Die Launen der Phantasie)*— remained unfinished, like most things begun in this period. I didn't even start on the play in which, according to my diary, I intended to "justify adultery under certain circumstances." *Jealousy because of a Dream (Eifersucht wegen eines Traumes)*, which I had noted down, after a personal, now forgotten experience, as "not a bad theme for a novella," was to prove its poetic value, which I must have sensed at the time, only decades later in the play, *The Veil of Beatrice (Der Schleier der Beatrice)*.

Although by May 1880, that is to say by my eighteenth birthday, I had inscribed in my diary twenty-three dramas as "finished" and thirteen as "begun," I was far from feeling particularly qualified or "chosen," and even though I occasionally resented the fact that people whom I considered beneath me looked upon me without further ado as their equal, the times when I doubted if I had any right to such arrogance were far more frequent. I can't explain the repeated lamentations in my diary over a boredom that was consuming me except as a misconceived expression of the deep-rooted uneasiness which arose in part from my uncertainty as to the way I was to take in life, but also from my guilty conscience. For whatever course I chose to take, the realization was constantly alive in me that I could be spending my time more cleverly and profitably; that both the profession to which I was dedicated

at present, as well as my avocation, which remained a constant
temptation, demanded a more serious and concentrated approach.
And it is quite possible that I tended to let this recognition suffice
without doing anything about it—a frequent and questionable
concomitant of self-observation.

My attitude, not so much to medicine as to the study of medicine, prevented an animated relationship with my colleagues. The
few I befriended in the beginning—especially the more diligent
ones—soon dropped me, if only because I would disappear for
hours, days, weeks at a time. In a few cases we met again on more
neutral ground, in a more congenial atmosphere. This neutral
ground was usually some coffee-house, in those days the Central,
where I would spend hours reading the papers, playing billiards
and dominoes, and, more rarely, chess, with a gray-bearded Polish
Jew called Tambour. The more easygoing atmosphere, in which
I felt light-hearted and altogether so much more at home, was the
artistic world, or whatever I considered to be just that, especially
when there was a Bohemian air about it. Then I was surrounded
by people of a very different caliber, who merged, only to part
again—friends of my *Gymnasium* days, new colleagues, chance
acquaintances and friends of my own choice, who attached themselves to me for a short or longer time, and now that we have
arrived at them I would like to mention first and at the same time
bid him farewell—Adolf Weizmann.

In the autumn that saw me entering the university, and after
numerous efforts on his part to get his certificate of educational
proficiency which would have qualified him for only one year of
military duty, Weizmann had to start his three years of compulsory military service in Olmütz. After that our friendship was
continued almost exclusively in letters. His, especially during the
first years, contained little beside complaints about his fate and
the fact that I didn't always attend promptly to the errands he
asked me to do for him, which were sometimes a nuisance; as
for instance the collecting of small sums owing to him, or the
procuring of money he needed to replace his rifle, which had
been stolen from his locker and for which he was liable, or the
books and magazines I was to send him. His letters also included
reproaches for my negligence and indifference, which were probably deserved. But when he came to Vienna on a short leave,

we always got along quite well. Thanks to his resourcefulness and adroitness, he was soon promoted to paymaster-sergeant, which took him to the various garrisons in the newly occupied province of Bosnia-Herzogovina. He was incredibly successful with all kinds of women, and although he never stopped complaining, seemed in the end quite pleased with army life. Sometimes he even thought of becoming a professional soldier, but when he was finally in a position to return to civilian life, after having served, for official reasons, a year longer than the normal period, he decided to try his luck traveling as a dealer in fur, which turned out to be unsteady work in more ways than one.

Whenever he had to stay in Vienna for any length of time, he looked me up. Then the friendship of our youth, which I had put behind me long ago—something he must have done too, without admitting it—came to life superficially, although I was increasingly displeased with the loudness of his behavior, which was somehow encouraged by his profession. His insatiability, as well as his lack of discrimination where women were concerned, increased; due I suppose in part to the fact that, after certain experiences in his army career, he felt he led a charmed life. In the end, however, he met his fate in the arms of a hotel chambermaid, and told me about it in despair when I went to meet him at the station one day, at his request. In the following year he was jailed twice for assault and rape, but if I am to believe what he told, didn't have too bad a time there. He was usually given the job of clerk in the prison office, where he enjoyed a certain amount of freedom, which he used to establish a tender relationship with the warden's wife and the female prisoners. In the spring of the year 1896, he walked into my room exhibiting obvious signs of paralysis in its early stages. He showed me his wallet, which I didn't think was too bountifully filled, yet he seemed to feel rich with its meager content. An hour later he called me up to tell me that he had spent three-and-a-half gulden for a seat for that evening's performance of *Liebelei*, something he seemed to consider a remarkable achievement. The following day my brother took him into his hospital to perform surgery for an ailment which was the sad result of one of his past love adventures, and six months later he died in an insane asylum, without my ever having seen him again.

Even in those days I considered Eugene Deimel a closer friend than Adolf Weizmann, and for a while he was my bosom companion. Our friendship dated back to our last *Gymnasium* years even though he was not in school with me to the end, for, like Wechsel and Weizmann, he was not to graduate. His father came from a Trieste family, was a retired civil servant and widower, and lived in Vienna with three or four sons and one daughter in very poor circumstances. I didn't know Eugene's brothers or sister, in fact I can't recall ever having visited him at home, yet I can still see the tall figure of his father, bathed in an aura of melancholy, which may be due to the fact that once Eugene brought with him the diary his aging father had kept in his youth. In it various love affairs were described, interspersed with highly revealing dots, which varied in number, and the Italian word *melanconia,* repeated over and over again like a refrain.

Eugene was a blond, lanky fellow, good-humored, light-hearted, and always ready for fun, some of it quite coarse. He preferred to spend his time in coffee-houses and taverns rather than in school, and his sentimentality seemed to include a consciousness of all the world's sorrow. He was a born vagabond yet not wholly indifferent to bourgeois traditions, a loafer with artistic aspirations, and in spite of all frivolity and apathy, a thoroughly honest, decent, and I would go so far as to say—noble character. He was strongly attracted to the theater. In him were combined, at least in concept, poet, actor and *habitué.* Since he was too poor to be the latter, he frequently got in as *clacqueur,* and I am quite shamelessly willing to confess that during my *Gymnasium* years I sat with him in the balcony of the Ringtheater several times on a ticket that had been handed to me by the director of the *clacqueurs,* with the obligation to vigorously applaud the great Italian mime, Rossi, which actually meant no sacrifice of my convictions.

Eugene satisfied his theatrical ambitions for the first time at the Matzleinsdorfertheater, which had once been the private theater of Prince Sulkovsky. Stage and auditorium were of such miniscule proportions that I could have touched the prompter's box from the proscenium loge. I was still a *Gymnasium* student when I had the pleasure of seeing my friend, who had not outgrown school but had fled from it, play two parts, that of a servant in *The Lady of the Camellias,* and the doctor of an insane asylum in *Marie-*

Anne, A Woman of the People. The parts were of no great importance but at least they had the advantage that the actor did
not have to pay the director a stipend. The actors playing leading
roles were taxed five to ten gulden. I don't know if Eugene was
ever called upon to indulge in this luxury; all I do know is that the
moment Director Niclas found it necessary to begin collecting
five gulden monthly from every member of the cast, Eugene had
to interrupt his career, at least for the time being. Meanwhile I
had been granted the opportunity to take a look at life in the
theater from the wings, so to speak, and I still like to think of the
gay morning hours during which I enjoyed a second breakfast in
a little tavern opposite the theater, in the company of several
actors. Among them the *bon vivant,* Richard Schulz, stands out
in my mind because of his exceptional gaiety and the fact that he
could eat an incredible number of cervelat sausage sandwiches;
and the enchanting ingenue, Fräulein Schubert, because of her
black curly hair. It was even granted me, on a beautiful summer's
day, to stroll along the shady walks of the Schwarzenberg Garden
with this dark-eyed, black-haired actress, a platonic tryst that was
never followed by a second meeting; in fact I never saw the lovely
creature or heard of her again.

My friend Eugene soon succeeded in rising to a position in the
theater which was not much more reputable but at least more
profitable, when he was permitted to work as an extra at the
Vienna Stadttheater for the salary of half-a-gulden, sometimes
even a whole gulden per evening. The only one of these performances that has remained with me was the one in which
Eugene, clad in ballroom elegance and wearing a very dubious
looking swallow-tailed coat, stood close to the footlights, a glass
of champagne in his hand, and after mumbling something unin-
telligible, toasted his host with remarkable naturalness, while I
sat in the orchestra at my father's side, trembling for fear that he
might recognize, in this miserable extra, my very best friend, for
whom he didn't have a good word to say, as was the case where
most of my friends were concerned. In Eugene's case his dispar-
agement was not entirely unjustified.

Eugene was unable to gain any more respect in the eyes of my
family when he read aloud to them several acts of *Zenobia,*
a play he had written and for which he had high hopes. However,

his evaluation of my talents was so high that he once took it upon himself to copy a clean version (which still exists) of the greater part of my monk drama. In the autumn of the year 1880, he moved to Munich, where at first he seemed to have better prospects. He became a collaborator of *Der Freie Landesbote,* a newspaper which had been under the management of the clerical-provincial administrator, Sigl, but under its new head, Bösl, followed a more liberal course. Eugene had a few friends in Munich who had encouraged him to make the move. Most prominent among them were a fat Baron Flotow and a blond Dr. Billinger, with whom we had spent many a wild night in Vienna when they had been staying there for amusement and study, for the most part in the notorious Café Laferl, where we once found ourselves at the same table with a troupe of musical clowns. They didn't forsake Eugene now but introduced him in their Munich circles. He consorted with painters and poets, mostly with those on whom good fortune had smiled as little as it had on him. In his letters a painter-poet, Adolf Paul, was vividly described, and again and again he would paraphrase a Goethe aphorism which he had changed pessimistically to read, "Every man, be he whoe'er he may, experiences his first joy on his last day." Meanwhile he had completed a new play, *Bar Kochba,* and had been led to believe that it might be accepted by the Hoftheater, a hope that was no more to be fulfilled than any of his earlier ones. I was flattered when he asked me to contribute to his paper and at last saw myself in print for the first time in *Der Freie Landesbote,* with a sort of philosophical dialogue for . . . no, against patriotism, and with "Love Song of a Ballerina" (*Liebeslied der Ballerine*), a moderately humorous poem which I was prudent enough to sign only with my initials. Eugene, whose financial situation was deteriorating rapidly, begged if he might use my first, and for some time to come my last, fee of ten marks, to which I understandably acquiesced. In the summer he returned to Vienna, disappointed, melancholy and a hypochondriac, due to the recent death of his third brother, who had died, as the two others had done at an earlier date, of tuberculosis. This didn't prevent him, in fact it may have induced him to overdo things at parties by heavy drinking and foolish pranks. For instance, after a shooting match in the Prater, which we had attended with a few other cronies, he decided to spend the

night under the Reichsbrücke, only to wake up the next morning
with a head swollen to twice its size because he had used an ant-
hill for a pillow. A platonic, sentimental love affair, of which more
later when it is connected with one of mine, had a dreary effect on
him; his material circumstances became increasingly desolate; a
money collection that was to make it possible for him to emigrate
to America brought only meager results, which was not surprising
since most of his close friends had nothing but their pocket money
to call their own. One winter morning I wanted to visit him in the
cheap hotel where he had taken a room. The clerk informed me in
a none too friendly fashion that my friend had disappeared a few
days ago without paying his bill. Only the suddenness of his departure surprised me. Soon his friends in Vienna received cards
from him, and after traveling back and forth all over Germany, to
what end was unclear, he finally boarded a ship in Antwerp,
bound for America.

Sparse but warm letters reached me, sometimes with interrup-
tions of months and years, and told casually of his bleak efforts
to make a living over there. He tried his luck at being kitchen boy,
salesman, factory worker, dishwasher, peddler, baker and cook,
until at last, with the help of a Bavarian peasant girl whom he had
met over the same hotel stove, he succeeded in starting his own
business, and as a delicatessen owner made a decent but never
very spectacular living. We continued to correspond, with long
intervals between letters, and on special occasions, such as outstanding family events (in his household, blessed as it was with
three daughters, there was no lack of romance); and when my
plays were presented in America, our exchange of letters would
become quite lively. We also had a lot to tell each other during
the war, until, in the winter of 1916 to 1917, all communication
between Austria and the United States was broken off and our
correspondence came to an end, hopefully only for the time being.
To this day, more than thirty-five years after seeing Eugene Deimel for the last time, I have preserved his personality, his mannerisms, yes, even his voice, as faithfully within me, as if we had
parted yesterday.

That I also confided my affairs of the heart to Eugene was natural during that period of one's youth in which one spontaneously
feels the need to confide in a close friend, and I soon found an

opportunity to introduce him to my beloved, and to the home of
her parents which I had been frequenting since my first university
years. I saw Fännchen often, but most of the time away from
home. Our favorite meeting place was the new Quai Park which
ran along the Danube canal and was called, in the vernacular, "the
Broom Park" because of its rather stunted trees. They didn't bother
us because we usually met in the dark evening hours, after the
piano lessons which Fännchen gave in the homes ·of various
friends. But with the coming of spring, the Rathauspark and
Volksgarten came into their own again and once, when we had
somehow lost our way, the little garden of the Officer's Hospital
was the scene for our still quite harmless embraces.

Fännchen's best friend at the time was the young girl I have
already mentioned casually as the sullen one. Her name was Ida
König. She wasn't nearly as pretty as Fännchen, but cleverer.
Somehow she seemed destined to fall in love with her friend's
lover and she often betrayed her feelings to me in her own facetiously disgruntled way. When Eugene joined our circle, a childishly mournful, but passionate relationship developed between him
and Ida, which she promptly broke off when he moved to Munich.
Her farewell note hurt him so deeply that he felt impelled to warn
me, in a letter, that I should let my Fännchen see as little as possible of a creature whose heartlessness had made him suffer so
profoundly.

I was attracted, more strongly than to Ida, to a cousin of Fännchen's who was four years older than she, Fanny Mütter, an appealing, truly charming girl who was training to be a singer. She
was blessed with a genuine gift for friendship such as occurs—at
any rate in such early years—perhaps only in the case of women
with no true erotic inclinations. It was she who was the gentle
mediator between Fännchen and me in the course of our frequent
misunderstandings and petty jealousies; she even graciously delivered our love messages and therefore sometimes became the
object of Fännchen's jealousy, not entirely without cause. Although she was totally lacking in any form of coquetry, even in
her relationship to me, I found in her the first female who offered
me a deep, one might almost say prophetic, understanding. She
believed in my gifts as a poet at a time when I was very much in
doubt about them; she scolded me in a friendly fashion for my

only too clearly evident peculiarities and incivilities, which were disturbing and retarding my development; she took my side against my envious and severe critics, later also against my father who persisted in the belief that his poetic talents had been far greater than mine and that nothing was ever going to become of me. I nearly always left her company feeling stronger and uplifted and a little bit in love, and confessed all this to her in a few affectedly sentimental letters, "To an Unknown," which I was tactful enough never to send off. She was strongly drawn to an ugly, tubercular pianist who died young; later she was tentatively engaged to a young doctor who jilted her to make a better match. She didn't remain long on the stage. She had a pretty voice which had been excellently trained by the famous German opera singer, Marchesi. She also had a nice talent for acting, but her total lack of passion, as well as a tendency to be phlegmatic, possibly also her undimmed purity of spirit, all may have been reasons why she broke off her career as an artist, where she could expect no laurels, and settled down to teaching singing. Here her musicality, patience and pedagogic tendencies found a profitable field. We shall come across her truly good and thoroughly unproblematic nature again in the course of these reminiscences.

Fanny Mütter's brother, a ne'er-do-well if ever there was one, whose cheerful impertinence broke all the bounds of moderation and refinement, was not exactly a necessary element in our easy-going circle; let us just say that he was ever present, and I was on good terms with him until something happened which was at the same time a minor crisis between my blonde Fännchen and me. One day she confessed to me—I don't know whether out of a sincere urge to bare the truth or because of a semi-conscious desire to revenge herself for my tendency to be unfaithful, which she surmised or suspected, perhaps also out of that exhibitionism of the soul which is frequently the motive for belated confessions of guilt—anyway, she told me that her cousin, when he was thirteen years old and she only ten, had taken advantage of her in a way she hadn't entirely understood at the time. It was a dreadful blow to me, and on the 27th of May 1882, I outlined the following words in black in my diary: "Today I experienced the most profound sorrow of my life." To the seducer I wrote a terse letter, informing him, without giving any reason, that I regretted having to break off relations with him for all time. He replied, probably quite sincerely, that he would of course bow to my decision even though it was totally incomprehensible to him. I can't recall whether there was ever any mention between us of this ridiculous exchange of letters, but since our relationship had always lacked any sort of intimacy and we continued to move in the same circles, it was soon restored. Not for long, though, because the rash young man's pranks soon took on aspects of criminality. Threatened with arrest for forgery, he fled to America. Thus I was at last able also to count a felon among the other dubious characters in my galaxy of friends. Many years later he was permitted to return home, not essentially changed in nature but in quite orderly circumstances. His good-humored, loud-mouthed, witty and swaggering personality had helped him to find a position and a wife. He traveled for an overseas pianola firm, settled down finally in Berlin and died, barely fifty years old.

My relationship to Fännchen didn't undergo any change either because of this "most profound sorrow of my life," but I made her atone for it in a not very noble fashion by repeated reproaches and constantly renewed forms of persecution. There had been no lack of discordant incidents in our relationship, nor of real and imaginary causes of dissent; and it is understandable that her parents didn't approve of our love affair, in spite of its innocence. A few months after I had been accepted in their home, I was told to stay away from it, thanks to the machinations of Fännchen's older brother, Rudolf, an insignificant, chronically ill-humored fellow who had once seen us kiss, and in a very businesslike letter written to me, revealed that he had "noticed the occurrence" and hadn't failed to report it to his parents. My banishment didn't last very long, nor my quarrel with Rudolf, who later committed suicide. I continued to be received in Fännchen's home in a friendly enough fashion, yet my visits remained unpopular, understandably, since there was a highly desirable plan to marry Fännchen off to a well-to-do relative, the banker Jacob Lawner, who was forty years old and very good-looking. She resisted the idea bravely, not that I encouraged her to do so; on the contrary, I advised her repeatedly, with precocious reasoning, probably also with the desire to free myself of all responsibility, not to reject such an apparently advantageous marriage without giving it some thought. For although

I shared with her the feeling that she was "developing intellectually under my influence," and was pleased when some of our
friends thought they could see a similarity between us—once I
even wrote tersely in my diary, probably without much conviction:
"Became engaged"—she wasn't thinking any more seriously than
I was of marriage since my faithfulness, at a time when I should
have felt attached, had held up far too weakly under quite a few
more or less serious temptations.

It was the various dances I attended, however, that began to
pose a real danger to our relationship. In the Crombé, the dancing
academy of the cultured middle-class, Fännchen was of course the
absolute leader; but as a girl of good family she could not accompany me to the dancing schools in the outlying districts of Vienna
which I attended, not solely for the purpose of learning how to
dance, and where I managed to score only a very moderate success. She also stayed away from the public balls which I now
began to attend. My debut took place, according to plan, at a small
physicians' gathering in the Grand Hotel. It was not a very happy
affair for me, since I was a passionate rather than a skillful dancer
and to my abiding shame fell full length on the floor toward the
end of the evening while partnering the tall daughter (in yellow)
of one of the doctors. But the incident couldn't cool my ardor
for dancing; on the contrary, for many a carnival season it remained my ambition to tear through the hall at every ball until
the last strains of the violins had faded and the lights had been
put out, if only because the final acceleration polka suited my
temperament and dilettantism much more than the six-step, which
I never did master completely.

Early in the year 1880, at one of my first balls, I made the acquaintance of a voluptuous, red-cheeked blonde, the daughter of
an innkeeeeper in Purkersdorf. After that we met on several winter
and spring evenings in the Weghuberpark; a year later again at
some balls, and it was without doubt only thanks to our inexperience—perhaps only to mine—that the caresses, which had already gone far on our first evening together, continued to remain
within quite innocent, albeit not entirely harmless limits; and
finally died without ever having burned full flame. Many years
later I saw her again while on an outing with my brother and a
friend, when we stopped at the country inn of her parents. She

was waiting on the guests and also served us our beers. When I asked her whether she remembered me, she nodded coolly, spoke my name, and, unmoved, turned away to wait on the other guests.

The part I played in another escapade shortly after that was even less heroic, although I remember the details more vividly than those of happier adventures. For some time now I had counted a *studiosus juris* from Czernowitz as one of my closer friends. He interested me probably because he wanted to be an actor, wrote poems, and had a youthful drama, entitled *Two Worlds*, milling around in his mind, or perhaps had already completed it . . . I can't exactly recall. On a November evening in the year 1881, on one of our walks through the suburban streets of the Neubau and Josefstadt districts, it so happened that we joined forces, after a few pleasantly received introductory flourishes, with two young girls. The designation *"süsses Mädel"* didn't exist in those days, but at least one of them could justifiably have claimed to be not only a sweet girl, but although hundreds of thousands might have preceded her, the *first* sweet girl, and I must have sensed that she was to be of great significance to me in my development as a poet, perhaps not as an individual but as a "conception." Otherwise it would be incomprehensible that on the same evening, immediately after our harmless walk together, I let myself go on about her in my diary in a most unusual fashion. She was a chorus girl at a theater which I chose to designate with three asterisks, more for belletristic reasons than out of a discretion which in this case would have been senseless. I described her as "the prototype of Viennese womanhood, with a bewitching figure, made for dancing; with lips that reminded me of Fännchen's (what pretty lips wouldn't have done so at the time?) made for kissing; eyes luminous and full of life, dressed simply, a *grisette* type—she sways a little when she walks, is lithe and unconcerned. Her voice is clear; she speaks vibrantly and naturally in the vernacular, and what she says is said as only she can say it —has to say it—that is to say, high-spiritedly and with a slight touch of haste. We're only young once, she says, with an unconcerned shrug, and is thinking: we shouldn't miss anything . . . and that is discernment, washed by the light colors of the south. Rash, with a defensive touch of coyness. She talks calmly about her lover with whom she broke off a few weeks ago, and chatters gaily, playfully, of how she fools all those who would like to take his place, but there is nothing French or passionately demonic about any of this; on the contrary, in a way the effect is humorous, as long as one isn't the one being fooled. And with all this, a curious air of domesticity, for instance the way she reprovingly said about her lover (did he possess you? I asked, naively doubting) that he played cards too much, and one had to be frugal, etc. The usual brothers and sisters, all living with their parents, the gossiping neighbors, every now and then an opening phrase, and then again a quite folksy melody. . . ."

A few evenings later the four of us were again strolling through the autumnal parks and streets and again Gusti talked about her lover who hadn't been her lover but had run around "with so many bad girls;" of an attempted suicide because of all the talk going on about her, with morphium, although she could have taken cyanide, she had some; "but you weren't all that tired of life," I added sardonically. Finally she voiced her probably well-grounded doubts about the virginity of her friend, Minna, who was walking a few steps ahead of us with my friend; a not very pretty girl and somehow repulsive to me. We stopped at a tavern where Leo began to hold forth. He was inclined to be loud and liked to hold the floor, and his manners were definitely questionable. He also distinguished himself as *farceur*, felt no qualms about telling dirty jokes and finally rendered a fairly explicit four-line verse—I shall never forget it—which not only didn't upset immodest Fräulein Minna, which was to be expected, but to my chagrin failed to dismay my so much more virtuous Fräulein Gusti; on the contrary, it seemed to amuse her inordinately. On the way home, Leo, intoxicated by his success, became increasingly bolder, and I couldn't help but notice that he was about to supplant me in the eyes of my appealing chorus girl from the theater of the three asterisks, and when we said goodbye at the front door of her house, she declared that at our next meeting she would make her final choice. I made good use, literally, of the time left me by this ultimatum. A folk-drama began to take shape in my mind with a girl like Gusti as protagonist. A girl seduced. Dancing school. A dealer in leather goods comes to board at the house. A household haphazardly thrown together. The blind faith of the parents. "I know it all so well," I wrote. "I feel at home everywhere, with everyone." Still a dozen years had to go by and much sorrow had to be experienced and inflicted before *The Girl at the Fountain* (*Fräul'n am Brunnen*), which was to be the title of my play about this girl, became Christine Weiring and her friend was transformed into Mizi Schlager in my play *Liebelei*.

All that remains now is to tell how this little adventure ended. The next time Leo, Gusti and I met, she pretended that she couldn't make up her mind. Finally we told her to designate the youth of her choice by a wave of the hand. "Hm," she said, "well . . . for all I care, the one on the right." Since I was on the left, there was nothing I could do but disappear into one of the side streets with the *noblesse* which seems to come to one automatically on such occasions. I never did find out, or perhaps I simply forgot how the affair between this first sweet girl, who by the irony of fate was not to be mine (fate likes to treat awkward people with irony), and my more fortunate friend developed. A more recent school of psychology would suspect that here we have a clear-cut case of the subconscious suppression of an unpleasant fact. If this should happen to be true, I can only regret that I didn't know how to perfect my talent for suppression in the years that lay ahead. Pepi Mütter, in whom I confided my failure, remarked facetiously that, "Leo's behavior suited her better so he was the better suitor!" Be that as it may, after this farewell evening I never saw Gusti again. Leo I would lose sight of for years at a time, yet he somehow managed to cross my path at certain periods in his life and seemed eager to resume our friendship, especially at the beginning of the 1890's, after he had completed a play, *The Athenian,* and was to enjoy a brief success when it was produced at the Burgtheater, a success which his shoulders proved too frail to carry. We shall come back to him and this event later.

I would like to mention a few other contemporaries of these first university years with whom I enjoyed friendships that began in a lively enough fashion but faded, some more quickly than others. I had high hopes for two attachments, entered into at the same time, to Heinrich Kahane and Sigmund Schneider. The former was a medical student, in the same class as myself, a brilliant but rather punctilious fellow who took his studies seriously. Schneider was a versatile but thoroughly superficial young man who, I believe, hadn't even been able to pass his *Gymnasium* finals.

His distinction was a certain dry, not altogether humorless men-dacity. Since the three of us were interested in poetizing, or at least in writing, we invested in a red leather notebook which was to be passed back and forth between us and be filled with our notes and aphorisms. But after each of us had inscribed his share (once I robbed my *Aegidius* for the purpose), our literary union was over; each of us tore his contribution out of the book and "aphorismed" on his own from then on. A "Club of Idealists" was to meet one evening in some tavern or other in the center of town. If I am not mistaken, the three of us decided to attend as the result of an advertisement in a newspaper. We waited for quite a while in the designated place, not without trepidation that the little cash we had might not suffice to pay our bill, but no fourth idealist appeared, and I suspect that the whole club existed only in the mind of our friend Sigmund, who liked to indulge in such mystifications. His guile expressed itself also on other occasions, for instance in connection with the shooting contest in the Prater, which I have already mentioned, where he suddenly decided to propose an inflammatory toast to the French Revolution at a table occupied by total strangers. This naturally turned out to be highly offensive. Neither he nor anyone else was too clear in their minds about what he was studying or what career he was going to choose. He busied himself with the study of medicine and philosophy, sketched, made music, wrote—all in an equally dilettantish fashion. Soon, as had been expected, he decided to be a journalist, and was the editor of an illustrated Vienna paper when he died at the age of fifty.

Heinrich Kahane went his prescribed way in a more orderly fashion. Today he is a highly successful doctor in a suburb of Vienna, but he has not given up his interest in philosophy. A paper on the theory of cognition, which unfortunately I have not yet had an opportunity to read, has been highly recommended to me by some very intelligent critics. Our intimate friendship, however, didn't last more than a year.

Among the colleagues of my first year as a medical student, with whom I chatted in lecture and study halls far more than I ever listened or worked, Richard Kohn (later Dr. Kerry), de-serves mention, also Landesmann, son of the poet Lorm, and finally the brother of the anatomist Otto Zuckerkandl, who later

became a famous urologist. Once, in the dissecting room, Landesmann tried his best to persuade me to join a dueling fraternity.
He belonged to one and was a formidable fencer. His reason was
that he thought a dueling scar would look well on me!

It was during these early years at the university that I happened
to come across Ludassy, son of the editor Gans von Ludassy, a
twenty-one-year-old youth whom I knew from earlier days. We
met at the Café Ruthmayr, a place where I preferred all too frequently to spend my time rather than attend to my studies in
lecture halls or laboratory. He had just returned from a prolonged
stay in Paris for the purpose of completing his studies in his native
city of Vienna. With his startling pallor, a complexion that could
almost have been called jaundiced, a dark Van Dyke beard, thick
curly hair and purposefully glowing eyes, he looked just as one
felt the Paris Bohemian of those days should look, and I had the
feeling that he chose to appear like this more for the effect it
would have when he returned to Vienna rather than as a direct
result of his stay in Paris. We soon settled down to a lively conversation. He told about Paris, the Latin Quarter, the friends he
had made and left behind. I was particularly interested in the
story of a young poet, who according to Ludassy's effective account had decided to commit suicide with his *inamorata* by an
overindulgence of sensual pleasure, the only result of which had
been that the two lovers had parted, thoroughly disgusted with
each other. On quite a few mornings after that, our conversation
was continued, more often than not at the same window table
at which I would wait in the evening for Fännchen to meet me,
at the appointed hour, from her home which was across the street.
Ludassy talked about his dramatic plans. The one that impressed
me most was produced later as *Jean qui rit*, and naturally I was
only too happy to find in him an understanding and grateful audience for my more or less undeveloped ideas. He always chose
his words carefully, expressing himself in a way that was almost
like the written word, and he had a habit of interspersing what
he had to say with astonishingly cynical remarks, for instance:
"I'd have you know that my father is an ass", hissing his "s's" in
an affected manner, and he would glare at you after such a statement with eyes that seemed to be probing, one might almost say

threatening you. Then he would suddenly and for no reason at all burst out laughing.

At first all this seemed to me less mannerism than the bizarre expression of his strange personality; and since a very essential element—the tendency toward further development—evidences itself only much later in life, out of a man's achievements, my overestimation of so promising and versatile a talent, which Ludassy undoubtedly displayed, may be readily understood; especially since it was arrived at by a flattered young man with similar aspirations. How impressed I was when some aphorisms of his were printed in the annual, *Dioscuren,* and were reprinted in a Sunday supplement and declared to be very witty by one of my father's colleagues! But I was fated to displease him quite soon through a rather ridiculous happening.

On occasional evenings I used to eat at a little inn with some of my harmless, easy-going friends, a group which included a few unimportant youths beside Deimel, Pichler and Pepi Mütter. Sometimes we would imitate student tavern-behavior, for no good reason, just for fun. Once—I can't recall how it came about —Ludassy had turned up and joined us at such a gathering, and I had the bright idea to laud his attributes, ambitions and achievements in an exaggeratedly comic fashion in a gay toast to our illustrious guest. I spoke of his professional studies in law and philosophy, of his lofty poetic plans and finally of his anonymous collaboration on the staff of the humorous journal, *The Flea (Der Floh),* for which he wrote a weekly satirical article on art and politics under the pseudonym of Kniebeiss von Bisamberg, a philosophical recluse; a fact which until now had been kept secret. Shortly before this I had come upon him one night at the Café Central, with a glass of absinthe on the table in front of him, staring with glazed eyes into a mirror, and he had responded to a question of mine, or perhaps only to a look, with the words, "I want to see what a fellow looks like who has made love five times (he used a more colloquial expression) and drunk two bottles of champagne."

As far as I can recall, it seems unlikely that I included this encounter in my toast, but I can't say for certain that I did not. Just the same, the rest of my indiscretions seemed to suffice for him to express his displeasure with me in the sharpest terms the next time we met. "You stripped me to the bone," he said, "stripped me in front of strangers," and he stuck to these words so categorically that all my justifications, even the sincere assurances of my best intentions, proved unavailing. In spite of his reaction I had every reason to believe even then that my toast had flattered rather than offended him; and as a matter of fact, for the time being nothing in our relationship changed.

Two friends of Ludassy's from an earlier time turned up now and then, and soon quite regularly, at the coffee-house table we frequented, both of them, like him, law students with literary interests. One of them, Gustave Frieberger, was a good-looking, slender young man with a chronically hoarse voice which somehow went perfectly with his refined, somewhat affected melancholy nature. The other, Fritz Schik, attracted attention to himself even in those days, at the age of twenty, by affecting the airs of a grumpy Viennese privy councillor. He fancied himself as a hypochondriac, an enemy of mankind and a crank; he resided in a house that belonged to his father, a wealthy attorney, where he occupied an entire floor all by himself. He never left his apartment without an overcoat, even on the hottest days, and wouldn't touch the handle of a door without gloves on. In the theater he had his likes and dislikes for and against certain actors, which were nearly always justified. He annoyed the waiters in restaurants and coffee-houses with the express purpose "of spoiling their enjoyment of life," and had a comically churlish, often paradoxical way of holding forth about God, the world and anything else he might have on his mind. He played his role, which was almost second-nature, so consistently that it was a pleasure to witness, as is the case with any successfully rounded-out performance. Of course character actors like this shouldn't remain on stage too long, much less try to monopolize it with their episodic personalities. If they do, it can happen to them, as it did to our friend Schik every now and then, that they become tiresome and the effect of their behavior in poor taste.

I considered Ludassy, Frieberger and Schik, all three of them only a few years older than I, a closed group, although in their relationship to each other they could hardly have been called close. I probably did so because they formed a quasi-audience for my literary efforts, and I enjoyed with them mutual recognition and criticism and serious encouragement to go on creating. But these friendships were also not meant to last. Scarcely begun, they soon cooled; yet a friendly tone was preserved which, however, increasingly lacked a deeper spiritual empathy as we approached the high point of our lives. This discrepancy between tone and content was to be expressed most clearly in my relationship to Ludassy, mainly because he became a distant relative of mine by marriage and because he didn't seem capable of accepting my later successes, which outdid his, with the desirable composure. If he didn't fulfill his promise, even as journalist, then the fact that he strove in the false direction, rather than too high, certainly played a part. However, since I have had ample opportunity to observe, in cases that touched me more closely, the unpleasant transformation brought about or at least clarified in one's character by disappointed ambitions, I do not wish to dwell any longer, especially not at this point, which I consider too early for such reflections, on an incident that was of such minor importance to the history of my life.

Between the other two members of our little group, imaginary and real rivalry did not manifest itself, at least not so openly. Frieberger, whose novella, *The Last Day of a Honeymoon*, had convinced me of his talent, and who gave me considerable cause for envy, not only because of his luck with women but also because he was in a position at the time to devote himself wholly to being a poet, soon found himself, as the husband of a penniless singer, dependent entirely on journalism. Since he wrote solely for the political and financial section of his paper, he may have found it easier to divest himself of his artistic ambitions than some of his fellow journalists, who compensated for their unfulfilled dreams by criticizing in their reviews the fulfilled or seemingly fulfilled dreams of the companions of their youth.

Fritz Schik, who at the beginning of our friendship had expressed the wish to write a play with me, decided in the end, after a few feebly-bizarre dramatic efforts of which I can recall only a one-act play entitled *Adam and Eve*, to concentrate on occasional critical reviews in the form of essays. When the new literary current from North Germany at last began to affect Vienna at the end of the eighties, he took part in the movement by adopting a progressively conservative, churlishly enthusiastic attitude; he ignored whatever the mood of the moment, his personal sympathies or antipathies or a true understanding of the arts, which was naturally his, demanded of him. Later, when he was forced into insecure, one might say distressing, circumstances because of a break with his father, he was offered a position as dramaturgist and technical adviser to the Hamburg director, Baron Berger. When Berger moved to the Burgtheater, he continued to employ Schik as his Berlin consultant. I shall come back to many a personal encounter with him.

I had Adolf Weizmann to thank for my acquaintance with Joseph Winter, who was a few years older than I and also a medical student, with an undeniable although not very spontaneous lyrical talent. I considered his gift superior to mine, certainly in its lyrical aspects, and since I felt drawn to him and somehow inwardly related, I was touched when once, while talking about his interesting fluctuation of moods as if he really had no right to such vagaries, he said in a rather resigned tone of voice, "And yet I am no genius; I just have talent." A few years later he won a one thousand gulden prize with his "Hymn of the Germans in Austria." Soon after that a volume of his poems was published which was very successful. Together with Richard von Kralik he published "Puppet Plays." His poetic star seemed to be ascendant only to decline all too soon. Since he had to earn his living as a tutor, he was late in getting his degree, after which, under the tutelage of Professor Billroth, he became a first-rate surgeon. Ambition continued to drive him, and after achieving the status of a multimillionaire by his marriage to a divorcee who happened to be exceptionally ugly, he could at last count himself a genius, at any rate in the art of living. He advanced to staff doctor, a rarity among reserve officers, and during the war, as head doctor of the hospital to which he had been assigned, worked tirelessly and successfully, never shunning material sacrifice, just as had been the case previously, when he had been organizer of an institution for cancer patients, all of which has to be appreciated all the more, whatever his motives may have been, because in the throes of his overworked condition, he succumbed to a heart ailment.

I was bound with even stronger, or let us say more intimate, ties during these first university years to another poetizing student of medicine—Fritz Kapper, in spite of the fact that he impressed me much less. Although he wrote poems, for the most part in the Baumbach style, and one of them, "God Greet Mistress Love Again," was even published in the illustrated magazine *Heimat,* I for my part decided at the time that he was never going to write anything worthwhile. In the year 1881 I went with him on my first holiday trip without my parents, and the fact that my father bade me farewell at the station with a glum expression, as if I were displaying a lack of filial respect, could not disturb my happy consciousness of at last being full-fledged. My most vivid memory of the eleven-day trip is of a hike from Gastein across the Nassfeld an the Austrian Alps to Mallnitz. I would probably have forgotten the fact that I devoured half a fried chicken at almost every meal, if it hadn't met with the disapproval of my parsimonious traveling companion every time I ordered it, since he seemed to feel he had to order and pay for the other half. Except for that we got along very well, and our relationship was not to change; in fact later, encouraged by a few circumstances to which we shall come in due course, it at times took on even an affectionate character. Like most of my friends of those days, whose aims were similar to mine, he soon gave up all dreams of poetry and immortality, and nothing could have been said against his sound standing as a doctor, father of a family and passably intelligent human being if he hadn't displayed the need, during even the most ordinary conversation, to raise himself to loftier heights, and seemed to feel in duty bound to attach remarks of a general and philosophical nature to even the most trivial concerns, which is so often the case with people desirous of convincing others, and themselves, that they have renounced things which it was never in their power to achieve.

Although I have to thank the young people just mentioned for many an inspiration, and however akin I may have felt to some of them, I was drawn with all my heart to a young man about whom I would have little to tell if I hadn't written in my diary, beside his name, "my favorite," and with the reading of these words found again in my memory the sympathy I once felt for him. His name was Hermann Löbl. I don't know how he became one of us nor why he happened to disappear from our midst a few years later. If I am not mistaken—and I am not entirely sure of this either—he was a businessman, and since he was a simple, quiet fellow, tactful, with no literary aspirations whatsoever, our friendship remained entirely free of those disturbances which are never missing between two people for whom life is not only element but also material, and who have based their lives more or less consciously not only on work and achievement but also on success and response. His nature may therefore have had a certain atmospheric effect on me like a healthy, pure, albeit not overly strong breath of fresh air in which I could recover from my own demands and those of my everyday surroundings. Characteristically only one of our many meetings has been preserved in my memory. It took place one morning on the Kärntnerstrasse. I felt the childish need to give him an account, very fast and much too loudly, of a little adventure of mine from a previous day, and he considered it necessary to tell me, gently, to lower my voice. I can also scarcely remember what he looked like, whereas the appearance of his younger brother, a totally negligible little man, is still clearly impressed on my mind: a traveler walking toward me on the outer Burgplatz, his red Baedeker in his hand, binoculars slung around his neck. Vienna was his home, yet Moni— which was the affectionate nickname we used rather than his more imposing real name, Solomon—had decided to spend his eight-day vacation like a genteel stranger, conscientiously seeing all the Vienna sights. I can't recall whether he had moved to a hotel for the purpose of playing his part consistently.

Among my more fleeting coffee-house acquaintances I remember a sympathetic billiard partner, a Herr Bachmann, a mature man who had lived in America and soon went back there, where Deimel was a cook in the same hotel in which Bachmann worked as a waiter.

Once, on the way home from a ball, a young man joined me who had made a name for himself in this rather less than exciting literary period, with a novella, *The Diary of an Idler* (*Das Tagebuch eines Verbummelten*). It had been published, with various classics, by the still quite exclusive Reclam Library. We talked animatedly in the café until the day dawned grayly. As the younger of the two and still entirely unknown, I again could feel that fate was treating me with a certain distinction, but my sympathies for this poet, who already looked famous to me, were gone the following day when he found it necessary to send me his publisher's flyer, listing his publications to date, without enclosing a word of explanation. Soon after that he wrote, asking me to join a then flourishing literary society in which he played a quite prominent part. I didn't accept his invitation, and with that our friendship was over. He was soon silenced as a poet and confined himself to publishing anthologies of selections for recitation.

That the mood of this evening, spent in such animated conversation, and not the content of our talk, which has been completely erased from my mind, has echoed in my memory for so long, is certainly due less to the effect on me of this young poet's personality than to the fact that he seemed to be a citizen of that other, nobler world to which I still had to fight for entry, or perhaps resign myself to the fact that it might be denied me. It was out of such doubts, which never left me, that I wrote a prologue to my monk drama, *Aegidius,* after I had finished it. The prologue opens with the words, "I pin my last hopes on this work." Coming from an eighteen-year-old, this judgment sounds a little premature, but in the end I pledged that if I had not deceived myself about the worthlessness of my life, I would enter "a quiet cell of the great cloister: that humdrum existence where mankind, so easily content, feels so miserably blissful," and I ended the prologue with the words:

> . . . Through the grille
> I can look down toward the wide free plain
> Stretched out below me, sunlit and beautiful,
> To where an enviable race of eternal children
> Frolic, happy in heart and spirit,
> In a never-ending play of their imaginations. . . .

With these comically touching and rather affected lines I was probably not only passing judgment on myself but in some vague way also trying to give myself absolution—a frequently admitted secondary aim of such judgments—an absolution I really needed much more in connection with the neglect of my medical studies.

Due to the fact that I had attended to medicine from the start in a highly desultory fashion, my interest could not be seriously or lastingly aroused, even where my predispositions—if they had been correctly channeled—would have found quite a few points of contact. My moods, to say nothing of my viewpoint, were soon influenced by the atmosphere of the halls in which the daily life of a medical student, even a not very industrious one, was played out. Before I entered the dissecting room for the first time, I had never seen a human corpse, but like all my colleagues I soon found out that the human body dead, if the observer is not moved by any personal relationship to the soul which has fled that body and especially when it is being demonstrated to a crowd of students in a sober hall of learning, solely as object, soon loses the dark, sinister character it seems to preserve for the sentimental layman (the layman as such is always sentimental). Yes, like my colleagues I too tended to exaggerate to some extent my indifference to the human creature become thing, as if in defense against just such lay sentimentality. But I never went so far in my cynicism as those who considered it something to be proud of when they munched roasted chestnuts with relish at the dissecting table, so to speak under the very nose of the corpse, a cynicism which may also spring from subconsciously logical considerations. At the head of the bed on which the dead man lies, even if the man who just breathed his last is unknown to you, stands Death, still a grandiose ghostly apparition. In the morgue he stalks like a pedantic schoolmaster whom the *baccalaureus* thinks he can deride. And only in infrequent moments, when the corpse apes the living man he once was in some grotesque motion or under a sudden light effect, does the composed, even the frivolous man involuntarily experience a feeling of embarrassment or fear.

The anatomical laboratory lay beside the dissecting room, and the relationship of the two to each other could be compared to that of church and sacristy, especially when the priestly eminent professor or one of his assistants stepped out of the room assigned to him, into the generally accessible ones, to mingle with the working or chattering students. By far the most interesting one of these assistants was Emil Zuckerkandl, a pale young man with a dark Van Dyke beard and black eyes, who in his robes looked exactly like one of the anatomists as depicted by Rembrandt. The almost legendary aura of his lively drink- and duel-happy fraternity days still wafted about him. He still enjoyed the reputation of being able to go straight from some night club or other, even from the arms of a beautiful woman, to his serious day's work, teaching and learning with incredible application until late in the evening. However, instead of letting him set me an example or at least taking advantage of his highly praised talents as an instructor by regularly attending his lectures, I preferred to let his romantically twilit figure, seen superficially from afar, inspire me to write a rather feeble poem which I called "Prosector." At about the same time I wrote a somewhat flat fantasy, *Spring Night in the Dissecting Room* (*Frühlingsnacht im Seziersaal*), which I never completed, and if I want to add the fragment, *Sebaldus*, already mentioned, then I have described everything for which the poet in me has the enigmatic, bleak impressions of anatomy to thank.

The atmosphere of the medical profession with which I was surrounded made impressions on me in other ways as well. I began to suffer from hypochondria, especially after I started to attend the clinical lecture halls and visit the hospital wards; and my awareness of this reaction probably played its part in alienating me from the areas that did most toward arousing it. Still, from time to time I could feel an honest professional interest struggling to life within me. Although I was disposed to classify my occasional hypochondriac emotions as "specific third-year manifestations," I already looked ahead with some apprehension to my maturer years, and wondered if I would ever have the strength to preserve my *joie de vivre* with a constantly more concentrated miasma of possible ailments all around me, which however did not prevent me from considering the publication of a book on natural philosophy in my fiftieth year.

It goes without saying that my father watched my activities and even more sharply the things I failed to do, with increasing displeasure. When I told him, in December, during my first university year, that I had passed my preliminary examination in mineralogy, with honors, a fact of which I informed him as we were passing the Stadttheater to which we were going together that evening, he cried out overjoyed, "What I would really like to do now is give you a kiss!" words that deeply touched me and my companion, Jacques Pichler. But from then on my father was to have only rare occasions for such expressions of fatherly satisfaction, although some of his reproaches were not entirely justified and a few of the vexations he suffered through me were all too exaggeratedly taken. It was quite impossible, for instance, to consider me a spendthrift, which was what he liked to call me, because I couldn't make do with my five gulden a week pocket money. When he insisted on reproaching me for coming home so late at night, with the declaration that he felt ashamed of my behavior in front of the caretaker, then he was only betraying again, as was his wont in pedagogic concerns, that he considered outer manifestations—what people might say—of disproportionate importance. Still I could understand, even if I objected to it, the displeasure, yes, even the anxiety of a man who had started at the bottom, and with only his own resources had risen to a status of esteem and prominence in his field, and to a satisfactory social position, and now saw the son he loved and considered talented showing signs of wavering at the outset of a career that had been prescribed and made easy for him, threatening to stray from it, even to losing his way, instead of moving steadily forward with at least some display of seriousness.

As an example of how I idled away my days, the description of one, told in my customary fashion, may serve as an example of many others: "13.2.80. Got up fairly late, as usual, and couldn't start anything much before nine, which was when my anatomy lecture began. After listening rather attentively to Langer's lecture on the larynx, I went over to the chemistry lab where I spent more time chatting with Richard Kohn than working. Then home, where I spent a quarter of an hour on zoology after which I worked on *Aegidius*, finally accompanied my brother on the piano. A Mozart sonata. After dinner, played the Wagner Faust overture with Mama, then off with Eugene to the Café Central where we played three games of chess. (I won the first, he won the second, the third was a draw.) Dillmann joined us just as I had to leave for the Maria-Theresienstrasse, the usual trysting spot. She came, we went to the Quai Park; spring heralded its arrival in our delightful chatter. Both of us were in a wonderful mood. She took my arm, it got darker and darker, and we frequently interrupted our conversation in the sweetest fashion with tender kisses. Then I met Kohn, spoke to Jacques, also to Eugene. Home again, I read Max Waldau's *According to Nature* (*Nach der Natur*), improvised on the piano and played cards and chess with my brother after a futile attempt to hypnotize him."

Sometimes I wrote in my diary in sentimental, humorous, blank verse. For instance, on June 27, 1880, the following lines:

> Life looks at me, although still young in years,
> With pale expression, and I fail to see
> What is intended to bring joy unto my soul,
> What still might come to lavish on my heart
> The jubilation of a lovelier life.
> In order not to pine away with boredom,
> I have decided to recount my day,
> (It was so cool, and so banal,) and tell
> The hollow tale, and so be rid of it.
> This evening I went walking in the gardens,
> Where people go for pleasure or for pain.
> A young girl, sitting on a bench, Fännchen her name,
> Her loving parents seated at her side.
> (They were the ones who did create the maid.)
> Words were exchanged, passed back and forth,
> But for the two of us there was a diff'rent feeling.
> Shyly, out of the corners of our eyes,
> Presentiments and recollections darted
> Forth from the faint glow of our furtive glances,
> To, fro, and daring not to linger,
> The all of me no longer rooted there
> But long since gone toward the Langegasse,
> Toward Vienna's Zuckerkandl-Kneipe.
> Forward—my coat slung o'er my shoulders,
> I strode, with one last lingering look
> At my girl flower and the flower she wore,
> A gift to signify my love and my devotion.
> Eugene, Jacques, Rudolf, all went with me;
> Soon we were lost in jollity and noise, in wildest drinking,
> Babel of voices, clapping hands and raucous singing,
> Which on the student ladder quickly rises
> To utter drunkenness. Weaved back and forth
> And swam in the most welcome pool. And yet
> One leaves such waters but to find oneself with simple cold,
> Which one then calls, with sheepish grin,
> A *Katzenjammer,* for e'en a cat
> On finding one in such condition
> Would have to groan and moan.
> I left. Tavern and witching-hour were over.

> Alone and lonely I wandered off to rouse myself
> Out of my semi-stupor, at a coffee-house.
> Chattered a while with some loose women, drank black coffee,
> Blew smoke into the sin-filled air,
> Told curious tales of curious journeys,
> Of how once shipwrecked, then again
> Roaming through jungles to New York,
> Lied my way thus through yet another hour
> Until at last, with hat perched rakishly on head,
> I hurried home. And since the night is gone,
> I sit here now, again faced with my papers,
> And write, lamenting. For lamentable 'tis
> To have on this earth naught of which it may be said,
> "This thing is mine. This thing I do delights me."

And continued in the same vein on the following day:

> In the fresh air, in kindly Nature,
> But in the company of those who neither
> Free nor kindly were—although beloved,
> I spent my yesterday. The Brühl,
> So beautiful, encircled us within
> The shadows of its woods, and with
> The sensuous scent of its wild flowers.
> I strolled through the green meadows,
> Holding a book which does divide all life
> In no time into cells. Its name is Botany.
> And all things blossoming around me
> Suddenly were naught but albumen, but wretched protoplasm.
> Then cosily I ate my cheese and butter
> And ham—the best—also salami,
> Must not forget to mention milk,
> Mixed with my coffee's pleasant black,
> Let it flow thoughtfully between my lips.
> Three pretty girls passed back and forth,
> And some prim misses, charming figures,
> Their pretty faces graced the terrace.

From all this it must be quite clear that I was not at all pleased with my behavior. My nervousness is clearly discernible, and it expressed itself in oversensitivity, defiance, yes, even in outbursts of rage which were accepted with patience at home. My father, although capable occasionally of flaring up, was actually a warm-hearted man who lacked only the gift of being able to lose himself, patiently and without bias, in the souls of others, even those of his closest relatives. But for that he might have been perfect. He was quite right in not wholly trusting his understanding of human nature, even if only subconsciously, and was therefore exceptionally dependent on opinions expressed in his presence, whatever the source, and listened so avidly to the talk and gossip going on around him that he frequently became their echo and of course changed with them. With people like this one can establish a relationship which may at times be most tender, yet has to remain a sentimental one, never a bond that is secured in the spirit. And since my mother was also filled with love for me without any true understanding, and, just as restless and far more absent-minded than my father, was entirely his creature, I was also unable to find in her—if ever I sought anything like this at home—any spiritual support. In spite of this I spent many bright and good hours in the home of my parents; in fact I would say that they by far outnumbered the bad ones, if for no other reason than that my father's profession did not leave him time to cope with domestic disagreements, and in these most mature and successful years of his life he was more easily engaged by a good mood than by disagreeable or melancholy matters. Our house was run along middle-class lines; still, in accordance with my father's generosity, on a quite lavish scale. Large parties were rarely given, yet a pleasant, at times quite formal social life was cultivated, and our teachers, my father's assistants and foreign doctors were frequently our guests at Sunday dinners.

We went to the theater often. Thanks to the circles in which some of my father's patients moved, we were frequently given free box seats for the Hoftheaters, and my father regularly received tickets for all the premières at the Stadttheater. Of course I profited by this too. To concerts I went either alone or with Mama, with whom I still played duets, so that I was gradually able to assimilate a quite widespread knowledge, especially of classical music.

It was on the occasion of a concert that I made my first public appearance on stage, even if only in a very modest role; namely I turned the pages for my teacher, Rückauf, who was accompanying the famous Schubert singer, Gustave Walter. It made a great impression on me when we withdrew to the Green Room with the other performers on the occasion of such a concert and saw an elegant young lady appear in the doorway, grasp Gustave Walter's hand in her white-gloved ones and press a fervent kiss on it, after which she disappeared, wordlessly, back into the auditorium. *That* is fame! I thought, not without a slight shiver.

Moritz Rosenthal was another musician whose acquaintance I made during this time. He had just stopped being considered a child prodigy and had given his first concert in Vienna as Royal Rumanian Court Pianist. He was a member of our coffee-house set; I think Pepi Mütter introduced him, the only celebrity among the Pichlers, Deimels, etc., and on the occasion of his first public appearance, we who had the honor of being his friends betook ourselves to the artist's room during practically every intermission to express our admiration. This swarming back and forth of very young men between auditorium and Green Room made a rather comical impression, and Max Kalbeck mentioned it, not without faintly anti-Semitic connotations, in his review. In spite of his fame and somewhat exaggeratedly satirical intellect, Rosenthal addressed us and we him with the informal "Du." From a letter of his to me, which I kept, I can see—as if I didn't know it myself—that at the time none of us were living on what could be called a grand scale. In the letter he sends me one gulden, called playfully a "floh," (from florin), to be passed on to another young man in our group. During the first year of our friendship we quarreled for some childish reason which I can't recall, but soon reconciled our differences. Shortly after, Rosenthal disappeared from our coffee-house circle, but our relationship lasted undisturbed for decades without any truly animated communication taking place between us, and in spite of our mutual esteem and occasional chats, without ever becoming truly intimate.

I have my friend Richard Horn to thank for my acquaintance with his uncle, the excellent pianist and charming composer, Ignaz Brüll, but also for a brief encounter with Anton Bruckner. Since it was a well-known fact that Bruckner sometimes liked to improvise on the organ for his visitors, Richard took me with him to Bruckner's apartment, where it was his purpose to have the composer certify his regular attendance at the counterpoint lectures he held at the university. Bruckner, who was not only a genius but also good-natured, didn't have to be coaxed by Richard, in whom he recognized a good student, and delighted us for a half-hour with his wonderful, transcendental playing. I never spoke to the great composer again, nor heard him play; but I saw him many times after that, when he would appear on stage after having been stormily demanded at the end of a performance of one of his symphonies, dressed in a suit that fitted him like a sack, to bow in a touchingly helpless manner before an amused audience, who in those days were sincerely enthusiastic only to a small extent.

I for my part remained true to myself and improvised on the piano rather than practiced it, and on the occasion of a journey, in a hotel in Zell am See, took it upon myself to play a joke on a few acquaintances who at first had listened to me with approval from the next room, by passing off a few of my own little inspirations as compositions of Raff or Bach. At first their undeserved praise flattered me, only to leave me, in the end, feeling ashamed.

It still never occurred to me to take my dilettantish musical talent seriously since I placed only very hesitant faith even in my gifts as a poet. The fact that my father shared my doubts—which of course I never confessed to him—was something that with my human and poetic nature I could not help but resent. Healthy pedagogic considerations were naturally at the bottom of his attitude toward my poetic aspirations, and for similar reasons he liked to see in me a definite talent for medicine, especially in the field of diagnosis, in which he may not have been so far wrong. What he would have liked to see most would have been for me to turn as soon as possible to his special field of laryngology. If, in spite of all this, he occasionally evidenced a degree of sympathy for my literary aspirations, it was inevitably occasioned by some outside cause. Sometimes, in spite of his misgivings, of which he himself wasn't at all sure, he may have spoken with the understandable vanity of a father's heart, in the artistic circles in which he moved as a doctor and socially, about his son who seemed dedicated to poetry; for he would come home with flattering signs of interest which portended a possible development of my talent. For instance, Charlotte Wolters once inquired about a play of mine—I must have said something idiotic about one of my comedies as a future

Burgtheater piece—and Sonnenthal also asked several times if he might read something I had written. Thus the ambition was awakened in me to submit a specimen of my art to such theatrical celebrities. After all, it was in their power to pave the way for a youthful author to the greatest German theater. Since I could see little hope for my two dramas, *Before the World* and *Aegidius;* and *Peters,* a modernized version of *Sebaldus,* which seemed the one most likely to be finished, had not pleased my father, I decided to rewrite completely an inadequate three-act comedy, *Out of Style,* as a one-act curtain-raiser. In this form I gave it to my father to present to his patient and friend, Adolf von Sonnenthal. A few days later my father returned the play to me with a letter from Sonnenthal, and I can still see the mocking, probing yet tender way he looked at me across the set table while I, instead of eating my dinner, read the letter which went as follows:

Dearest Friend! I read your Arthur's play and must admit that in spite of the innumerable flaws, I came across more talent than I am accustomed to finding in such dilettantish efforts. This, I am afraid, does not mean much but only shows that your Arthur has learned more than some others I know who write plays. But from here to a true dramatic competence is a long, long way; and I see no justification, from this trial piece, in encouraging him to take up such a profession. This is my honest opinion which I know stands in no need of your corroboration. My most cordial greetings to you and your son Arthur from your faithful, A. Sonnenthal.

I can't remember if at the time I grasped the justice of this judgment which, when one takes the quality of my trial effort into consideration, could be considered too mild rather than too severe. I don't think I did, for then I would never have dared to present this eminent master with the feeble effort only a few days before. At any rate, the letter had a quite different effect on me than my father—who had undoubtedly planned the whole thing with Sonnenthal—had expected or desired, for immediately on leaving the table I took myself off to the Café Central, and in a corner, by artificial lighting, began to write a new play called *Modern Youth.* It starts off with a young poet who has read his novella aloud to a medical-Mephistophelian friend who rejects it. I let the curtain rise cannily during the criticism, *not* during the reading. The friend advises the disgruntled poet to give up his adored blonde beloved and to acquire a real *inamorata,* and to mingle with different kinds of people than heretofore; and a meaningful vista is opened up on what was called in those days, "the wild life."

With this clandestine response to Sonnenthal's letter, the matter was temporarily closed. It would not have convinced him of my vocation any more than my harmless one-act play had done. The material itself lived on in me for some time, and if anyone wanted to have a bit of literary history fun, he would find in the dramatic and prose fragments which remain of *Modern Youth,* certain traces of Anatol.

I have told so much about my negligence in the field of medicine, that this could easily be read as the story of a hopelessly indolent scholar; I must therefore not conceal the fact that in the course of my third year as a medical student I dutifully passed my first oral examination, just like my more industrious colleagues. I got through my two *practica* with little honor. Langer, because of my laryngological father, decided to examine me on the bone structure of the larynx; still I just barely passed in anatomy. In physiology, although better prepared, I had only the indulgence of Professor Brücke, who was usually feared, to thank for my passing grade. I was so afraid, justifiably, of the theoretical examination that my father, at my request, went to the dean, who happened that year to be Langer, to ask if I might withdraw; but instead of allowing me to take the examination at a later date, my father came home with Langer's friendly assurances to be courageous and to appear for the *theoreticum* on the appointed day. And so, on a beautiful summer morning, feeling slightly nauseated and accompanied by my father, I betook myself via the burgeoning Ringstrasse to the green table of the stern gentlemen in the so-called "armory." And it went off splendidly, beyond all expectations. In anatomy and chemistry my rather questionable courage was rewarded with honors. In physiology I did quite well, but my answers to the questions on physical science were so lacking in sophistication that Professor Lang, an outstanding scholar and notoriously boring teacher, whose lectures were very irregularly attended by even the most conscientious students, said in his reedy voice, "It seems to me, Herr Kandidat, that you are trying to make fun of me." This I could honestly and vehemently deny. Professor Lang, as was customary with him, let mercy rule over justice and thus it came to pass that after the results had been announced I was able to look forward, before the commencement of my fourth university year, to an undimmed vacation.

When one looks back on one's life in later years, the various segments seem to follow one upon the other like the chapters of a novel, separated with skillful intent. But I don't think I can draw this separating line at any other point in my life so decisively as in this summer of the year 1882, in which I completed my twentieth year, passed my first oral examination, ordered my army uniform and destroyed my old diaries; not however before having carefully copied the most essential parts.

Book Four

July 1882 to May 1885

IN THE SUMMER of 1882, just as we had done for the first time ten years before, we again traveled to Switzerland; this time via Ragaz and Davos to Pontresina, over the Bernina Pass and the Stilfser Joch to Meran, and finally by way of Innsbruck to our native Salzkammergut, to Gmunden, Ischl and Aussee. The entire trip, in the usual parental tempo, didn't take more than three weeks, and soon after our return, on the first of October, I reported at the Garnisonsspital No. 1 for my year of military service.

The medical students' corps to which I now belonged was not thought very much of from a military point of view, just as the army doctors were not considered combatants in those days, therefore not actually soldiers. They didn't even have any punitive rights over their subordinates; the officers in the medical corps attended to that. In a rather feeble witticism, the medical students were called "Moses dragoons," and there is no denying that some of them, especially the Hungarian and Polish Jews, left much to be desired in respect to military bearing and appearance. And then there were those—one finds them among Jews of all nations—who in their officers' uniforms behaved from the first day in such a martial and swashbuckling fashion, as if they had been at least cadets or veteran officers in a hussar regiment. Even if I could not be classified in this brilliant category, my uniform suited me quite well, and only now did I begin to pay some attention to my appearance which had at times shown a tendency to foppishness. Up to this time I had chosen to dress rather pretentiously, like an artist—my hair fairly long, wide-brimmed so-called Rembrandt hats, soft fluttering cravats, and although I was quite decently clad, as the son of a good bourgeois home should be, I was not what one would have called a well-groomed young man. In this respect our upbringing had been somewhat neglected. In those days the care of one's physical appearance was not given the attention, literally or figuratively, that is bestowed on it today. As was the case in most city apartments, even the more modern and elegant ones, ours did not have a bathroom until we finally had one installed. Before that we did what most middle-class families did —once a week a bathhouse employee brought in a large wooden tub which was filled with hot water, in which, one after the other, Papa, Mama, we children and finally the servants, disported ourselves as best we could. Any more elaborate grooming, such as proper care of the nails, was given even less consideration, and our idea of good table manners was so vague that in the years to come, well meaning friends had to draw my attention—to my shame—to quite a few acts of ill-breeding on my part; things which I, my brother and sister had been permitted to indulge in at home because they simply hadn't been noticed. As for physical exercise and agility—my father took a dim view of both; and since sport in the hygienic, social and especially in the purely competitive sense was appreciated in those days in only a few select circles (to be overevaluated and exaggerated later, partly out of conviction but also out of snobbery and to the detriment of more intellectual diversions), any tendencies we may have had in this direction were all too often doomed to atrophy or to be developed too late and therefore imperfectly. Actually the only thing that was widely practiced was that most primitive and least costly of sports— gymnastics; but since the subject was not compulsory in the *Gymnasium* and my father had absolutely no use for it, I was never urged to take the course and didn't mind at all having to miss it. Fencing was another story. Even my father had to admit that a future soldier and reserve officer should know how to handle a sword, so, with passing interest and without putting myself out in the slightest, I took a course with fencing-master Domaschintzky, a gray-bearded, genial, savage giant. A little later I learned the rudiments of riding at Von Tippelt's academy, but although I did occasionally ride in the Wienerwald with friends who were more accomplished equestrians, and later even dared to undertake such outings in the vicinity of London, I could accept the slightly derogatory designation of "Sunday rider" as flattery rather than as ridicule. I was just as indifferent to ice skating, which I found too much of a bother and which took more time than it gave me pleasure. For a few winters I let myself be persuaded onto the rink to please some young ladies but promptly gave up the sport as soon as these persuasions ceased. That a young man who intended to be a doctor and who was expected to marry well should know how to dance was so self-evident that here at least I did not have to overcome any opposition at home, and actually, dancing remained the only sport in which I indulged wholeheartedly and without any outside pressure.

I had scarcely donned my uniform—it was as if I or my fate had been waiting for such a banal cue—when I began to aim more consciously for what is designated—all too heroically—as "conquests." During the past year my relationship to the opposite sex had taken on an increasingly lively, yet at the same time more impersonal, character; and only a pretty sixteen-year-old blonde with delicate features stands out from the list of trivial fifteen-minute encounters.

Her name was Helene; she came from North Germany, I think from Berlin, and was staying in Vienna, she said, on a pleasure trip with her lover. One of my acquaintances, who was a little older, a little more experienced and a little better-off than I, bore the cost of the dinner the four of us enjoyed at the home of the friendly arranger of the modest party, also of everything we enjoyed after that. On the following day a young lady, who looked a lot like Helene, passed me, seated in a *fiacre* beside an elegantly dressed gentleman. Since the entire rather mediocre episode could only profit by a romantic ending, I decided that the pair trotting by were my blonde partner of the preceding night and her deceived lover.

Nor was the second couple missing in my first amorous adventure as a soldier. Among my comrades there was a certain Hiero Stössel, a short, fat, pimply, dreadfully ugly but not stupid fellow, whose capacity for lying was astounding and marked him as problematic, which may suffice as reason or excuse for my consorting with him. At the time he was having a love affair with the daughter of a retired major, a Hungarian aristocrat. This strange girl would enter into intimate relationships only with army medical students—one finds specialization in every field—but with each one only briefly. And so she appeared one evening at the gate of the hospital where Hiero and I were waiting for her, with a companion who was not at all pretty. This was the first time Hiero had seen the girl, just as it was my first sight of the major's daughter. In spite of the fact that she was quite poorly dressed, with pleasant but pallid and slightly dissipated features, there was a certain air of nobility about her. She turned at once, as had been arranged, to me, and without any further formalities we repaired to one of those dismal little inns where the guests change more than once daily. Although Irma and I had an inordinately good time, there were no further meetings; and after the rather startling information I received later concerning her way of life and state of health, facts of which I am sure Hiero had not been ignorant, I considered myself fortunate to have got away so lightly with this first and last hour of love with the major's daughter.

During my first year in the army, my colleague and second cousin, Louis Mandl, proved to be a more pleasant companion than Hiero, who was really distasteful. Because of our kinship I had been at home in Louis's house since childhood, and had therefore also known his father for a long time. Dr. Ferdinand Mandl had emigrated from Rumania, married a wealthy woman, and, while still a young man, had contracted a blennorrheal conjunctivitis while making a gynecological examination, and within a few days had gone totally blind. When there could be no more doubt, also in the mind of the sick man, that his tragic condition was incurable, the famous ophthalmologist Arlt left at the patient's bedside, as if by chance, a small bottle of the atropine which had now become useless, in the expectation—as he admitted later—that his unfortunate patient and former pupil would know how to use the poison for a purpose other than the one of healing, which had had to be abandoned. But the blind doctor, husband and father of several sons, decided, after a bitter inner conflict, to live on for his family and profession. His infirmity, far from damaging his practice, gradually gained for him the reputation of a miracle doctor, especially among his countrymen and co-religionists. The trust put in him by those seeking help, which bordered on adoration, the tender love bestowed on him by his family, and the respect with which he was treated, even by outsiders, certainly helped him to bear his fate with resignation and dignity, yes, in the unfathomable correlation of things, even as god–sent, with the purpose perhaps of contributing to the salvation of other sufferers. He always wore a black patch over one eye, his gray hair flowing around his head, and a long patriarchal beard, and such a gentle yet at the same time priestly glow played about his noble features that even those who were very ill dared to hope that they would find in his proximity, if not actual healing then at least a magnificent example of spiritual composure.

Of his three brothers, two were merchants who dealt on the stock exchange in grain. I have already mentioned one, Ludwig, who was married to a younger sister of my mother; the other, Bernard, I met only fleetingly. Stranger than these two was the youngest brother, Ignatz, who turned to politics after leading a rather unstable and unsuccessful life as tutor and doctor of medicine. As Vienna councilman, his functioning was vociferous rather than productive. He was active, without any justification whatsoever, as an anti-corruptionist, and to begin with formed, together with Dr. Lueger, what might be termed a party of their own. Soon they were joined by other rather questionable ethicists, and the anti-corruption democratic party soon developed into the anti-Semitic wing of the city administration, not because more corrupt elements were to be found among the Jewish population than among those of other faiths, but because it seemed more easily explicable to the masses and therefore promised a quicker political success, to denounce as corrupt a strictly defined group of human beings, especially the Jews, who seemed destined for the role even without the "yellow mark" they once had had to wear. This seemed preferable to the more troublesome method of ferreting out a few suspicious creatures from various other classes and religions and delivering them up case by case to the morally indignant.

As soon as anti-Semitism had succeeded in revealing itself clearly and had prevailed, Ignatz Mandl was one of its first victims; while his former friend and comrade in battle, Lueger, without a glance at his fallen friend, moved on the prescribed path of his promising future at the end of which beckoned the longed-for goal of his aspirations—the dignity of the mayoralty. Although he understood so well how to exploit the lowest instincts of the masses and the general political atmosphere to further his own ends, at heart, even at the height of his popularity, he was no more anti-Semitic than he had been in the days when he had played tarot at the home of Dr. Ferdinand Mandl, with his brother Ignatz and other Jews. There were and still are people who thought it was to his credit that even during the period of his most pro-nounced anti-Semitism he preserved a certain preference for a great many Jews and didn't try to conceal it, but as far as I am concerned, this has always seemed to me the strongest evidence of his moral questionability. Or are the so-called differentiations between the demands of political partisanship, on the one hand, and one's own private, humane convictions, experiences and sym-pathies on the other really so clean-cut as the designation im-plies? I would say no, just the opposite; that for the pure in heart it is impossible to make such differentiations, much less be pleased with them.

In those days however, and specifically in December 1882, it was neither Lueger nor any of the other tarot players to whom I paid much attention; what attracted me to the home of my col-league Louis, beside his many pretty cousins who turned up, especially on Sundays and holidays, was a young lady who helped in the household and was companion to Fräulein Nancy. She had been accepted in the family like a foster daughter and lived with them on a footing of complete equality. Else von Kolsch came from an impoverished Polish aristocratic family; she was still quite pretty, very sensible and fairly well-educated; a serious girl, almost reserved. One evening—before this we had exchanged only a few words and rarely conversed without witnesses—we met by chance on the stairs and after a few trivial, completely conventional phrases, were suddenly in each other's arms, a silent mutual prom-ise which was fulfilled a few days later without any reminder pass-ing between us. Now for the first time I could enjoy the ever-charming experience of seeing a creature, who only a few hours before had lain at my side, unreservedly mine, in the company of people who knew nothing and were never to know about our affair, behaving toward me in an innocent and ladylike fashion.

That afternoon we had lain on rumpled pillows, nibbling chocolate chestnuts and other sweets, only to sit opposite each other at the table on the same evening, well-behaved and all buttoned-up, exchanging words of exaggerated simplicity, which of course were not lacking in innuendo, words that made us blush unseen or smile, and drinking to each other with looks that no one was supposed to notice. As farewell I would kiss her beloved little hand as if . . . or as I put it in the poem I dedicated to this episode, "As if I had never kissed your throat." These glances which no one was supposed to notice, and other gentler signs of our secret understanding, may have eluded those who could see, but they did not escape the blind doctor. Whether it was a friendly fatherly feeling or perhaps to some extent the vague, helpless jealousy of the aging man that made him suddenly "seeing" and induced him to speak to Else in serious, gentle admonition; or whether she, in remorse or subconsciously cruel, confessed to him more than he had sensed or guessed, were considerations which didn't bother me very much at the time. But Else was deeply moved by the ingratiating and solicitous words of the revered blind man and declared that from then on she would be my friend only, a decision which, after having succeeded several times in shaking it, I countered with a poem that I never showed her and in which I concluded with the rather impertinent lines, "This garter, too, I do return to thee. Early this morn I found it in my bed." So I bade her farewell for the time being, my heart all the lighter because I had never really been in love with her, and a new, gayer happiness was awaiting me, in fact was already holding me captive.

It happened toward the end of the carnival season. I accompanied my friend Louis to a small gathering in the suburbs which a pretty coffee-house owner's wife had urged him to attend. He was less passionately involved, according to my observations in the coffee-house where the whole thing had started, than she was. The Three Angels Hall in which the "house ball" was to take place —that was what such festivities were called even if any outsider could buy a cheap ticket at the desk—was not distinguished by splendor or refinement but rather by an atmosphere of old-fashioned geniality. In the main hall there was dancing and in the tavern rooms on either side the town notables sat eating and drinking, dressed in their Sunday-best—fathers, mothers and other relatives, most of them from a quite well-to-do middle-class milieu. Everywhere the smell of beer and cigars mingled with the scent of flowers and various perfumes spread by the dancing daughters in their light and colorful summer dresses. Although there was no lack of native sons and other suburban dandies among the dancers, still we two military men in our officers' uniforms, which here were shorn of the odium of Moses dragoonship, entered the scene—I won't go so far as to say like princes from a fairy tale land but certainly like beings from another, loftier world. Regardless of whether the established gentlemen and experienced dancers eyed us with respect or displeasure, the only smart thing for us to do was to mingle with the crowd as affably as possible and disappear in it. I lost no time in asking a pretty little blonde to dance with me, and while walking up and down with her during a pause, we suddenly found ourselves in one of the adjacent rooms which looked like an enormous storage place, with a long bare table and some chairs, end side up. It was unlit and was probably used on other occasions for private club meetings. Here our conversation took on such a lively character that we left the room a few minutes later feeling a lot closer than we had on entering it. We repeated the visit in every intermission and also occasionally spent some time at the tavern table where Anni's father, a short, gray-bearded gentleman, dressed in his best Sunday coat, sat watching the young people amuse themselves while methodically drinking one glass of beer after the other and smoking a cigar in a long white holder; seated at his side was Anni's mother, whom I can't remember at all. They didn't seem in the least concerned to see their daughter, always with the same young man for a partner, disappear from their view, even from the dance hall itself, for shorter or longer periods of time. I can't report whether Louis was enjoying himself as much with the coffee-house owner's wife as I was with my chance acquaintance, in fact I don't even know if the lady in question ever turned up at the ball. All the characters from this lovely carnival night are like shadows among whom I can see myself and golden-haired Anni, the only living creatures, floating by or kissing and embracing in dark corners, while her gray bearded father is satisfied to sit, solemn and sleepy, his cigar cold, a glass of beer on the table in front of him, in an apathetic and remote minor role.

That Anni, in spite of her innocent little face and childlike figure was not altogether inexperienced was something about which I could have no illusions after the unhesitating way she had responded to my caresses during the first hours of our acquaintance; and a few days later, on our first evening walk together, she confessed, with the semi-honesty which is somehow unavoidable in the preliminary stages of such a relationship and which at the time seems to be just one more attraction, that she had been quite intimate with several men but truly loved and still loved only one, the conductor of a small orchestra that played in taverns for dancing and entertainment. He was quite popular at the time and was married. Courtesy of this suburban Don Juan she had become pregnant and had chosen in good time to put a drastic end to her condition. With this distressing episode as warning, and by temperament driven constantly into new love adventures, she belonged to that category of sorry females who are doomed to live from month to month, fluctuating between rashness and fear. Since rashness was the stronger element in her nature, our relationship, which only lasted a short time, ran its course serenely except for a few hectic days during which she swore—a vow soon broken—never to be mine again. I, for my part, felt completely free of responsibility, and in spite of the fact that I was fairly seriously involved, was not yet tortured, as on later occasions, by jealousy of the past and future. The few hours granted me in Anni's arms count therefore not as the most passionate but perhaps as the pleasantest and gayest memories of my youth, and were I obliged, in a bad "examination" dream, to designate to a pedantic professor of literature one of the girls I have known as the archetype of the "sweet girl," that could only be little golden-haired Anni, whom I recognized and with whom I got along so well during the first waltz at a family ball in the Three Angels Hall; who was tarnished but without sin, innocent without virginity, passably honest yet just a little bit deceitful, nearly always in good spirits yet occasionally with a fleeting frown of anxiety on her forehead, not exactly a success as the daughter of a respectable bourgeois home but as a sweetheart the most respectable and unselfish creature imaginable. And even if she had just finished being the tender, exuberant beloved, blissfully lost in the magic hour spent in the cosy, well-heated little room into which she always followed me after a first slight hesitation, she had only to walk down the dimly-lighted stairs, through the half-dark entryway and out of the secluded twilit side street into the sobering glare of the lamps on the main thoroughfare, and plunge into the swarming crowd of businessmen, pedestrians and people hurrying home, to be transformed into an unobtrusive, conventional little Fräulein with insouciant eyes, among so many others just like her. And I am sure that a quarter of an hour later, she would appear at the family table, a little late but innocently merry and spreading merriment all around her, the good little, bad little daughter, bringing with her—regardless of whether anyone believed it or not—greetings from the shopkeeper where she had stopped to buy something, or from a friend with whom, as usual, she had stayed too late, chatting. And if her mother noticed, while her attractive child ate heartily the meal that had had to be warmed up for her, that her braids weren't pinned up just the way they had been that afternoon when she had been in such a hurry to leave right after the coffee had been served, she preferred not to make any obvious remarks or ask any questions, but with a glance at her husband—always such a trusting father, who was about to stick his cigar into its white paper holder—would think, with a trace of sadness possibly, but hardly with regret, of bygone times when she had been young and perhaps also a sweet girl.

On a beautiful afternoon in early spring it so happened that I waited in vain for Anni at the usual street corner, and with that the story ended. When I met her by chance in the autumn of that same year, she declared that she had only been late and I had left too soon. We chose not to bring up the question why, after this abortive meeting, neither of us had written a word to each other, and she gave me to understand, with that three-quarter honesty which is customary after the termination of such love affairs but which by then has lost its charm, that she was having an affair with somebody else. I never saw her again, but ten or twelve years later, when I was telling a friend of mine about various past love affairs, and mentioned Anni and where she lived, he recognized in her a young lady with whom an acquaintance of his had had and was still having a serious affair.

The few poems I wrote to Anni or rather, about her—for in this case too I placed no value on being considered a poet by my beloved—wouldn't be worth mentioning if they hadn't been my first efforts to write in the folk idiom; and the artificiality of my endeavor was betrayed by the fact that in the refrain I felt impelled to call my sweet Viennese girl, not Anni—"Annerl" would have been even better—but "Ännchen," as if she had been a native, not of Vienna's Wieden, Kettenbrücken or Schleifmühlgasse, but of Tharau or Berlin. I never received a letter from her but have kept a photograph in which a white lace veil gives her a theatrical appearance which doesn't suit her at all, and one feels like addressing her neither as Anni nor Ännchen, but as Annette, perhaps even "Beatrice" would seem more appropriate. But of what use are pictures? What use would letters be if one had them? Of what avail are descriptions and reports? Now that I have come to the end of my tale—and how often this is still to happen to me—I realize that I have told nothing actually about her.

She was followed by Theresa, the much courted cashier of my favorite café, where I played billiards in the morning, cards in the afternoon, billiards and cards in the evening and cards and billiards at night. I was probably correct in my suspicion that there was a liaison between her and the pay waiter, who was a *roué* and looked a lot more elegant than most of the steady customers he served, from whom he liked to borrow money. One afternoon, on the way to the coffee-house, I happened to meet Theresa, who was just leaving. We quickly conveyed to each other what was on our minds, understood each other perfectly, and after a drive through the Prater in a closed *fiacre*, spent the evening merrily in an even more secluded spot. She was very pretty and liked to hum, more often than I considered necessary, a popular operetta song, "Love requires endless study; who loves but once is a fuddy-duddy." The next time—it was a bright spring day from which we had fled into the twilight of drawn curtains —she was in a sentimental mood and sighed on my shoulder, "At last I've found somebody I could really like, just when I have to

leave." For she had given up her position at the coffee-house and
a few days later left for her home town, an event that was followed shortly afterward by the departure of the elegant pay
waiter who had been noticed lately whispering meaningfully with
her at the cashier desk. He left numerous creditors behind; thanks
however to the meagerness of my allowance, which had prevented
me from acceding to his requests, I had no cause to lament his
departure. I paid my debt of gratitude to Theresa in one of those
Heine style poems which I evidently felt in duty bound to produce in those days, not so much for the benefit of my beloveds as
for my own.

All these minor love affairs did not occupy my mind to any
great extent and didn't actually absorb much of my time. Billiards
and cards filled in more and more useless hours with the result
that few were left for lectures and study. Nor could my duties at
the military hospital be rated as advancing my medical career.
During the first months I was assigned to the morgue where I
attended autopsies, and when it was my turn, had to keep the
records. The departmental head, an army doctor in charge of
pathological anatomy, did nothing to inspire the participation of
his subordinates in scientific subject matter. Half of the students
assigned to the morgue were free of duty every second week; then
all they had to do was put in a daily appearance at the hospital,
and like all the others, receive "the order of the day," with its
usual inconsequential items. Two months later I was moved to
the department of Staff-doctor Professor Chvostek, a capable practitioner, active researcher and heavy drinker. At the time he was
specializing in research on inflammation of the portal vein and
was therefore eager to discover among the soldiers under his care
as many cases as possible of this rare disease. I can't remember
whether any of the autopsies ever corroborated his diagnosis, but
now I was faced for the first time with one of those cases of monomania which may well be termed the professional sickness of
scientifically ambitious second- and third-rate doctors. After the
death of the famous internist, Bamberger, Chvostek had flattered
himself with the hope that he might become the great doctor's
successor. When Nothnagel was called from Jena to fill the vacant
chair, our staff-doctor made no effort to conceal his poor opinion
of the new director, and liked to be entertained by stories of his

presumed failures in diagnosis and similar more or less well-founded hospital gossip. Several of my comrades knew how to curry favor with such talebearing, and even I, who wasn't at all cut out for ingratiating myself with anyone, decided one day that I could please my chief with the information that Nothnagel had diagnosed a case of pleurisy but the autopsy had resulted in a verdict of hydrothorax. "He's a devil," said Chvostek casually, which wasn't exactly correct; but his reaction made me realize the pettiness of my action more efficaciously than any success of my little effort might have done, by infusing me with a salutary feeling of shame which may well have affected me for the rest of my life.

While in the army, it was impossible to attend university lectures regularly, but even the hours from twelve to two, which was when my more diligent comrades went to hear Späth on obstetrics, I usually spent, with a few others, eating my lunch so that nothing could prevent me from wielding my billiard cue at two. We had a table reserved for us regularly at the Riedhof, where Louis Mandl and I were rarely missing. Armin Petschek, a good, capable student, today district doctor in Vienna, and Sigmund Dynes, an industrious agreeable fellow who stayed in the army and rose to the rank of top staff-doctor, usually also partook of this midday meal with us. The only civilian in our midst was Theodore Friedmann who was destined to become the prototype for Dr. Friedrich Witte in my *Fairy Tale* (*Das Märchen*), of which neither of us had any idea at the time. Like Louis Mandl and myself, he was a doctor's son (his father was director of the hydropathic institute in Gainfarn), a handsome, quite elegant and pleasant young man, not particularly ambitious and only moderately gifted. I have not been able to forget a remark of his from those days, less because of its significance than for the impression it made on us. We were talking about dueling, and all of us, without exactly feeling that we were supporters of the tradition as a matter of principle, but more out of the general spirit of those student days and especially as inductees and future reserve officers, stressed our willingness to give satisfaction if it were demanded. Theodore was the only one who declared that under no circumstances would he duel, and in answer to our question: why, replied with a smile—because he was a coward. It was not so much the unestablished fact of his cowardice that astonished us, as the courage it took to confess it, something we weren't ready to admit at the time, not to him nor to ourselves. None of us were brawlers nor were any of us expert duelers, yet there wasn't one among us who would have tried to evade a student duel or any other kind of duel, if the prevailing rules of conduct made it unavoidable.

The question was very topical at the time for us young men, especially for the Jews among us, since anti-Semitism was spreading rapidly in student circles. The German-national associations, or *Burschenschaften,* had already started to expel all Jews and Jewish descendants, and conflicts during the so-called "promenade" on Saturday mornings, and during student carousals, also street fights, were not rare in those days between the anti-Semitic student corps and the radical-liberal *Landsmannschaften,* formed by those coming from the same native areas, some of which were predominantly Jewish. (Dueling corps with a solely Jewish membership did not as yet exist in those days.) Provocations between individuals in lecture halls, corridors and laboratories were daily occurrences. This was one of the reasons why many Jewish students considered it necessary to become exceptionally expert and dangerous fencers. Tired of waiting for the opponent's effrontery and insults, they quite frequently behaved in a provocative fashion, and their superiority in dueling, which was becoming an increasing embarrassment, was certainly the main reason for the priceless Waidhofen manifesto with which the German-Austrian student body declared all Jews once and for all incapable of giving satisfaction. I have no intention of omitting the exact words of this decree; it went like this:

Every son of a Jewish mother, every human being in whose veins flows Jewish blood, is from the day of his birth without honor and void of all the more refined emotions. He cannot differentiate between what is dirty and what is clean. He is ethically subhuman. Friendly intercourse with a Jew is therefore dishonorable; any association with him has to be avoided. It is impossible to insult a Jew; a Jew cannot therefore demand satisfaction for any suffered insult.

The decree was not declared official until a few years later but the spirit that sponsored it and the sentiments it expressed existed at the time I am describing here, at the beginning of the eighties therefore, and the practical conclusions were drawn on both sides simultaneously. It wasn't always possible, when actual insults had been exchanged and especially when officer honor could not be made to agree with student behavior, to apply the Waidhofen principles as strictly as their followers would have liked; but the spirit of these principles, the idea—if one may call it that— triumphed all along the line, and as is common knowledge, not only along these lines.

One of the Jewish students who belonged to a German-national fraternity before the changes just mentioned, was Theodore Herzl. I can remember seeing him with his blue student's cap and black walking-stick with the ivory handle and F.V.C. (*Floriat Vivat Crescat*) engraved on it, parading in step with his fraternity brothers. That they eventually expelled him, or, as the students called it, "bounced" him, was undoubtedly the first motivation that transformed this German-national student and spokesman in the Academic Debating Hall (where we had stared at each other contemptuously one evening at a meeting, without however knowing each other personally), into the perhaps more enthusiastic than convinced Zionist, as which he lives on in posterity.

In the institutions of higher learning, anti-Semitism was naturally not altogether satisfied with these auspicious reforms in the areas of student behavior and questions of honor, areas in which theoretical racial speculations and in a sense therefore the dominance of an idea could still be considered excusable; but they succeeded in enforcing their bias also on societies that had nothing to do with philosophy or politics, nor with the phantom of the honor of rank, there where solely humanitarian ends were being served. There was a club at the university which had the function of lending aid to needy, industrious medical students by a monthly contribution of from two to five gulden. The way things stood, those who profited by these sums, which came mainly from Jewish pockets, were for the most part Jews from Hungary, also a few from Bohemia and Moravia. Granted that they were not always good to look at, but they were hard-working, sometimes very talented young men and certainly unfortunate devils who had starved in the ghettos of their homeland and now continued to suffer hunger in the big city. The distribution of these subsidies was undertaken by a committee composed of two members of each university year, to which I had belonged from my first semester. Every year a general meeting took place at which the committee gave its report, which was usually accepted by the full assembly without further debate. It was, I believe, during my year in the army, perhaps a year before, that the German-national element demanded that from now on only Germans were to receive such financial aid, no Hungarians or Slavs, which was to say—no Jewish students. This was followed by a stormy discussion, interpellations, invectives, cries for order, in short the whole farce of a parliamentary scandal in miniature. The baptized Jew was of course represented among the speakers of the Christian-German Party, and with the false objectivity of the renegade knew so cleverly how to defend the viewpoint of his wretched but, in all probability, sincerely convinced fellow members, whose favor he was trying to curry, that he became the butt of a slogan that was popular at the time: "Anti-Semitism did not succeed until the Jews began to sponsor it." Although this first attack was not entirely successful, the one after that was. I and my liberal colleagues on the committee lost their mandate, and a thoroughly anti-Semitic committee was chosen. My personal successor was a serious medical student in the same year as myself, called Mausetschläger, a puffy, pale, Tyrolese peasant who was destined to die of galloping consumption before the completion of his education. His appearance flows together in my mind with that of another student whom I had to treat for scarlet fever a few years later, in the Standthartner clinic. When I met him in the hospital garden a few days after his recovery, he seemed to feel in duty bound, as a staunch advocate of the Waidhofen manifesto, to walk past me without a greeting. A joining of these two figures produced the student, Hochroitzpointner, who plays a rather characteristic role in my comedy, *Professor Bernhardi.*

I am not cognizant in any detail of the fate of this society for the subsidization of medical students, but the disturbance was by no means ended with this first decisive victory of the anti-Semitic elements in it. During later meetings there were scuffles, and when once, or more often than that, some anti-Semitic students belabored their Jewish colleagues with sticks and clubs, and the latter, after conferring among themselves, withdrew, the society was officially dissolved. I don't know if it was reconstituted later, and if so, under what conditions.

Among the army medical students, as in almost every unit of those serving for one year only—and where not?—there was a, let us say here too, clean-cut division between Gentiles and Jews, or, since the national factor was being stressed more and more, between the Aryan and Semitic elements, and any private socializing was very narrowly circumscribed. Of the staff doctors scarcely one was amiably disposed toward the Jews, but among the younger assistants and head doctors, in so far as they were not Jewish, only a few expressed their sentiments with undesirable clarity; not that any of us took it very much to heart. One of these gentlemen—his name was Rudroff—hoped once to vent his spleen on me and a few of my comrades by ordering us to report, because we had been late for our appointments several times, a violation which could have netted us several weeks of confinement to barracks. I promptly filed a request, in my name and the names of my comrades, with our senior medical officer, Staff-doctor Chvostek, begging him to quash the complaint, to which he acquiesced promptly and without further ado. I reported this along strictly official channels to Assistant Doctor Rudroff, second-in-command, who was extremely annoyed and inquired of Chvostek whether his leniency toward us could be termed correct, which Chvostek, who abhorred all military chicanery, took as an affront, and to our delight the whole affair ended with a reprimand for Rudroff. As a matter of fact, I can state quite categorically that the most efficient army doctors thought least of making a display of militancy, whereas the so-called *Kommissknöpfe*, or military pedants among them were nearly all ignoramuses. Of course there were a few who knew how to combine a fair amount of knowledge with more moderate military behavior, and these were the men who were most popular, as for instance the regimental doctors Gschirhakl and Trnka. The latter, like Chvostek an internist, was my immediate superior for a few months and favored me to some extent, causing Gschirhakl to call me jokingly "the adjutant."

I did my best to remain in the department for internal medicine. Staff-doctor Matzal, under whom I served for a time, was an internist, so-called, but he was possessed of an indolence and incompetence which made itself felt in all scientific and military matters. Those who maintained that for him no ailments existed beside *catarrhus pulmonum* and *catarrhus ventriculi*, were exaggerating, and the fact that he crossed out the diagnosis *ulcus rotundum* (a round ulcer), which an overly eager student had dared to write on the chart, with the notation, "We don't go in for anything like that," is nothing but a maliciously invented anecdote; yet both anecdote and exaggeration came pretty close to the truth. One of the men who tried to compensate for his mediocrity as a doctor by rude army behavior was the regimental doctor Guido von Török, head of the surgical department, who probably because of this crude propensity had been ordered to drill us, exercises for which only a few summer afternoon hours had been reserved. Since I had been granted a fourteen-day vacation at the beginning of July, I asked for and received dispensation from the last hour of drill on the afternoon preceding my departure. During a pause in the exercises, I stepped out of line, and referring to my permit, asked the regimental doctor for permission to retire. My request was granted, but the churlish "Go to the devil!" with which Dr. Guido von Török dismissed me echoed on in my mind for a long time with an almost exaggerated symbolic power, as if not only the miserable nature of a negligible individual, but a whole human class, yes, a whole epoch, had found expression in this unreasonable, ill-bred, barracks outburst.

During this year I became a steady visitor at the races. Actually it was not so much a sporting interest that drew me to the Freudenau, nor were the results on the board the only or even the main attraction. That lay far more in the whole marvelous atmosphere of elegance, amusement and grace which appealed to my senses. The landscape and how it was peopled held their especial charms for me; the track with its hurdles and ditches, a white fence all around it, circumscribed in the distance by woods; the lean jockeys seated on their noble horses with the flaring nostrils, their shiny bright silk blouses puffed by the wind; their red, blue and gold sashes; the crowds—a dark mass thinning out and lost on the outskirts of the raceway; and above all this whirring, murmuring, fluttering, surging—a pale blue sky with its little white clouds spread out above the crowns of the Prater trees all the way to the Hungarian flatlands; and added to all this, a peculiar almost intoxicating *mélange* of hay, stall and meadow smells mixed with every variation of exotic perfumes. No wonder that from one time to the next one would long for the magic of this scene and these smells, and for the cool damp air that even on more humid days blew from the invisible Danube flowing nearby, through this field of gaiety. More often than not I would find myself, with my friends, in the so-called "gulden" seats, with other bourgeois citizens, students, salesmen, bank clerks and their ladies—for the most part harmless folk for whom the races were a Sunday pleasure and sport, much like any other; or with habitual second or third rate bettors. But sometimes, when money was scarce, I could be found in the twenty-kreuzer section, amid the lower classes, if that's the way one wants to put it; among which, however, the more well-to-do elements were also quite numerous. Sometimes, for instance if one had won the last time round and arrived, not by train but in a *fiacre*, galloping down the Hauptallee, one could be seen strolling in the enclosure, wearing a yellow top coat— until Derby Day of course with a top hat—binoculars slung around one's neck, among counts, bankers, bookies, cavalry officers, crooks and ardent followers of the sport, to say nothing of their hybrid varieties, feeling as if one belonged, and slightly overcome by snobbishness, one would look with a measure of contempt, as if at a strange far-off world, at those pitiful or comic creatures who had to make do with the cheaper seats, or, *sans* necessity, were perfectly satisfied with them. But wherever one happened to be, whether in the enclosure or in the "gulden" seats or among the common people, one felt united with those who belonged there. One knew the colors of the stables, the pedigrees of the horses, had one's favorites among the owners, the riders, the racers, knew all about their chances for the day and placed one's bets, a dilettantish and insouciant gambler, on the outsider rather than the favorite, always in the hope that this was the race that would make one a rich man.

But however restless and exciting and interspersed with a breath of the forbidden, all this was only preparation or echo. Truly precious and mysterious were the minutes in which the entire meaning of all the commotion was to be fulfilled, in which the landscape, as if designed with artistic intent, became wings and backdrop for a marvelous drama in which one was almost participant, watching the race with a heart beating fast, following it with one's binoculars, among the galloping horses always keeping the one in sight on which one had set one's money, oh, sometimes one's last gulden! Even when it was left behind, unable to extricate itself from the pack, yes, even a hundred yards before the winning post, and if it was running last and the jockey had given up, never, as if one's wishes had wings, did one relinquish the hope that it might yet come in first. And often, when it came in second, third or fourth, one tried to tell oneself that it had been ahead of the others, or that at least there had been a tie, until at last, on the big board beside the judges' box, the lights of which could be seen from far off, the number of the actual winner was posted, irrevocable and annihilating. Ah well, so one had been unlucky as usual, but the next race would reimburse one's losses ten- or twentyfold. The only dreadful thing was when one had sacrificed the last of one's fortune, and this time for something that had actually been dubious from the start, and along came a race in which one could tell the winner with mathematical certainty, or still better, prophesy intuitively which horse would win. Could any other horse possibly come in first, in the race that was just being announced, but this brown-black stallion, "Lord Byron" out of "Kiss Me Quick"? Just take a look at him, my friends, a horse that was treacherously held back some time ago by a bribed jockey, on which, by the way, one had bet (and lost) every time it had run, yes, since its first race; a horse that today would bring its faithful followers their well-earned satisfaction. And still worse, when one tried to borrow ten, five, two gulden from a good friend, from another whom one had only recently helped out, from a third, who had just been lucky, until there was nothing left to do but give up hope of placing a bet oneself and had to settle all too magnanimously for persuading, for imploring one's less enthusiastic friends to place their money, all of it, everything they had with them on this dead certain horse which would pay ten times as much! Only to reap nothing but scorn and derision for one's unselfish advice, just because one had been wrong a while before in a similar case. But worst of all, when the horses were assembled at the gate and one saw one's favorite, the most magnificent one, the triumph to come streaming from its dashing nostrils, and the red flag was lowered and the racers started to gallop and one's favorite broke away miraculously from the pack and took the lead at once, surging forward, ten, fifteen, twenty lengths ahead of all the others, and two minutes later, reins hanging slack, ripped past the winning post to the jubilation of the few fortunates who had betted on it, yes, that was undoubtedly the worst moment of all, almost literally painful.

So there one stood with one's empty pockets, a bitter smile playing about one's lips, with nothing left but the pitiful satisfaction of strolling from one hardhearted foolish friend to the other and hissing into their ears, "So . . . what did I tell you?" Fifteen times one's money, a hundred and fifty to ten, seventy-five to five, even thirty to two . . . in any case a sum that could have meant a lot, above all a basis for the next race, for if one had bet twenty, naturally on the outsider, who according to the law of consecutives had to win, moreover this one was a steeplechase and one always had luck with a steeplechase, and in the last race (a steeplechase), the winner had again paid double the money, or perhaps ten to one; nothing was more likely than that one would have left the racecourse a few hundred gulden to the good. And the money would have meant Havana cigars, dinner at Leidinger's, a *fiacre*, an orchestra seat at the Wiednertheater, first row, a priceless cravat, and above all—money for the next time. That was the most important thing.

Sometimes, oh, rarely enough, luck smiled on me to such an extent that one or two of these dreams could be modestly fulfilled. On the whole though, the racetrack treated me just as unfavorably as every other form of gambling, so that today it still puzzles me how I could possibly have managed during this army year and the few that were to follow, to continue pursuing my way of life without getting into serious financial difficulties. Seen from afar, with my meager allowance which was usually spent, theoretically, in advance, and always heavily encumbered by debts, I really was to some extent a "five-gulden *roué*," which was what Hermann Bahr called the hero of my first book, not entirely correctly; and quite a few of my cronies—at this point I guess I can call them that—didn't look much better when seen close up, even if one or two of them could be categorized as above the five-gulden status.

Among these friends of mine, the most remarkable one, whom this sarcastic designation also doesn't exactly fit, was Richard

Tausenau, a law student whom I described in my diary a few weeks before going into the army, in the racing jargon of those days, as "my most intimate friend by three lengths." He had been in my class in the *Gymnasium*, but we hadn't really become close until the holidays between our first and second year at the university. His Mariahilf bourgeois blood was one-quarter Jewish. His grand- or great-grandfather or great-uncle had played a somewhat obscure role as demagogue or *agent provocateur* in the 1848 days; he may even have been fated to fight out in his own heart, with tragic cognizance, the eternal struggle between conservatism and revolution, as happens more frequently than the admirers or exaggerators of staunchness of character realize or care to admit, and which can lead to all sorts of serious and dangerous misunderstandings. His great-grandson or great-grandnephew, who had never known him, couldn't provide me with any details. ·

At the *Gymnasium* Tausenau had been one of the less brilliant students. He had scarcely entered the university when he became a member of "Silesia," a German-national dueling corps, wore his cap jauntily on the side of his head, caroused and dueled, in emulation of his *couleur* brothers, but left the society after receiving his first dueling scar on the forehead, which seemed to have been the main purpose of his participation in student dueling glory. Nobody objected to his leaving; because of his Jewish blood it was even encouraged, if not requested. Soon after that he joined the Vienna Hausregiment, the *Hoch und Deutschmeister*, for his one year of service, which was also typical of him. Again he wore his cap jauntily on the side of his head, just as he had worn his student's cap the year before. Costumed to live and carouse in every respect above his means, he became more negligent about paying his gambling debts than was customary even in our lax little group, indulged himself indiscriminately with females of all categories, even though his luck with women of refinement was enviable and legendary, until he met his fate, as his colleagues of the médical profession had predicted, in the arms of an unregistered prostitute. The seriousness of his illness, which a relative, the fashionable track doctor August Schwarz had first considered fairly harmless, was to make itself felt only later. I can still hear the strange short laugh, so typical of Richard whenever things were critical, that I was to hear often as time went by, with which he confessed the distressing circumstances to me.

From a medical viewpoint the illness ran a relatively mild course; Richard didn't let the misfortune trouble him particularly and as soon as possible resumed his old way of life in every respect. As chance would have it, about six months after his temporary recovery, we met, in the Prater, the poor, pale and thoroughly unattractive woman who had precipitated the disease, and my friend Richard, void of all resentment, greeted the fateful creature like a sympathetic acquaintance and soon bade me adieu to spend the evening and probably the night with her. But somehow it was impossible to be angry with him because his rashness was rooted in a melancholy-cynical feeling for the world in general, a melancholy that glittered with a cynicism that was most strongly expressed whenever he saw it confirmed as the result of his own frivolous behavior; and his tendency to incur debts and to indulge in all sorts of slightly shady actions that were even worse, emanated from his inclination toward an aristocratic way of life, which may occasionally have been lacking in grandeur but which never degenerated into ludicrous snobbery. Without ever appearing or behaving like a dandy, he was the one in our group who came closest to a true, although at times shabby, elegance. He was not what one would have called a handsome man, yet his lithe, slender figure, his narrow features, his pale, in a way too-small face with its black Van Dyke beard, made him look interesting, although not always pleasant. For his mocking way of looking at you, which was never quite open and in the background of which unclarified things seemed to lie hidden, aroused suspicion in those who didn't know him well and a slight sense of caution even in his friends. Sometimes he admired a certain aristocratic impertinence in a person more than I could understand or even forgive; for instance, he once told me with something akin to relish about the shameless behavior of a young count who had entered a box in some place of amusement or other to converse in an intimate fashion with the lady in it, with nothing but a scornful glance at her bourgeois escort, seated at her side, fuming and helpless.

It must be fairly obvious that I had to feel strongly attracted to

Richard as probably the most problematic human being with
whom I had ever established contact, but that he was also more
closely drawn to me than to anyone else was surprising. For I
couldn't begin to satisfy him in elegance—the one human attribute
for which he had unbounded admiration; nor was I sufficiently
dashing—a trait he also rated highly; nor was I affluent, which
was sometimes an incentive for him to enter into a more intimate
relationship. But he was perhaps the first person who recognized,
or at least sensed, not only the essential aspects of my talent but
also the specific and in the last analysis not altogether unproblematic aspects of my personality, and this may have been what attracted him to me. Without any real interest in literary matters,
he took what one might call prophetic pleasure in a few of my
poems, which I felt disposed to show him in some coffee-house
corner or other, the only member of my innocuous little group of
men-of-the-world with whom I felt so inclined. He liked them,
probably more for their mystical-spiritual content than for their
poetic quality. In his love affairs he was more the collector than the
seeker, absolutely unscrupulous, and for someone who aspired to
being a gentleman, too indiscreet; and in this he did not change.

These were the years during which, for reasons which may be
readily understood, he could scarcely have been called at the
height of his powers as a lover; and even in our circles, whose
members couldn't boast of all too many romantic or passionate
experiences, he no longer played the role of conqueror. Thus he
appears as an episodic figure among the half-dozen or so young
men who assembled one evening to play roulette in the apartment
of a certain Herr Wilhelm Ostersetzer, a totally insignificant young
bank clerk with a fairly good income but beyond that neither too
well educated nor clever nor particularly good-looking; it may
be said though that he dressed fashionably. I would probably have
made the acquaintance of this clerk, or as we students liked to call
the type—this "jerk," where I met the few others like him that I
knew, namely at the races. At this particular party there were
three girls. One was called Betty and was the sweetheart of Arthur
Horner, who was also present, a mediocre but pleasant enough
fellow, already at that time highly versed in racing matters, who
was later to enjoy quite a reputation as bookmaker on the Austrian tracks. The two other girls were sisters, nothing better

though than the daughters of a caretaker, although no ordinary caretaker but the one in charge of the huge Mölkerhof in the Schottengasse, and they looked like something better. Minna, the oldest, who was Wilhelm Ostersetzer's choice, was a pretty, pale, strapping girl who conjured up the words "snappy" and "pert," with which her personality was completely described. Her younger sister, Toni, was also pale and well-built but not so pretty and less pleasant, also less glib in word and spirit, and although neatly dressed was not as smart as her sister, Minna, whose behavior already seemed to foreshadow the future fashion model.

After the game, the whole crowd, which included our old friend Pepi Mütter and the pianist Rosenthal, moved on to the Stephanskeller where most of us were in pretty good spirits, except the two official lovers, Arthur and Wilhelm, who grew increasingly jealous and bad-tempered. Toni paid especially tender attention to me. On the following evening I had just started out on a routine inspection of the officers' hospital, when a private came to me and reported that a gentleman with two ladies were expecting me at the nearby inn, "Zum Grünen Jäger." With a total disregard for discipline, I left, and at the "Grünen Jäger" found Richard Tausenau, not with the two sisters from the Mölkerhof, whose last name, Faust, was surprising, considering their status in life— but with a pockmarked yet otherwise pretty and buxom Fräulein Mitzi and Arthur Horner's flame, enjoying a frugal supper; and, to my dismay, at a table exactly opposite, Regimental Doctor Gschirhakl with a glass of beer in front of him. He responded to my smart salute with impeccable but somewhat ironic amiability. Of course I couldn't stay long, and Richard and his two ladies, one of whom had been intended for me, accompanied me back to the hospital gates. That evening Betty became Richard's sweetheart. It was just one of those youthful escapades, but ten years later, when I had to treat Betty for a quite serious throat tumor (she had meanwhile married Arthur Horner, although Wilhelm Ostersetzer had informed him of her infidelity and he had complained bitterly about Richard's unscrupulous behavior), and twenty years later, when Arthur Horner came shuffling toward me on a street in the Cottage district, a stammering paralytic, and told me that he was on his way to pay his daily visit to his ex-wife Betty, from whom he had been divorced long ago, I couldn't help but recall that evening long past which had probably laid the foundation for all their misfortune. And the sentence came to my mind which I once wrote down, "We always have to see the dagger glitter before we can grasp that a murder has been committed," and added, for my own edification, "We see it glitter so often, but instead of wresting it from the hand of the murderer, are content to warn him softly that he really shouldn't do anything like that, unless we are too indifferent and indolent for even such admonition."

As a matter of fact, though, it would have been nothing short of Philistine if in those days we had taken things seriously, the consequences of which—if they were to take place at all—lay in the far distant future and a few days later, Richard, Wilhelm and I were sitting at Tökes', a Hungarian restaurant for a change, laughing ourselves nearly sick over the funny story of faithless Betty and cuckolded Arthur.

Meanwhile Toni, whom I hadn't seen since that roulette evening, had begun to play a certain role in my life, and one evening I went to the Volksgarten where I knew she liked to go with her sister and their friends. But instead of Toni I found Fännchen, and there was nothing I could do but walk up and down the summery lanes of the park with her and one of her cousins, a bachelor of about forty. Herr Eduard Mütter was a fat, good-natured little man, a bit of a jokester with twinkling eyes, and he had taken it upon himself for some time now to act as Fännchen's providence, or at least to function as her guardian angel. Whenever he caught me alone, he would try to impress upon me how unhappy Fännchen was about me and that it was heartless of me to cause suffering to such a dear, good girl, all of which flattered me without persuading me in the direction he felt to be right, which would have been the worst one of all. On this day too, and in Fännchen's presence, he played the confidant who could permit himself a thing or two, and got in a few of his friendly little matchmaker innuendos while Fännchen, who could be perfectly natural in front of the good man, behaved in a sadly-in-love and jealously tender manner, which was habitual with her. However, once I had astutely talked them right out of the Volksgarten and to the door of their house, I bade them farewell and hurried back to the park where I found more desirable and jollier company, namely the sisters from the Mölkerhof, accompanied by Wilhelm and Richard. The five of us drove to Döbling and had a gay dinner *al fresco.* On the following Sunday we undertook an outing that was just as merry, across the Kahlenberg to Klosterneuburg, and on our way home, in the railway compartment, feeling the pleasant aftereffects of the sweet *vin de paille* from the cloister cellar and half-asleep on Toni's shoulder, I was quite ready to believe all sorts of things she said, which before Kahlenberg and the cloister cellar I would have smiled at with my usual skepticism. And so our relationship developed gradually but promisingly under the disapproving eyes of sister Minna, who didn't approve, for practical, rather than for moral reasons, of her sister entering into a more intimate relationship with a one-year inductee who was dependent on a meager allowance, and therefore did her best never to leave us alone. Sometimes, though, when the four of us happened to be sitting in the Rathauspark on a humid summer night, Minna would show just as little resistance as Toni, who still couldn't make up her mind whether she should let me have "the ultimate gift of love," mainly because she was afraid of her father—the perfect and rarely equaled prototype of a caretaker —who had sworn to turn out of the house any daughter of his who might so far forget herself.

In the meantime I had been assigned for a few weeks, as dictated by official regulations for army medical students, to the troops, to be precise, to the Mollinary Regiment—brown jackets, black revers. It proved to be quite fatiguing to report at four A.M. in the barracks square and march up the Galizinberg to Aspern after spending the preceding evening with friends (male and female) in coffee-houses, listening to folk singers, and ending up finally in the dark of night on some garden bench or other in endlessly passionate embraces. It must therefore be understandable that one spent many an afternoon sleeping or in a twilit mood in a coffee-house corner with one's melancholy-cynical friend whose blood harbored a mysterious disease and who never had any money, conversing, all dissipation past, all exhilaration spent, on subjects that included all the world's sorrows, during which conversations the word "dreary" turned up again and again in a hundred variations. That Toni eventually became mine did nothing to glorify or uplift my spirit and the idea that I was supposed to believe that of which she so persistently assured me, and which I never ceased to doubt, made me no prouder or happier, for the simple reason that deluding physiological arguments never succeeded in overcoming my well-grounded distrust of the soul. Actually we were happiest when we were alone together, either in a cosy little room, with Toni wrapped in my army coat, my cap perched on her disheveled hair, sitting opposite me as we ate our dinner, or enjoying a mild summer evening on the paths of the park where I had so often strolled in more charming and innocent company. However, I grew increasingly averse to the other couple, Wilhelm and Minna, from whom we could only rarely free ourselves. I couldn't abide Wilhelm, who with his total lack of intellectualism was truly a bore, and Minna treated him with such unconcealed contempt that I began to doubt that they were really having an affair. But then again Toni's charms, which I had never found all that irresistible, paled to such an extent that I began to prefer her vulgar but certainly more jolly sister, whereupon I decided that I had never been in love with Toni in the first place, only jealous of her, and that my life with her excited rather than inspired me. Of course such dismal moments alternated with some that were brighter. Then the distasteful group with which I had somehow become involved would recede and no longer affect me as living individuals, but almost as if they had dissolved into an ambiance. This happened one evening at a supper party in Wilhelm's apartment. I was seated at the piano, improvising, oblivious to the others, my eyes closed, my head leaning against Toni's bosom, and was intoxicated by wine, music and kisses. No! *Could have been* intoxicated. For it was quite clear to me even in moments such as these, that superlatives were uncalled-for, that even my most fervent declarations of love were half-conscious lies, and that I was destined for another nobler creature than one as ordinary as Toni, in spite of her several charming attributes. And in my sorrow I deplored what I was later to experience much more deeply, "If only that which in the course of our development is episodic could be recognized at the time and according to its merits, as episode. But in the end one lives for the moment and lets it suffice."

But then again there were the gay, or at any rate cheerful evenings, and we five-gulden *roués*, soldiers or civilians, really deserved a somewhat higher rating when we could be seen, with our ladies, seated in a smart carriage, tearing off to the Casino Zögernitz in Döbling, where at a crowded table in the packed tavern garden, we listened to Kuzel Leopoldine, or to Mirzl, who was all the rage, or to the sometimes sentimental, sometimes humorous couplets and duets of the famous folksinging couple, Seidl and Wiesberg. I can still hear the *estamtam* verses that were so popular at the time, and for a certain reason remember one word for word. It went like this:

> Estamtam, estamtam, ay and juchay,
> And ay and juchay.
> The city-hall tower has no ventilation,
> But windows that cost all of three-thousand gulden.
> Ay and juchay—juchay!

On the following day I was to take my officer's examination, and one of the standard questions in hygiene, a subject for which I was not at all prepared, was on ventilation equipment. I therefore took the verse as a sign, hurriedly studied the chapter in question before going to sleep and was in fact examined on ventilation the following day. Since the test was a formality and one's appointment to assistant or full-fledged doctor upon getting one's degree was as good as assured to any medical student who wasn't guilty of a misdemeanor, I do not expect my *estamtam* experience to be interpreted as a tale with a moral.

At the beginning of September I bade Toni a tender farewell before leaving for three-day maneuvers, which were to take place not far from Vienna in the neighborhood of Fischamend. A few episodes, not of any actual importance in the sparkling contours of my youthful memories, have remained with me—our quarters for the night, on straw pallets in an attic in Maria Elend, which I shared with two comrades—Hiero Stössel and Wassing, who at the time was still called Wassertrilling; the village square, veiled gray by the dawn; myself, one of the first up, shivering and half-asleep; and in front of the door, Colonel von Pittel in his brown uniform with the black revers, his riding whip in his hand, and the utterly unmilitary friendliness with which he asked me if I had slept well for which I thanked him, *gehorsamst*, more touched than my formal response could imply. I remember too a midday pause on a green meadow surrounded by a few sparse towering trees; the sound of trumpets in the distance; and finally a vast field, covered with troops—the scene of the decisive battle, for which none of those taking part had the slightest understanding and we medical students were entirely superfluous. With not a soul to command us, we wandered aimlessly back and forth, lost, in all probability in full range of a hail of bullets. Since the colossal battle showed no sign of ending, and we were not only bored but soon began to feel hungry, I suggested to my comrades, Stössel, Wassertrilling and Petschek, that we desert. In military march step and protected by our white arm bands with the red cross, we marched across the field on which the incomprehensible battle was surging back and forth and finally passed through the enemy lines, where they took as little notice of us as our side had done, past the sentries who treated us with the same indifference, until we came to an inn on the Reichsstrasse, on the road to Vienna, where the host led us through the over-crowded main dining room, which had probably been "taken" by the troops, into a small private room. There we found only one other guest, who to our considerable shock turned out to be no other than the anti-Semitic Czech head doctor of our regiment, who could not have been accused of any fondness for us "Moses dragoons." However, he seemed to have fled the chaos of battle just as illegally as we had and moreover had quite evidently already quenched his thirst with quite a few glasses of wine. With comradely joviality he invited us to sit down and eat at his table, and one of us was even permitted to drive home with him in a little wagon pulled by dogs, I can't remember whether on the big drum or in its place. I had to walk quite a distance in the glaring sun until I reached the Central Cemetery and from there rode into town, fast asleep in the horse-drawn trolley. The next morning, in barracks, I was informed that I had the honor of belonging to the victorious army.

Although it was by no means longing for Toni that had lured me home ahead of time from such glorious regions, still I met her that same evening in the Volksgarten and for a few more evenings after that, yet in spite of the fact that we were alone, I could not seem to be completely happy with her. I don't think I am wrong in ascribing the blame for this to the hypochondriac element in my nature and the capital of mistrust that went with it, which paid dividends in the form of self-torture and the desire to torture others, but I was also irked by the fact that I was wasting my time, my thoughts, my finest emotions on a creature who was basically insignificant, and with prophetic anxiety asked myself what would happen to me when faced with a true passion. When Toni refused me out of fear of the possible consequences, or, after giving in to me, tormented me with her anxiety; after scenes of despair, melancholy, bitterness, and finally increasingly sobered by Toni's constant complaints about the aimlessness of our affair, I gradually loosened the ties that bound me to her, or let it happen that she loosened them, and shortly after my return to civilian life she bade me a final farewell with the promise to write. When she did nothing of the sort, I took it upon myself to look her up once more, for the sole purpose of explaining to her that she was no better and no worse than ninety-nine women out of a hundred, in other words that she was a quite normal little beast; but instead I seemed to have been satisfied to confide this bit of enlightenment to my diary, which in the end did me some good too. About six months later I ran across her at a party. It was near the end of the carnival season, and after we had danced past each other several times, I had a good friend of mine introduce us formally, for fun. He was her latest lover, for whom, as I learned from him, she had put on the same little act of virginity or semi-virginity, which she had played for me a few months before. Some weeks later I saw her again, in a coffee-house, this time with her sister and a few other young people. I drank to them from my table, then followed them to their house where the men who were with them departed politely, after which I enjoyed a very nice hour with the two girls who seemed definitely to be on a downhill path. We repaired to the Rathauspark where we planned all sorts of fun, none of which was ever consummated. I never saw Toni again and her sister only several years later at a small *soirée* in a fashionable dress shop where she worked as a salesgirl and was highly thought of by the woman who employed her. At the first possible opportunity she whispered to me that I shouldn't mention our past relationship to a soul.

Already during my army year I entered gently into all sorts of more delicate relationships with various young girls from better homes, or let us say girls who were better chaperoned, between the affairs just mentioned; sometimes they even encroached on them; and if I had been more audacious or artful, and if my horror of complications and responsibility hadn't been so acute, I am sure that one or the other of these affinities could have developed into a true love affair. On the other hand I think that in those days, in the solid Jewish bourgeois circles in which I moved for the most part, such friendships rarely flourished beyond certain permissible limits, not because the girls were less sensual or more innocent than they are today but because the whole social ambiance of the middle-class had been barely touched, philosophically or literally, by more modern and ethically freer points of view. Upbringing, manners, and possibilities for meeting and of developing freer relationships were less advantageous. For the young girl with no sure prospects of marriage, perhaps even without any secret marital hopes, who today decides, after due consideration of all practical precautions, to give her all to her beloved man or youth, such a decision would not have been possible in the times about which I am writing. The born conqueror or seducer always knows how to triumph over the morals of a certain social class, even over the spirit of an epoch, but I was usually satisfied with the adventure that met me half-way, although I sometimes scorned that which was offered too cheaply with the thought that such things were frequently paid for most dearly.

Thus it happened, on a November afternoon, shortly after the termination of my year of military service that, with Richard, I accompanied a very pretty chorus girl from the Wiednertheater to her apartment, where we decided to draw lots for the favor of the young lady who was undecided rather than demure. I was the winner. But since she had told me the name of her lover, a Hungarian aristocrat, and his doctor's indiscretion had previously informed me as to the condition of his health, and when, with my arm around her neck, I by chance touched a gland which according to my medical knowledge felt highly suspicious, I nobly waived the prize I had won and left it to my friend, who, fortunately or unfortunately was in no more danger from this direction. I for my part went off to a nearby coffee-house where, under the impression of this disappointing experience I began to write a

Arthur Schnitzler with his parents

The house in the Praterstrasse where Schnitzler was born

Dr. Philipp Markbreiter, his maternal grandfather who was also a doctor

His father, Professor Johann Schnitzler

The three Schnitzler children: (from left) Julius, Arthur, and Gisela

The young Arthur, aged sixteen—"A slight contempt
for everything conventionally termed elegant."

Schnitzler with his close friends, Louis Friedman (center),
and Richard Tausenau (right) in 1885

Fännchen (Franziska Reich) as she appeared in 1882

Arthur as an officer in the medical corps:
"My uniform suited me quite well."

Schnitzler at the time he met his first "sweet girl"

Jeanette Heger in 1887

His good friend and writer, Richard Tausenau

Schnitzler with Fritz Kapper

The Thalhof Hotel at Reichenau; as Peter Altenberg noted
in the lefthand corner: "The hotel of my marvelous childhood days!"

Frau Olga Waissnix

Arthur Schnitzler about 1890

scene which for the first time gives a faint hint of the man-of-the-world tone of *Anatol*. Months or years later I finished it; called the whole thing, with scornful irony, *Faithfulness (Treue)*, and placed it with the many other manuscripts I have kept, not with pride in my poetic beginnings but rather with a sort of auto-biographical pedantry.

I have already mentioned that I often met cousins of my cousin, Louis Mandl, at public and private dances and at his house, the pretty half- and full-grown daughters of the Adlers, who had been blessed with thirteen or fourteen children. Even if all of them were not present, a good quarter-dozen were always to be found there, all of them in love with their pretty, gentle and platonically pasha-like cousin who lisped when he spoke; or perhaps, to put it more specifically, they had made him the object of their eroticism. But this objectification was by no means exclusive, nor so strong that it didn't flicker and radiate from their prurient little souls in every direction, and two of them especially—Gisela and Emma —left less to be desired in their willingness toward me than I did when it came to exploiting the opportunity. On one of these sociable evenings at the home of the blind old doctor, things must have been a little more lively and abandoned than usual, of course in look and word only, for on the way home I spoke to my friend Petschek, probably in a rather sententious and slightly derogatory tone, about the behavior of the young ladies at the party we had just left. A few days later I noticed that my friend, colleague and cousin Louis responded in a rather dour and alien fashion to the cordial look with which I greeted him from bench to bench before the lecture. Immediately after it was over, when I asked him why, I was astonished, not so much by the fact that Petschek had repeated my remarks with which he had seemed in complete accord during our conversation, but that Louis, in his capacity as cousin of the young ladies and son of the host, seemed upset by them. He soon recovered when I assured him that what I had said in fun had been completely misunderstood, and if this small difference between us, which was so quickly and satisfactorily settled, had not somehow remained with me, I wouldn't be able to recall the foolish remarks I made; in fact if someone had attributed them to me I would have said they were malicious invention, for it was so little a part of my nature, then and now, to

display any moral indignation, especially not if the modest cause
had to a certain extent worked to my advantage.

A few weeks after my return to civilian life, on the tenth of
November 1883, I jotted down in my diary, with the brevity of a
chronicle, some historical and highly personal facts, as follows:
"Luther's 400th birthday—my grandfather's fiftieth anniversary
as a doctor—game of ninepins, arranged by Leopold Rosenberg
—animated evening at Richard's house—attend all lectures on
time, except ophthalmology," and in between, the comment:
"Gisela F.'s lips are sweet."

This Gisela Freistadt was a pretty Jewish girl who, with her
family, was at home literally and figuratively on the outskirts of
the ghetto. We would meet for walks in the evening, at various
parties, and I also visited her in her humble middle-class home.
Her parents had two children beside Gisela—a second daughter,
sixteen years old and prettier than Gisela, and an older son, a bank
clerk who was usually jobless, with a bent for getting in debt and
a tendency to fraud, which soon brought him into conflict with
the courts. Customarily Jewish parents, especially those in such
lowly, almost needy circumstances, have no greater desire than
to marry off their daughters as soon as possible. I was therefore
not surprised when Gisela informed me one day that a wine
merchant from Leoben, whom she couldn't abide, was asking for
her hand in marriage; nor did it astonish me to receive, a few
days later, the announcement of her engagement to him. On
Carnival Sunday, accompanied by my friend Jacques Pichler, who
on this occasion again popped up like a jack-in-the-box, I paid
my congratulatory visit and presented her with a bouquet of
violets. "They are faded," she cried, whereupon I felt impelled to
reply in the florid style of the times, "Like your love for me, my
Fräulein." She informed me in a whisper that this wasn't so, not
at all, and when I visited her again a few weeks later, she sighed,
her arms around my neck in a darkened room, "If only I could
love my fiancé half as much as I love you." The fiancé, more often
than not, was in Leoben; her parents, since the marriage was
assured, had nothing to say against my visits; her brother, Szigo,
also seemed to have no qualms about his sister's honor, so it was
certainly neither scruples of caution or conscience, but indifference, rather, and convenience, that kept me from conducting this

pleasant little adventure to its destined conclusion. The wedding was to take place on the twenty-second of April, and as a preliminary celebration there was an afternoon outing in the Prater on the preceding Sunday, in which the bridal couple, the bride's brother, Jacques, and I participated. The groom, an unprepossessing fellow, in appearance and behavior quite the little Jewish merchant from the provinces, boring and unsuspecting, didn't seem to mind that I never left his future wife's side and didn't seem to notice, as it grew dark, that our fingers were intertwined and we were whispering to each other tenderly. Finally we trooped off to a café in the city and on a twilit spiral staircase, Gisela and I forgot her fiancé and the rest of the world in a long kiss.

The fact that Else von Kolsch turned up in Vienna again, totally free now of the virtuous attitude that had been the cause of our separation the year before, may perhaps count as an excuse for the fact that I let the days following the Prater outing pass without using them to good advantage as far as Gisela was concerned, but on the wedding day I stood in temple, facing her, while she exchanged rings with the groom, and that evening I personally conveyed my congratulations to the couple. Before the bride left her parental home with her husband, she promised me letters, and more and better things than letters. In the anteroom, all dressed to leave, she embraced her attractive sister and cried bitterly. When the young couple had finally left, I could no longer control my anger—I doubt very much if it was pain—and fled into an empty room where I stamped my feet in a bit of play-acting for my own benefit, and for Mela's who had followed me; then I sat down gloomily in a corner of the room, my hand over my eyes. Mela, smiling through her tears, took my hand, pulled it gently from my face, and I kissed hers. That was all, but a few days later her mother begged me, in a polite letter, "to stop visiting them because of all the gossip." Her wish was understandable since Mela was not yet engaged.

Now it would be nice if I could close with the words: I never saw either of these charming sisters again, but that would unfortunately not coincide with the facts. Some years later, after Gisela had written me a few anonymous letters and had finally made herself known to me as their author, and we had met occasionally in coffee-houses and for walks, she turned up during my office hours under the pretext of suffering from pains in the throat. By now she was the mother of several Leoben children, a good housewife but quite evidently ready and willing to keep the promise made on her wedding day. But she had long ago ceased to please me. Her boring, banal way of speaking, which was not free of jargon, only served to further cool my ardor, and I withdrew into my medical profession so successfully that her visits soon ceased. A few years later Mela turned up. She too was unhappily married and the mother of several children, and stood on the threshold of a theatrical career. Since by that time I had already embarked on my literary life, her visit had the objective of arousing in me the interest to do something for her, in return for which she would not have hesitated for a moment to express her gratitude in every conceivable way. She was still very pretty and slightly made up, but although, in anticipation of her future as an artist, she apparently had accepted an advance of sorts in sinfulness, and had even adopted a stage name, she still looked like a rather poor middle-class girl. In her case too I was sufficiently indifferent and cautious not to make up for what I had missed a decade before. The wise old saying, "Never put off until tomorrow . . ." is nowhere so valid as in affairs of the heart.

I find a few other names inscribed in my diary at about the same time, for instance "Charlotte," a voluptuous blonde who came from a similar milieu as the two sisters. I wouldn't say that I remember her as cold, but she was certainly more respectable and reserved, always rather touchy, and, without any right to it, quite jealous. She too soon married and had about half a dozen children. Somehow I kept coming across her, finally as a fat, faded and careworn old woman. Every now and then she would ask me for tickets to one of my plays and was terribly hurt when I couldn't fulfill her wish or failed to reply to her letters, which resulted in bitter complaints about my "insulting ignorance." Indeed, our style never changes, in matters great or small. But I seem to have forgotten all about "pretty black-eyed Agnes," with whom, according to my diary, I could have entered into "a charming suburban idyll," and I have no idea what Fräulein Rosa even looked like, from whom I once received a letter in which she wrote of her great love, and also a few lines about marriage. Fännchen, too, didn't disappear entirely from my life. I met her fre-

quently at balls, and even if we hadn't seen each other for weeks
and scarcely given each other a thought, still we would find ourselves on the balcony of the *Sophien-* or *Blumensäle,* kissing passionately, and she would assure me that I would be the death of
her, a declaration which I accepted with the pride of adolescent
youth, mildly flattered, and didn't take any more seriously than
it was intended.

At the same time as my affair with Gisela Freistadt, I was having
another, on a spiritually higher level, with gentle, ash-blonde
Charlotte Heit, to whose family I had been introduced two years
before. Her father was a well-to-do businessman and as president
of a Jewish burial organization participated in the funerals of
all the wealthier Jewish families, which undoubtedly betrayed
solemn inclinations but ones I found hard to understand. Charlotte's mother was a quiet, boringly dignified woman, and the
entire household was run on decorously homelike lines, but in
consideration of the two daughters, of whom Charlotte, the oldest,
was of marriageable age, was at the same time gay and sociable.
I expressed my impression of the first visit with the words, "The
daughter of the house, a beautiful girl—a few dear people—the
cigars could have been better."

In respect to the latter one was rather spoiled in those days, and
we young dancers, whose allowances rarely sufficed for Havanas,
considered it in no way dishonorable, during a ball, to let a few,
sometimes quite a few cigars disappear from their brown boxes
into the pockets of our dress suits, this beside the one we had enjoyed with our dinner, and would boast about this little act of
pilfering even in front of our host. However, the poor quality of
the cigars evidently didn't stop me from visiting the Heit house,
where I was provided with stimulation of a loftier nature. We
read *Julius Caesar* aloud, taking different parts; presented the one-
act comedy, *Ambition in the Kitchen,* in which I played the father;
also *Dead Man,* by Hans Sachs, for which I happened to be ill-
prepared and had to read my part with my back to the audience,
which didn't seem to mar our success. But not until two years
later, by which time my sister had become a close friend of Charlotte's, did I become a more frequent guest and begin to get along
better and better with Charlotte, who was not what one would
call vivacious, but intellectually attractive and clever, and I en-

joyed her as a dinner partner just as much as I liked to dance with her. Once, during dinner, after she had told me the innocent, naive story of her first love, which was now a thing of the past, I felt impelled to reciprocate with similar proof of my confidence; so our hearts had practically found each other, before the next rehearsals (this time for the French curtain-raiser, *A Cup of Tea*) could exert their oft-proven matchmaking powers. I played Henri; Charlotte, naturally, my wife; and the comic role of Camouflet fell to Ferdinand Neumann, a pleasant, absent-minded, sociable fellow who had been my companion two years before at the modest orgy in the Kärntnerhof. I still owed him my share of that expenditure and never did pay it.

The Heit house was not the only one where I let my feeble thespian talents shine. The year before I had appeared twice at Horn's in a rather vulgar farce, *Two Deaf Men,* once as the young hero who pretends to be deaf, the second time as the old man who is healed of his deafness by a miraculous cure. Henri, in *A Cup of Tea,* was an excellent role, for here I was given an opportunity to imitate the Burgtheater actor Ernst Hartmann, with which I could always be sure of success at any social gathering, without the help of any further theatrical props. Charlotte had even less talent than I, but she looked beautiful, and Ferdinand Neumann achieved the desired comic effect because he had no acting talent at all. We could therefore not complain of any lack of enthusiasm on the part of our goodhumored audiences. The pleasantest part of the evening, however, at any rate for me, was the supper, during which I of course sat beside my "cup of tea" Hermante; and the champagne, perhaps also her success as an actress, would lure words to her lips, the frankness of which would have startled her under more ordinary circumstances. In the course of the conversation she asked me what I thought her ideal person would be like. I said this, I said that; probably nothing more profound than such a question demands, until she suddenly cut off any further profundities on my part by saying, "If only you were a few years older, I'd marry you on the spot."

When dinner was over, I remained at her side, the dancing began and she whispered in my ear, "I've never danced with anyone the way I dance with you." And how did I behave during all this? was the question I asked myself on the following morning when

I wrote in my diary, which here reads a little more affectedly than was usual during this entire unsure rather than impure period of my life, and is moreover interspersed with French novel phraseology, perhaps because I considered the German language, in which after all I wanted to be a poet, too good for such trivia. And I gave myself the reply, "Have no idea. I think, in love, yet feeling dreadfully calm." And that I was, to the depths of my soul; and Charlotte too, after the intoxication of champagne and amateur theatricals had worn off, was her usual well-behaved self again, although she was over-friendly when I visited their house the next time and made no efforts to hide her regret over her imminent departure. She was leaving for Arco with her mother, and while she was away I didn't give her absence much thought because now it was Gisela Freistadt's turn. But Charlotte came back, Gisela married and was gone, and on a beautiful day in May, in the company of a few friendly families, I was at last able to involve Charlotte in a more intimate conversation. I don't recall the goal of the outing nor what we had to say to each other, and I would have no memory at all of this lovely spring day, in the magic and scents of which two young hearts were happy, just as I haven't the faintest memory of a few other days similarly spent, if the following words about it weren't inscribed in my diary, "Everything went according to plan and developed to the point where my reserved egoism and her shyness called a halt." Thus, in these pages, sweet romantic effusions alternate constantly with statements as dry as official documents.

A few days later we celebrated Charlotte's eighteenth birthday. It was a beautiful, warm, summery afternoon. I stood with her and a few others on the balcony of their city apartment from which one could look down at the meager landscaping which was doing its best to simulate a bit of nature between the high, unadorned houses of the Rudolfsplatz, and it was only too clear to me that I wasn't feeling anything at all. At dinner I sat beside her, and as usual during the conversation, our spirits gently merged. Afterward there was dancing, and while I was walking up and down the salon with her, arm in arm between two waltzes, I let fall a remark that came from my head rather than from my heart, and which sounded precocious considering the meager, albeit crowded experiences of my youth, to the effect that I thought I would never marry because I was much too jealous and couldn't demand of any woman that she be faithful to me for more than two years without subjecting her to great emotional strain; for surely during that time somebody would come along with far better physical and mental qualifications. Charlotte replied excitedly, "You're just talking yourself into that. I'm sure your wife would remain faithful to you." "That's what you think today," I said, as another dancer led her away. But a few minutes later she came up to me and said softly, "You shouldn't have said that. Not today." I felt confused. "It's an *idée fixe* with me," I said, in an effort to apologize. "Maybe I'm a fool."

We sat down in a quiet corner. From a conversation going on nearby the word "suicide" drifted across to us and I picked it up. With my urge for logic and probably with the purpose of putting myself in a position that conflicted with the other person, I pleaded zealously for man's right to end his own life whenever he chose and without consideration for others. Charlotte took the opposite view, and after our discussion had run on for quite some time, she turned to me and in her gentle way said, "Look, Arthur, after all the things you have told me this evening, I can no longer hope to marry the one man who could make me happy, yet I am not going to kill myself. I shall try to live on at the side of another man whom I certainly shall not love."

I wouldn't swear to the fact that, as inscribed in a suspiciously romanticized way in my diary, I didn't speak another word for the rest of the evening, but I don't doubt for a moment that I didn't counter with anything sensible and probably wasn't capable of replying at all, and I can't decide now whether it was caution rather than indifference, on purpose or by chance, that for some time after that I did not see Charlotte again. Anyway, she soon moved with her family to Vöslau, and during the first days of July I paid them a formal visit there, accompanied by my brother, and found Charlotte charming and friendly. A few weeks later I left for Ischl, where we had rented a pretty apartment on the Stefanie Quay. It was my intention to prepare for my finals in the relaxing atmosphere of this summer resort. When I opened my trunk I saw a letter which I certainly hadn't put there. It was open, a letter from Charlotte to my sister, which the latter had quite evidently smuggled in with my things and which contained nothing but one long outburst of passion, concerning the object of which there could be no doubt. I remained fairly untouched by it and cannot even justify this lethargy of my heart with the fleeting, semi-platonic relationship to another female whom I had met shortly before my departure for Ischl. The only thing I have to say about her is that "impertinently enough," as emphasized in my diary, she was also called Charlotte. But I can remember clearly that it was during this summer that we young men would wander around avid for the easy conquest, without however being able to report that I was particularly lucky; in fact, a pretty chambermaid seems to have driven me almost to despair with her calculating coyness.

Shortly after our return, my good grandmother, whose noticeable lapses of memory had caused us anxiety already in Ischl, suffered a stroke. For a week she lay unconscious. I was just feeling her pulse when she breathed her last, after having opened her eyes a moment before and looked up in a most touching manner, as if she suddenly knew those standing around her and was bidding them farewell. It was my duty to inform my grandfather of her demise. He had been pacing restlessly up and down his room for hours and now received the news of her death with a mute, almost irritated nod of his head. And I had seen a human being die for the first time.

The sad event, even though I personally soon got over it, darkened the atmosphere at home considerably. The imminence of my examinations didn't help to improve the mood, and it was without any deep feeling of sympathy that I learned that Charlotte had become melancholy, was walking in her sleep, cried a great deal, and in spite of all good advice, refused to move elsewhere. On a late November day, my sister came suddenly to my room and declared that I was in love with Charlotte and should marry her. A few days later Richard Tausenau turned up. Usually he paid little attention to affairs of the heart that bordered on the legitimate, but now he produced a letter, written by an intimate friend of Charlotte's, in which she begged him to persuade me to visit the girl. He would be doing a good deed if he did.

I remained strong, or weak, according to one's viewpoint, and did not go to see Charlotte. One day, during the carnival season, I found out that she was going to the Merchants' Ball. To see her again on neutral ground was an opportunity I didn't want to miss, or did other attractions perhaps play a part? I don't know. Anyway, I donned my dress suit, and while we were getting ready for the *Sofiensaal*, my brother informed me that the other day a young lady had told him the true reason behind Charlotte's illness. After our visit to Vöslau, her mother had suddenly asked her if she was in love with me, and after Charlotte's full confession, had tried desperately to make clear to the girl that I did not come into question as a husband. After this altercation, which evidently destroyed all Charlotte's hopes far more effectively than my remarks at her birthday party or my behavior since then, she had fallen into this melancholy condition which I was hearing about now for the "n-th" time, and in which I was apparently going to find her an hour from now, and after so many months, at the *Sofiensaal*.

Our reunion seemed to make no impression on her. A sad rigid smile played about her lips; she spoke slowly, tonelessly, wearily, and whatever I chose to talk about, her smile remained dimmed, her conversation apathetic, her gaze distant and void of expression, but what I found most strange was the way she danced. Whether with me or with another partner, she floated and glided as if asleep. Only sometimes, when she passed me in the arms of another, she would glance at me with a look filled with intimacy and sadness, as if she had awakened for a few seconds out of a dream, only to sink back into it again.

A few days after this she left for Venice and a few weeks later she returned, according to what she told my sister, refreshed and happy. So she didn't have to "marry to get well again," as I had silently wished for her, nobly-cynical, during my impression of her at the ball. She had been completely restored for some time when she gave her dear gentle hand, that same year, to an attractive and efficient young manufacturer and entered into a promising marriage, a promise which, according to all signs, was to be completely fulfilled.

My friend and comrade, Hiero Stössel, was also an occasional guest at the Heit house, a fact that wouldn't be worth mentioning if this were not the place to report on an example of his mendacity, which was perhaps the worst experience of its kind in my whole life. He had introduced a Dr. Joseph Zeisler, also a good friend of mine, into the Heit home, and one day the latter took me aside to inform me, with the condition that on my honor I promise not to draw any consequences from his revelation, that Hiero had confided to him that he was having an affair with Charlotte. When he had sensed the doctor's doubt, he had tried to confirm the story by citing all sorts of details, even the name of the hotel where he allegedly took her. The slanderous revelation was so incredibly foolish for anyone who knew the family, the girl, to say nothing of the slanderer, that after a momentary outburst of fury I had to agree with Zeisler, who felt one should let the matter pass rather than lend it importance by treating it seriously, and as would then be inevitable, have it spread, which could only be highly embarrassing for the innocent party concerned. So I contented myself with the satisfaction of seeing the miserable braggart (who happened to be an excellent fencer and altogether what is termed "a gay young blade,") horribly embarrassed and terrified when Dr. Zeisler, one evening in a café, began to quiz him about his alleged luck with women, with allusions that bordered on betrayal, until he finally forced Hiero to implore him, the "Herr Oberarzt," not to forget the discretion he had sworn to respect.

Frankly I have the feeling that to individuals like Hiero Stössel the important thing is the lie itself, not so much that it should be believed. At times there seems to be a purpose behind their behavior, most frequently the satisfaction of vanity, but that is often secondary. Such stupid fellows accept the advantages that occasionally accrue from their lying, without the anticipation of such a reward having been the decisive factor. That is and remains the irresistible compulsion itself which, like any compulsive delusions or behavior in the case of others, may occasionally be corrected or regulated according to the man's mentality or character, but can rarely be overcome.

After the marriage I saw Charlotte Heit again a few times, but always from afar and fleetingly, and I don't believe I ever spoke to her again. I never regretted the fact that my attitude toward her love had been so lukewarm nor that I had been so reserved in response to her marriage plans. Moreover I don't believe that my parents would have agreed to my becoming engaged to her, since I was dependent on my father's support until

I got my degree and for years after that, also because of the fact
that although she was considered a fairly good match, she was
certainly not a brilliant one. And I think it is quite possible that
considerations such as these also influenced my behavior, even if
only incidentally, for I can recall that about that time I was surprised by a decision of my Uncle Felix. Instead of marrying the
beautiful and wealthy daughter of a Paris banker, who would
have been delighted to marry him, he brought home as his wife a
practically poverty-stricken girl, his cousin Julie, whom I have
already mentioned. And my astonishment, which I can remember so well, is proof not only of how deeply I was still rooted in
those days in a practical bourgeois point of view, the atmosphere
of which I was breathing, but also of the fact that I still knew
nothing, absolutely nothing about love in a higher sense, nor had
as yet any understanding for it.

The verses I composed in those days and titled with the names
of my constantly changing greater or lesser flames, were devoid
of any deeper feeling without compensating for the lack by any
poetic merit, and I seemed to be satisfied, beside a few excep-
tions, with the adoption of an ironically skeptical, superciliously
witty tone, induced admittedly by the ladies extolled in them.
The rest of my literary efforts, from my year in the army to the
attainment of my degree and for a while after that, seem hardly
worth mentioning even as concomitants to the development of
my intellect. The material of *Modern Youth* continued to hold
my interest without anything actually coming of it. A novelistic
skit, *The Feast* (*Festmahl*,) which tried to describe, sentimentally
and without humor, a poetizing dramatist, a failure of a man,
waiting in vain for his guests, was not only completed but was
read aloud to a few friends, singly, among them the pianist,
Rosenthal, and was submitted to the *Neue Freie Presse* through
the mediation of Tausenau, who professed to having some sort
of journalistic connections there. This effort was just as unsuccessful as the previous submission of a few of my poems to the magazine, *Fliegende Blätter*. These little disappointments were no
great blow to me since during this time my confidence in my
inner calling had in no way increased.

My attitude toward the medical profession had also remained
unsure and wavering, and it was just the ever more pressing

necessity to study which at one moment would cause me to reject it violently only to be tempted and stirred by it to the depths of my being on other occasions. I think I realize this more definitely today, after so many decades, than I did then, because my emotional relationship to medicine, untrammeled by outside compulsions or any practical activity, has been able to develop into a purity that could almost be called experimental. With this I don't even want to rate especially high my interest in mental illness, which was the only concern definitely alive in me in those days, since it was rooted in the poetic and belletristic aspects of my nature rather than in my medical pursuits. In any case it was internal medicine, with all its ramifications, which attracted me far more than surgery, toward which I felt a mixture of reticence and repugnance, and it was this aspect of medicine with which my tendency to hypochondria so often came into almost pathological conflict. I attended lectures, as a rule irregularly, and neglected those on surgery, with Albert and Billroth, to an even greater extent than those on internal medicine, with Nothnagel. I tried to make up for the former lapse by attending the obligatory courses in surgical procedure. I didn't appear any more regularly for Späth's lectures at the obstetrics clinic, and the opthalmologist, Stellwag, didn't see me very often in his classroom—a minor thing I had against him was the fact that he wore tan shoes with a Prince Albert coat. The same applies to the theoretical courses.

To pass my finals I realized that I would have to bone up on every subject thoroughly. When the time came I therefore chose the company of my more conscientious colleagues and went over the various subjects with them. Of inestimable value in this respect, also for Louis Mandl, who during the years had developed into a highly industrious scholar, was the assistance of a medical student who was considered one of the most brilliant in our class—my future brother-in-law, Marcus Hajek. A few years before he had been introduced into our home, with references— an anemic youth from Temesvar, and from then on had been a guest at our midday dinners several times a week. His gift for the natural sciences was outstanding, his diligence and frugality were admirable, and since he was so far ahead of us we looked upon him as a teacher rather than as a fellow student. But since

bad company may corrupt even the best habits, he soon became
not only our comrade in learning and study, but also our crony
at cards, and one night we were frivolous and unscrupulous
enough to let him lose to us youths, who were so much better off,
all his examination money, which he had saved up laboriously by
tutoring. This did not prevent him from getting his degree several
months ahead of us, with honors in every subject, and he was
just as honorable about paying his gambling debts without being
dunned for them.

I too came out of the examinations better than I had dared
hope or deserved. On October 21, 1884, I passed my *practicum*
in pathological anatomy; on November 22, internal medicine; on
November 28, my second theoretical examination, in part with
honors. In the spring of 1885, I completed the practicals in
gynecology, opthalmology and surgery, and on May 28, my third
and last theoretical oral examination. On the thirtieth of May I
graduated, with Louis Mandl, Armin Petschek and ten other colleagues, and received my degree as doctor of medicine. My mood
on one of those days in May, during which I was readying myself for the last examinations, has been inscribed in my diary with
such veracity and is so characteristically expressed, that I think
it should bring this chapter to a close. Written under the date
May 7 is the following:

I forget totally what and who I am and with that realize that I am
not moving in the right direction. I don't think that my objectivity
could have got lost because of my aversion to the examinations, which
is understandable (the day after tomorrow I have one, and two weeks
later, I hope, the last), but I have the definite feeling that, apart from
the possible material advantages, it was idiocy on my part, ethically
speaking, to study medicine. But now I am one of the crowd. Added
to all this there is, first and foremost, my indolence; secondly, and
probably an even greater disadvantage, my disgraceful hypochondria
which this miserable branch of knowledge—miserable in its direction
and what it reveals—has brought with it. I often feel absolutely flat-
tened out. My nervous system simply isn't equal to such a profusion
of depressing and at the same time esthetically debilitating affects. I
don't know yet, don't know today, as I stand (supposedly) in the flower
of my young intellectual powers, whether there is a true gift within me
for the art of writing; I know only that with every fiber of my being
and with my noblest thoughts I gravitate toward it and experience

something akin to nostalgia for this calling. This I feel clearly and have never felt it more clearly than now, stuck as I am up to my neck in medicine. Is it possible that I might be elastic enough, in due course, to spring back? Something is developing within me that looks like melancholy, yet I do have a certain sympathy for the creature that represents me so that I sometimes think it would be a pity if he were to go to waste. But there really isn't anything in my life that could uplift me. I must admit that my vanity occasionally and quite intensively resents the fact that so many people with whom my way of life and my student years have brought me into contact, seem to feel that they are my equals, and it never occurs to them that I might belong in a quite different category. If one of them (and so often they are very nice people) should by chance read these lines he would probably think: the fellow is even more arrogant than I thought. And yet how are they supposed to know that something is going on inside me of which they couldn't possibly have any idea. After all, in recent months even I have forgotten all about it, and in the end it may all boil down to a form of megalomania. Today I feel even less clear about all these things than I did in the past, for that which I am supposed to be I most certainly am not, in fact, perhaps even less so. Well, the time is approaching in which I shall have to achieve some sort of assurance concerning myself. Just wait, young men, I shall yet learn to fathom you!

Very often during these years of voyage on the dark seas of life I was tempted to let sink a plummet or even an anchor, without being at all sure that on its way to the elements of my nature it might not bury itself in a deceptive sandbank or become entangled in some mysterious aquatic vine.

Book Five

❃❀❃❀❃❀❃❀❃❀❃

May 1885 to April 1886

MY FINAL EXAMINATIONS, especially the third *theoreticum*, which brought the series to a close, did not make too excessive demands on a candidate like myself, who was only mildly ambitious; my time therefore, during those days in May, was not occupied wholly by my studies; enough remained for my habitual walks and all sorts of other activities. On one such occasion, two days before my last oral examination, it so happened that on one of the paths in the Volksgarten, a young girl, Jewish, with a face that had character rather than beauty, accosted me casually by whispering my name in passing. In reply to my question as to how she knew me, she replied that she had seen me at the Polyclinic when she had accompanied a friend there, who was ill. She introduced herself as a prospective actress, and demonstrated her talent to me on the occasion of our next meeting by threatening, in bed, to strangle herself with her black hair, which she had let down; a threat that was histrionic rather than hysterical. Her embarrassing behavior resulted in my terminating our relationship as quickly as possible, which was facilitated by the fact that Pepita, which was what she called herself, left for a summer engagement as chorus girl at a theater in the Austrian provinces. From there she pursued me, at first with passionate, extortionary letters in which she threatened, among other things, to shoot herself in front of my apartment, but after the receipt of a sum of money that was compatible with my resources, she desisted from carry-

ing out her grim intention and soon let me know, in a more cheerful letter, that she was on tour as dancer-singer, with which I
had finally heard the last of her. This adventure, which left a
bad after-taste, stands wretchedly and ridiculously on the threshold of my years as a doctor.

On my first holiday after obtaining my degree I did various
things. On a brief trip to Hungary with my brother, at the end of
June, I recall a tour of the night clubs of Budapest under highly
expert guidance. We rose from the lowest type to the highest and
were thus able to gain what one might call a constabulary view
of the secret public nooks and crannies of that capital city. Of
the night's impressions I have preserved most clearly the picture
of a dark little garden surrounded by high, windowless walls,
where kitchen smells and all sorts of sweet perfumes were won-
derfully mixed, and half-naked women disappeared from time to
time with unscrupulous gentlemen into the not entirely sound-
proof shrubbery. On the following day we visited relatives on
Lake Balaton and returned to Vienna the same day, exhausted
rather than enriched.

We spent the first half of June with our mother at the Thalhof
Hotel in Reichenau, the same place from which, in the long past
years of my boyhood, I had wanted to undertake the conquest of
the world with my friend Felix Sonnenthal, dressed as devils.
This time I would have been satisfied with a more modest conquest. A pretty, flirtatious widow inflamed my heart with jealousy
rather than love, and I shall never forget the mocking, oh, so
female look with which Frau Betty came back from a stroll in
the woods with my brother, who I felt was being grossly favored,
and greeted her pining admirer, who, on a bench near the house,
book in hand, had been waiting with agonized impatience for
their return. I was fully aware of the illusory, one might almost
say sick tenor of my feelings without this insight having the
slightest alleviating effect on my abject misery.

During our stay in Reichenau, my sister developed a case of
pleurisy, which my father, who was little inclined to think of any
illness in his immediate surroundings, much less in the family, as
even a possibility, had to admit was present. The case was a
light one, but the raw evening air that swept in on us from the
narrow valley leading to the Schneeberg was detrimental to her

convalescence; we therefore returned to Vienna as soon as was feasible. My passion for Frau Betty began to wane already on the train and disappeared completely in a very short time once I was home again; whereas I retained a permanent affection for a sweet dessert which she had ordered daily—a chocolate-strawberry torte with whipped cream, which we had named for the charming lady with the sweet tooth.

The Hungarian outing and our brief stay in Reichenau were only the opening phases of my actual first long vacation trip as a doctor, which began in the middle of August. I was accompanied by a young friend, Max Weinberg, the son of a rich Rumanian, retired and a widower but still very much a man-of-the-world, who had moved to Vienna years before with his children. Max, who had attended the *Gymnasium* with my brother, was a good-natured, pleasant, not particularly smart young man, by nature absent-minded and hasty and always ready for harmless fun which he was prone to accompany, regardless of whether he was jokester or audience, by foolish, one might almost say idiotic, laughter. That I happened to single him out as my traveling companion—not that I was particularly selective in my choice of companionship in those days—was probably because his father was in a position to provide him with the money for the journey. Moreover, with all his failings, I had no objection to him as a traveling companion just because of his innocuousness, and on the fourteen-day trip, which took us from Ischl over Innsbruck, Zürich, Lucerne and the Gotthard Pass to the Italian lakes and Milan, we got along famously. In Milan I met my family, as had been arranged. The joy of our meeting was dimmed slightly by the fact that right away I had to ask my father for a few hundred francs, which I had lost at gambling in the Lucerne casino and now owed Max, who had been luckier. From Milan the journey went on, via Innsbruck back to Ischl, and on the last day of August, home to Vienna.

At the beginning of September I entered the Allgemeine Krankenhaus as intern, at first in the department for internal medicine under Dr. Standthartner, who had just as fine a reputation in Viennese society as music lover and Wagner enthusiast (Wagner had often stayed with him in Vienna), as he enjoyed as a doctor. The duties of an intern at that city hospital were fairly narrowly circumscribed and I had no inclination whatsoever to broaden them. After I had participated with a greater or lesser degree of attentiveness in the morning round of bedside visits, and had charted and completed as many case histories as was required of me, off I went, usually to a coffee-house, to read the papers or play a game of skittle-pool on the billiard table with some acquaintance or other, in those days more often than not with an elderly gentleman called Wolf, preferably the so-called game of *kalakaux,* which with its tricky rules appealed to the gambler in me. Around noon I would put in an appearance at the Polyclinic where I sat in on lectures by neuro-pathologist Professor Benedikt, who was as erudite as he was conceited, and delivered his stimulating talks, which were spiced with anecdotes and occasionally founded more on fantasy than scientific fact, in a curious drawl. Benedikt was one of my father's closest and— which isn't always the same thing—most loyal friends, of whom he had fewer than he realized or would have cared to admit. The Polyclinic itself was in part the creation and certainly the most important element in my father's life, a project and at the same time a cause in which his most intrinsic qualities had been developed, expressed and had prevailed; and it seems to me that at this point in my story, when I may be seen passing in a secondary role across the threshold of an institution which meant so much to my father, also to me at certain periods in my life, it would be proper to briefly describe its beginnings. In the following account I have used excerpts from some articles by my father, and his colleague, Professor Reuss.

The Polyclinic was founded in the year 1872 by twelve young doctors, my father among them, whose purpose it was to escape the trying conditions for visiting doctors at the state clinics by creating a place of their own to teach, to learn and to heal. They rented a courtyard apartment in one of the old houses on the Wipplingerstrasse, and only two years later had to move into larger quarters on the Oppolzergasse because of the growing number of patients and students. The authorities were cooperative, there was no lack of patrons, and when a prince of the royal house, the admirable Archduke Rainer, decided to sponsor the institution, the most favorable conditions for its undisturbed and flourishing development seemed assured. Suddenly, especially among the general practitioners, who at the time were suffering financially from the after-effects of the 1873 stock market crash, complaints, accusations, suspicions and slander could be heard, which, with the support of partisan journalism gradually took on the character of a thoroughly unscrupulous agitation. It was claimed that the Polyclinic spelled the ruination of the general practitioner since well-to-do patients were also being treated there; actually it was nothing but an advertising agency for the doctors who had founded it; the apparently official statistics of the number of patients and students were fradulent; and the presence in the center of town of this assembly-point for the sick posed a serious danger to the health of the entire city as a future breeding ground for epidemics. Appeals were made to the authorities to close the institute; subsidies were withdrawn; the number of patrons decreased, until in the end the Polyclinic itself, which had reached the point where it was willing to close its doors but was being induced by Archduke Rainer to hold out, requested an investigation of the censorious grievances, an appeal that ended, naturally, in the complete vindication of the questionable institute.

Things quieted down, the Polyclinic continued to flourish and became a valuable component of the medical faculty, not only academically but also in so far as the general practitioners were concerned. In the year 1880 it moved into a house on the Schwarz-spanierstrasse which had been built expressly for the purpose by one of its members, the pediatrician Professor Monti. During this struggle it was primarily my father who, as editor of the *Medizinische Presse*, astutely and spiritedly represented the cause of the institute of which he was co-founder and director, and very little time had passed before it became necessary for him to take up the struggle again. This time he was parrying not only the professional jealousy of the less successful practitioners (which was excusable), and the superstitious fear of the simple-minded —grievances which would have had to come to nothing when faced with sensible considerations, to say nothing of official investigations (or would a transposition of latter and former be more correct?) but he also had to cope with the petty and miserable intrigues which had been hatched in the college of medical professors itself, where the attitude toward the young doctors of the Polyclinic had been anything but friendly or even honest at the time of the earlier struggle.

For quite some time, a few of the "old guard" had watched with displeasure the ever prouder flourishing of the clinic, the growing fame of several of its lecturers and titular professors, and especially their increasingly extensive practices, until at last they decided to take steps openly against the dangerous rival. After lengthy debates, a resolution was passed at a faculty meeting which declared that—first, the society of Polyclinic doctors was interfering with the functions of the academic council by announcing their lecture programs through their own (Polyclinical) management; second (for some formal reasons that were absolutely incomprehensible) they had no right to call their organization a Polyclinic; finally, and so to say officially, the fear was expressed that the Polyclinic, which even (perish the thought!) was striving to found its own hospital, might possibly develop a second "free" university, which could not be tolerated under any circumstances. From the incredible and fumbling formulation of these accusations, the last of which was tantamount to an indignant appreciation of what the clinic was capable of accomplishing, it became quite clear that this was the best (or worst) they could do, and that the true causes for the latent enmity of the college against the Polyclinic were of a caliber one would not have liked to attribute to friend or enemy, nor even admit to oneself. My father, at the end of an excellent rejoinder, which appeared in the *Medizinische Presse* early in 1886, gently pointed out these more or less hidden or disavowed motives when he wrote of "certain currents that occasionally sweep along even the most intelligent groups," and of "a spirit of intolerance that is spreading also in the medical faculty since it is no longer controlled by the spirit of Rokitansky," of impulses therefore that are present in every struggle between rivals, today as in those days, more often than not with an elementary shamelessness. Here I would like to add that Theodore Billroth was the only one who voted against the resolution and stood up decisively for the Polyclinic; at his side, naturally, was Benedikt, who at the time represented the associate professors.

This spirit of intolerance had not yet succeeded in penetrating the Polyclinic itself. Jews and Christians (the latter admittedly in the minority) were still working peacefully together and stood unanimously opposed to their adversaries, who in this case again were unable to do the institute any significant harm, and had to continue to be satisfied with intriguing from case to case against anyone who happened to offer a target.

My father was tirelessly active not only in the field of journalistic polemics, but in association with others (some of whom, it must be admitted, later opposed him), was also increasingly concerned with soliciting funds for the institute which he considered, and had every right to consider, more and more his creation.

At the time mentioned here, that is to say in the middle of the 1880's, my father was at the height of his career. As one of the leading laryngologists, his practice still included for the most part singers and actors, but he was also favored as consultant in the wealthiest bourgeois circles, among members of the aristocracy, the court, and was even called in occasionally by foreign princely personages. Innumerable families were pleased to see him as their house doctor, and because of his amiable, slightly ironic way of conversing, also liked to listen to him. His extraordinary popularity was due mainly to the soothing effect of his optimistic outlook, his good-naturedness which verged on benevolence, and his *noblesse* in monetary matters, which some of his patients, especially the artists among them, knew how to exploit. In spite of the fact that he was absorbed by his practice, he neglected neither his scientific research nor his literary obligations, and published numerous short articles, most of them with casuistic content, which in his clear fluid style gave evidence of his diagnostic acumen, his vision as a therapeutist and the speed with which he could come to a decision. Even if he could not be considered a very thorough researcher, still he was recognized as an excellent observer and summarizer, and although he led the way up no entirely new paths, he was always close behind those who did; and sometimes, with the adaptability and ease of his happy nature, moved so fast behind the new achievement as if eager to demonstrate the speed with which he could assimilate rather than the value of the latest discovery itself.

I for my part soon gained the impression that in spite of all public honors earned, he had not gone as far in the absolute sense, as scholar or doctor, as might have been granted him with a full development of his wealth of capabilities. He was prevented from such a development, and with it the attainment of highest possible achievement and of truly great heights, by a lack of that profound seriousness which is predicted by objectivity, imperturbability and patience. He possessed all of these qualities to some degree, but not sufficiently; they served him from time to time but were not rooted in him as immutable components of his personality. His activities therefore, from a severe standpoint, were at times touched by a measure of superficiality and his personality by something almost akin to frivolity.

My impression that he was not always absolutely meticulous when it came to the sterilization of instruments, for instance the cleansing of the mirror after use, things like that, as I would have considered necessary, may have been due to the fact that he belonged to an older school and I to the younger one, in which one had been raised on aseptic principles. But I could also not reconcile with my conceptions of medical discretion his habit of leaving the office records, in which the diagnosis was entered beside the name of the patient, on his writing desk, not locked up; nor (although this I witnessed only once), how he jokingly hinted at the sexual inferiority of one of his patients, which had come to his knowledge as the result of his treatment of the man, to a coquettish young woman whom the patient was courting. I also found very characteristic his reaction on an occasion when I had something to tell him which I was anxious to have kept secret, and asked him to give me his word of honor in the matter. Not only did he refuse, but he seemed annoyed, not so much, I am sure, because he was hurt by my distrust but rather because he considered my request, and discretion and word of honor generally speaking, in rather poor taste. That he was not entirely free from vanity may scarcely count as a failing in a man who had made a brilliant name for himself professionally, had achieved a highly favored position socially, and in the prime of his life could point with pride to the fact that his beginnings had been poor and limited, and that he had only his talent, industriousness and energy to thank for everything he had achieved. In the years to come some of his patients, especially those in so-called high society, were to leave him, and the brightness of his name was to be somewhat dimmed, for which not only the pressure of younger, more recently successful specialists was to blame but also, beside the general laws that govern the aging man, the rapidly increasing power of those currents which, as explained in the aforementioned polemic, "occasionally sweep along even the most intelligent groups," to which I would like to add— especially when they choose to accelerate the current with some strong oar-strokes of their own.

Even before receiving my degree I had had frequent opportunities to observe my father as a doctor in his department at the Polyclinic. I had watched him dealing with native and foreign— mainly English and American—students, and with his patients, who here belonged wholly to the needier classes, and had come to recognize in him an exceptional teacher and an equally diligent and humane doctor. Now that I had my degree, I was permitted to substitute for him occasionally during his office hours. My knowledge—to say nothing of my experience—was not what one could have called of the highest order, but at least I did know when it was my duty to pass on the responsibility to someone better equipped to deal with it. My professional manner was sufficiently adroit, even if I did not try to compete with the amiability, at any rate not the imperturbable amiability which my father could display, particularly when he sent me to one of his "houses" as substitute, which in those days didn't happen often. Then I was only too anxious to let the people in question notice that I had no desire to force myself upon them, and my reserve may at times have had the effect of arrogance, especially when I had reason to suspect that I was being received and treated with condescension, or what was worse—with a gentle irony, only as my father's son.

At first my activity as a privately practicing doctor was naturally fairly limited, and I continued to lead my former student life—a young man of good family, spending a few hours of his day at the city hospital and Polyclinic, or in the laboratory for pathological histology, going regularly to the theater, concerts, parties, spending a great deal too much of his time with friends in coffee-houses, and still living on a parental allowance which of course never sufficed.

These friends could be divided, as had always been the case, into groups that were not very sharply defined and which tended to merge. Together with Richard Tausenau, I had of late attached myself more closely to one of our former *Gymnasium* friends, Louis Friedmann, who with his younger brother, Max, was managing the machine factory of his deceased father—the liberal representative Alexander Friedmann—while their younger brother, Emil, an odd fellow who was shy of life in the big city, lived near Vienna, in Baden, his back turned on work and business, his days spent studying philosophy and playing chess. Louis and Max, however, lived what could have been called bachelors' lives in the Tabor district, in a house of their own which stood next door to the factory. I can't recall ever having met their mother in their home. She lived on another floor and soon married again, or may have already remarried at the time.

Louis and Max were highly efficient businessmen. Louis was more involved with the technical and inventive aspects, whereas Max's talents lay in the administrative and practical side. The latter was more cautious, the former more enterprising, but both were as smart as they were honest so that in spite of occasional differences, the factory soon prospered under their joint leadership, and in their special domain—the manufacture of locomotive injectors—developed into one of the most outstanding manufactories of its kind in Austria and Hungary. Both of them, sons of a Jewish father and a Gentile mother, were physically very well-built, especially Louis, who was a strikingly handsome young man of medium height, slim, always impeccably dressed, and he moved with an attractive indolence. He was exceptionally talented for sports, and enjoyed a reputation as Alpine climber that went far beyond the borders of his native land. He had won numerous prizes for ice skating and was moreover a fencer of repute, even if in this respect he could not equal his younger brother, who was a master at it. It is understandable that two such personalities, especially Louis, in whom smartness, elegance and affluence were so pleasantly combined without a trace of ostentation or foppishness, were bound to appeal to my friend Richard, but I also got along very well with the brothers, especially with Louis. We had already spent quite a few evenings together during the preceding winter, and in a humorous poem entitled "Elephant," have preserved one of them, on which

Richard and Louis were each accompanied by a pretty young thing but I as the "elephant," got off better than these unfortunate animals usually do.

During the winter of 1885–86, Richard and I were in the habit of meeting at Friedmann's almost every Sunday, in the late afternoon. After some talk, we would dine in a restaurant in town, and then proceed to visit a place of amusement, perhaps a music hall, or only a coffee-house, where a game of billiards usually concluded the evening. Neither of the brothers, especially Louis, cared to gamble. It didn't interest them, and they were clever enough to realize that, as the only capitalists in our circle, they would have been at a definite disadvantage with us for partners.

Beside Richard and myself, a blond young geologist called Geyer frequently joined us on these Sunday afternoons. He was not very well off and could satisfy our demands for elegance to only a modest degree, but he was always in good spirits, free yet irreproachable in his behavior, reliable and without pretensions, in short one of those rare comrades who one could be sure would never remain owing a kreuzer or be guilty of any lack of tact. Between him and Louis Friedmann the type of friendship developed which in its complete lack of materialism and egoism was a credit to both of them and spread a clean, purifying atmosphere all around them. Karl Diener, with his sharp tongue and dry wit, who was later professor of geology at the University of Vienna, also turned up occasionally at the Tabor; he was not nearly as likable as his colleague Geyer, at least not as far as I was concerned, in spite of his intellectual eminence. An unimportant but more popular figure in our midst was Hermann Eissler, friend of our *Gymnasium* years, whose hospitable home Richard, Louis and I had frequented once, mainly because of his not exactly pretty but quite interesting older sister, Laura. He was a droll little fellow, who enjoyed telling jokes just as much as letting his friends make fun of him. We chose to see his relationship to his sister's governess in a humorous light and talked freely about it, but there was never anything unseemly about the detailed honesty of his accounts, nor were our thoughtless comments ever tinged with embarrassment, not at the time nor later in retrospect, to such an extent did this good-natured, wildly ugly fellow exude an atmosphere in which everything always resolves itself harmlessly. We called him "Stop Ignatz," which was how he liked to admonish himself, and this was also how he signed his photograph, as if it had been a maxim.

At times other young people joined us, comrades from Louis Friedmann's years in the army, or sporting friends, as for instance young Diamantidi, son of the famous mountain climber, and Cavalry Lieutenant Millanich; but however and wherever we happened to meet, the gathering, in spite of occasionally very high spirits, never included any worldly or daredevil characteristics, and the female element was represented, if at all, then exclusively by Louis' sweetheart, slender, gentle, beautiful Fräulein Valeska. Louis, however, looked upon love dispassionately and thoroughly egotistically, as a pleasant way of passing time, and was to develop into a collector of women and a professional conqueror only after his marriage. He was a sportsman therefore also on an erotic level, had already tired of his mistress and at first tried to get rid of her by being cool and neglecting her, without being actually cruel.

One winter Sunday, as we were leaving the Tabor district with the intention of strolling through the streets as was our wont, in the direction of Leidinger's, our favorite restaurant, Fräulein Valeska appeared suddenly, beautiful and gentle as ever. But her love, displayed with such humility, seemed to touch us rather than her bored lover, who in a politely rejecting, amiably disdainful manner conveyed to her in his high-pitched yet soft, slightly insulting yet seductive voice that tonight she was *de trop*. She followed us down the street. Louis, without paying any further attention to his sweetheart, went on ahead with the others; Max and I brought up the rear with Valeska, who was having difficulty controlling her tears; and we felt rather sorry for her.

I can't remember whether the plan we carried out that evening had been thought up by us ahead of time or whether it came about by a series of chances; the fact is that Max and I succeeded in establishing Fräulein Valeska at Leidinger's, with a quite handsome coachman, in a *cabinet particulier*, directly opposite the one in which our group was dining, and that one of us, pretending to be surprised, hesitantly told Louis about it, as if we had just found out about it ourselves as we had passed the door, which by chance had been open. Shortly after that, either by our request, or perhaps it was Louis who had asked her to come in, Valeska walked into the room where we were dining, to be followed a few minutes later by the coachman, who came storming in like a wild man and could easily have passed as the son of a good solid suburban family. Faithfully he carried out the orders which we conspirators had given him, made a fearful fuss and behaved as if he had every intention of retrieving his dinner partner. And now it was priceless to see Louis, insulted in the pride of his manhood, disposing of his unworthy rival with diabolical scorn, punishing Valeska with unutterable contempt, and trying to act the ironical superior until, probably because of the ill-timed laughter of those of us who were in the know, he began to notice that he had been tricked, and the whole prank petered out without a proper finale. As a matter of fact it never did have any appreciable consequences, because Valeska wandered off home, not only without her coachman but also without Louis, who did however continue his affair with her for a few months longer.

At the time, in spite of his origin, Louis was a convinced anti-Semite and was determined to remain single, or at least have no children, so that the hated Jewish blood flowing in his veins from his father's side might not be propagated. It gave me, who had often argued the point with him, a certain satisfaction when once, in a train compartment, while pretending to be asleep, I overheard a conversation between several Alpinists who were talking about their fellow club member who was not present; and one of them, with all due respect of Friedmann's achievements in the field of mountain climbing, voiced his antipathy with the observation that, as a matter of principle, he simply couldn't stand Jews. I don't know why I never told Louis, not at the time nor later, about this experience.

Another group of friends—and I call them that in the lightest and most hollow sense of the word—were those I met in the summer in Ischl. Here a quasi-community spirit was less the result of an appreciation of nature and *Wanderlust*, which was satisfied in minor outings and walks, than due again to those accursed games of chance, for which there was even more time and opportunity in a resort than there was in Vienna. Among my "makao" and "poker" companions there was a fellow called Benvenisti, whom I also met occasionally in town. He was a chemist, from an affluent Spagnuoli family, who after the recent death of his father, was living with his mother and sisters. Good-natured, rather limited but pleasant, he enjoyed entertaining his friends, especially when they happened to be cavalry officers and sporting types. Consorting with them seemed to flatter him. Altogether he squandered his share of his father's estate in a most foolhardy fashion. I can recall a drinking session at Sacher's, after the races, for which I appeared late and found my friend, already quite drunk, among his boon companions, who were making up to his sweetheart, a pretty blonde called Heli, in a highly uninhibited manner, to which he—although he couldn't possibly have liked it—responded with his habitual, foolish laughter. As for me, I knew practically no one present and certainly had no friends in the group, beside Benvenisti, and nobody, as I could tell from the coolness with which I was received, seemed overly pleased to see me, so I left when they started to play baccarat for quite high stakes, a game I couldn't have joined in anyway, during which Benvenisti, whom we called Nixl, was certainly fated to be the goat, on that night as always. He had become a heavy drinker less by inclination than out of snobbery, and therefore went to extremes to such an extent that once, on the verge of delirium tremens because the *concierge* had kept him waiting too long, he had begun shooting off his revolver wildly in the house entrance, which almost got him into trouble with the police. When the time for the hangover came, he was receptive to my warnings and admonitions and promised to re-form, only to scatter all good resolutions to the wind a few hours later.

One day, at the urgent advice of his guardian or mother, he decided to give up his senseless and costly life in Vienna and accepted a position in a chemical factory in Lodz. Heli was to join him there as soon as possible. He left me, for whom he seemed to nurture a special fondness which I reciprocated for reasons I can't explain, in charge of Heli during the short period of their separation. Previous to this I had frequently visited Heli with him. She lived with her mother in one modest room in the Rotenturmstrasse, and I had sometimes been witness to quarrels between her and Nixl, during which the latter had deemed it necessary to remind his tempestuous sweetheart of the world from which she came, in fact from what kind of a house he had brought her up to his social level. She was a very pretty, graceful, thoroughly depraved little creature, the born *cocotte;* and while Nixl was in Lodz and I appeared at the Rotenturmstrasse more often than was actually necessary, to inquire about the wellbeing of my "ward," it cannot be said that her principles and certainly not mine, but solely my sense of caution (which here was well-grounded on a few things I happened to know about her), always made me feel that the right thing to do was to extricate myself at the last, or the one before the last moment.

Nixl had hardly been gone fourteen days when he sent me some money with the request to buy all sorts of things for Heli, which she would need for the journey to Lodz and her stay there, to put her on the train and speed her off into the arms of her yearning lover. However, since Heli had no desire whatsoever to be sped off, Nixl decided to come and get her himself, and sent me a telegram asking me to meet him at the North Station at a specified time, with Heli. Both of us were there, but instead of welcoming her lover in a friendly, or at least polite fashion, Heli behaved in such an ill-mannered and bad-tempered way toward him from the moment he stepped off the train, also in the cab and after they reached her home, and to me with a friendliness that was quite obviously premeditated, that Nixl sat there looking more and more perplexed and unhappy. I finally managed to convey to him, at a moment when I felt we were unobserved and before he could get around to questioning me, that I couldn't understand Heli's behavior any more than he could, and that during his absence absolutely nothing had taken place between her and me, something that was obviously on his mind. He declared that he didn't doubt my words for a moment, and a few days later left for Lodz, with Heli, only to return to Vienna with her a few weeks later, evidently on much better terms than had prevailed between them before. But at this point I felt that the right thing to do was withdraw, if for no other reason than that some good friends of his were anxious to nourish his distrust of me, or seriously to arouse it.

Toward the end of the winter he had to fight a duel with one of his drinking and gambling friends, a lieutenant in a hussar regiment, because the latter had insulted Nixl's family with anti-Semitic remarks. On the morning of the duel, I received a letter from him in which he begged me, in the case of his death, to inform his relatives and above all, Heli, and to look after his forsaken sweetheart, whom, by the way, he had left financially secure. If by twelve o'clock I hadn't heard from him, I should consider the time to fulfill my mission had come. In a state of excitement which was apparently endurable—a game of billiards seemed to calm me down further—probably because I never doubted for a moment that the result of the duel would be in Nixl's favor, I waited, as prearranged, at the Arkadencafé for the hour of noon to arrive. A few minutes before the appointed time, Nixl, in hunter's dress, which he had had to wear to deceive his mother and sisters, came bouncing in, in a rare good mood, embraced me and informed me that the duel had ended in "no decision," with which his will and the codicil that concerned Heli, became obsolete *pro tem,* and increasingly so since he managed to run through the rest of his inheritance in the ensuing months and finally found himself forced to find a job in Lodz, or anywhere else. From then on our meetings were sporadic, and his relationship to Heli ended in all probability with the expiration of his bank account. He didn't go very far in business and I believe his finances improved with his marriage, a few years later, to an aging opera singer.

Heli, however, now embarked definitely on the career for which she had always been destined, or perhaps simply resumed it, became a truly *grande cocotte,* and could boast, like some of the greater and lesser lights in her profession, of a fleeting relationship with King Milan of Serbia, of which she didn't hesitate to inform me when she met me a few years later in front of the opera house, pale, very fair, rouged, and with big, blue, gem earrings.

Beside all these student-bachelor goings-on, friendships with more respectable females were not neglected, and during the carnival season, which, as is well known, is not always celebrated strictly according to the calendar, these achieved their own specific charm and purpose. Already in years gone by, I had found, beside Charlotte, a certain Fräulein Helene Herz the most attrac-

tive among the young society ladies, and in the winter of 1885–
86, as far as I was concerned, she had no rival. Of all the young
girls who until now had interested me and reciprocated my interest, she was not only the most beautiful but also—and this was
her specific charm—the most virginal in appearance and personality; and looking back I can't see her slender, delicate, well-
proportioned figure dressed in any other way but in airy white
tulle, neck and shoulders bare—a swaying, untouched apparition.
She had a way of speaking that was all her own—fast, free, not
very intellectual but usually sensible, even if not always quite
coherent. Her voice was dark, sometimes a trifle broken; her black
eyes, with their long lashes, would at one moment be sparkling
only to be dimmed almost at once by her lowered lids, which however did not seem to be a secret sign of inner restlessness but
rather the expression of a certain hastiness and absent-mindedness
in her nature. But all this verged so closely on the pathological,
that although I was strongly attracted to Helene, and she unmistakably favored me above all the rest of her admirers, I was never
really able to let myself go with her.

A pretty brunette from the same but not quite so affluent circles,
less inhibited and more mature, and with a good sense of humor,
Anni Holitscher, was in love with Peter Altenberg, who in those
days was still called Richard Engländer; and since she had decided that there was a strange inner resemblance between me and
him, a ray of her affinity for him fell upon me. Just as for the
European, at a superficial glance, all Negroes look alike, to a young
girl who has not had much experience with the breed, one poet
might at first impress her as being exactly like the other. Strangely
enough, in this case the parallel happened to be justified, although
at the time neither Peter nor I had appeared in public as poets,
and in more remote circles weren't even suspected of harboring
such ambitions. Peter had a reputation for being a witty, odd
fellow, and behaved, in a way I couldn't feel was quite genuine,
rather like a professional neurotic, something I once told him
without his taking offense. I don't know if up to that time he had
written a single line, and whatever may have leaked out concerning my literary efforts certainly wasn't being taken seriously.
Again and again it fell to that unique girl, Fanni Mütter, to en-

courage and exhort me to turn to my proper vocation, to which I didn't seem sufficiently dedicated.

During this year too, my spirits were uplifted only rarely by any creations of my own, or by the urge to create. I had the artistic impressions made by the theater and concerts to thank for my best inspirations; yes, even for quite a few presentiments concerning my own, still so unrevealed nature, all of which resulted in various good but rather vague intentions. Among these impressions, Rubinstein's seven-cycle piano concerts remain unforgettable.

This is not to say that I was completely idle as a writer. A novella with which I was preoccupied that winter, however amateurish it turned out to be in the end, deserves brief consideration because of its basic idea, since at a time before Ibsen was recognized in Germany, it dealt with the problem of tainted heredity, which runs spectrally through it in a rationally romantic manner. The plot goes as follows: A young poet with neuropathic tendencies, friend of a doctor, loves a young girl from a similarly burdened family. The doctor, who to his sorrow has recognized the inadequacy of all medical wisdom long ago, desires to fulfill a certain obligation, as doctor, at least in this one case; and with the next generation in mind, he is determined to prevent the two from getting married. At first he lacks the cruel courage to persuade his friend, with scientific reasoning, not to join forces with the girl; but when she throws herself at the doctor in a fit of hysteria, he feels it his duty, or perhaps, to put it more correctly, he takes this opportunity to warn his friend of Ella, not as someone sick, but as a girl who won't be faithful. Benno, stricken, explains that the warning comes too late. A few days before he had started an affair with his fiancée, and for that reason is determined to keep his promise of marriage. He leaves town with her hurriedly; Dr. Flimmer sails for some time on the high seas as ship's doctor, returns home, practices for a while, but then gives up his practice to become tutor to the crown prince. On one of their occasional walks in the garden, he tells the crown prince about this sad experience of his youth. The young man is a melancholic, and broods over the problem of happiness. On the day on which the prince's father, a gay man-of-the-world, is about to celebrate the twenty-five-year jubilee of his reign, his son goes mad. He steps out onto the balcony of the palace and makes a speech to the crowd assembled below, addressed to humanity, in which he assures mankind of his love and pleads that it should be reciprocated. At his bedside, and in the belief that the boy is unconscious, the father tells his son's tutor that Marcel is not his son but the child of another, a man who had caught the prince making love to his wife and had exacted from him, under threat of death, the promise to raise his son, recently born, as the crown prince. Sensing the truth, Dr. Flimmer wants to know the name of this strange, jealous man, and deeply moved, hears as reply the name of the problematic friend of his youth. The prince leaves the room, Marcel has heard everything, thanks the doctor with the words, "Oh noble man, you wanted to preserve me from the misfortune of having to live," and with that slips finally into insanity.

Another, just as hopeless poetic work, even if not quite so childishly confused, also deals with the problem of heredity, albeit in a much lighter and still quite unconscious fashion. To complete the parallel, in it a twenty-five-year jubilee also plays a part. It is the festival play which I wrote for the sixth of January 1886, on which day my father was celebrating the twenty-fifth anniversary of his doctorate and of his activities in the editorial offices of the *Wiener Medizinische Presse,* very formally, which was how he wanted it. Around noon, in dress suit and wearing all his medals, he stood in the drawing room, surrounded by members of the family, his assistants and friends, receiving awards and listening to addresses to which he replied in short, clear, extemporaneous speeches, which I am sure were well prepared in advance, and in which references were not lacking to the struggles he had experienced for his beloved Polyclinic, which were by no means ended. To be sure, the festivities on this day represented not only the triumph of his vanity but also a justifiable pride in everything he had accomplished and created, not only to enhance his fame but also for the well-being of mankind. And actually one should grant a man who has so continually suffered the attacks and enmity of those who were envious and wished him ill, the right once to hear the services he has rendered confirmed loudly and for all the world to hear, without any critical dissonance. Since the press was also present, taking down all speeches in shorthand, the necessary echo was amply taken care of.

On the same evening my festival play was presented before an audience which the newspapers, which took cognizance also of this, had every reason to call illustrious. Beside famous thespians and singers such as Charlotte Wolters, Adolf Sonnenthal and Gustave Walter, there were also present Prince Ferdinand von Koburg (the future King of Bulgaria); Count Mensdorff (later ambassador to England); Cathedral Provost Marschall, member of the board of trustees of the Polyclinic; and Princess Metternich. My play, which my Uncle Edmund Markbreiter had helped me to produce, was in three scenes: the first played in the Riedhof and showed my father as a young doctor, surrounded by colleagues and students, whom he was informing of the fact that he had become engaged. The second introduced him as editor, young husband and doctor, without his patients; in the third he appeared as that which he had meanwhile become, as professor and privy councillor among his patients. I played my father, Gisela appeared as his wife, our mother, and in a supporting role my Uncle Peter von Suppé played a lazy student. Various other parts were divided among divers cousins, male and female, and friends, among whom my cousin Olga Mandl, as a conservatory student, and Fritz Fürst in an impersonation of Sonnenthal, were outstanding. The latter was intended as a joke which, strangely enough, slightly offended the famous actor. Rather cheap gags animated the friendly audience to a merriment and applause which this totally humorless little effort of mine, whipped up by me rather unfeelingly, definitely didn't call for.

As I read novella and festival play today, I am not so much surprised by the apparent lack of any sign of poetic or even literary talent (after beginnings which, in *Aegidius*, for instance, had shown some promise), but even more by the intellectual immaturity evident in these efforts, which in the case of a twenty-four-year-old man, who had been precocious in his youth, make an absolutely absurd impression.

This festival, or "absurd," play was followed by dinner for over a hundred guests, and by toasts—serious and humorous—among which that of Dr. Urbantschitsch was received with the most enthusiasm; and the celebrant replied tirelessly and always in the correct tone. Thus the day, with its honors and joys must certainly have been one of the happiest in my father's life. Even I did not remain unmoved, although I couldn't quite grasp what exceptional amusement such festivities could offer to a wise and active man.

The winter passed, a moderately busy one with quite a few diversions and a lot of distraction, and during the carnival season there was, as usual, plenty of dancing. At a masked ball, costumed as a Viennese ragamuffin, I found my not-forgotten but only neglected Fännchen, who had chosen to come dressed as a laundress, so that on this evening we went exceptionally well together.

At one of the private balls which I attended, after having waited in vain for a so-called "adventure," I had the good fortune to please the French governess of the house, but she was my beloved for only one afternoon because, first of all, she was engaged; secondly, I wasn't the only one with whom she was deceiving her fiancé; and finally she had only one day off every second week, reasons enough for her to be sparing with her time.

During Lent and approaching springtime, the entertainments, which this year were unusually numerous, didn't seem to want to end. Rehearsals for a rather infantile play by a friend of my youth, Emil Brüll, had just begun. It was to be presented early in April, and I was to play the part of a grocer. Suddenly an event which, although it had been creeping up on me for some time, still seemed to descend upon me unexpectedly, not only brought my participation in these rehearsals to an end, but with its threatening features interrupted my entire way of life. Since the beginning of the year, a gland on the left side of my neck had begun to swell noticeably and gradually, yet relatively quickly to the size of a child's fist.

As happens at times to hypochondriacs—just because they are hypochondriacs—I at first didn't take the thing seriously, although as a doctor I certainly should have done so from the start. I treated it with tincture of iodine and compresses, but otherwise didn't let it upset my life in the slightest. My father, as was his way, would have preferred to ignore any inconveniencing or troubling fact, such as that a member of his family and of all people his son, could be really ill, but in the end he let my colleague, Marcus

Hayek, who in the meantime had become secretly engaged to my sister and visited our home frequently, persuade him to consult Professor Albert. One afternoon toward the end of March, I went to the office of this excellent surgeon with my father, and at first tried to induce him to give a mild diagnosis by assuring him that in my opinion a decayed tooth was the cause of the swollen gland, something I naturally wasn't at all sure of, and an opinion which the professor rejected almost rudely. He said that for the present he was against surgery, although he could feel fluctuations at one particular spot, but he insisted that for the time being I discontinue any work at the hospital, admonished me to live sensibly, and recommended that, beside a strict diet, I spend a few weeks in the south. Thereupon I felt impelled to ask if he considered the ailment tuberculosis, to which he replied simply, "I advise you to live as if it were." This I considered clear enough, also apparently for my father, who remained with Professor Albert for a while after I had left the office while I proceeded downstairs, shedding tears for no one to see. But this depression didn't last long. A quarter-hour later I was seated in the dimly lighted, smoke-filled Arkadencafé, playing poker with a few friends, among them Louis Mandl and Richard Tausenau, and contrary to the usual course of things, was extraordinarily lucky, in fact once held four kings in my hand.

Next morning I said goodbye to my amiable chief, Dr. Standthartner, in whose department I had probably caught the infection. With a friendly, worried expression he wished me a speedy recovery, after which I spent a few more days in Vienna, even went to a party given at the Polyclinic, looking pale with a black scarf around my neck, and after returning the script of my role in *My Mausi* to the author, with my regrets, I set out, on one of the last days of March, on my prescribed journey south.

The preceding summer in Reichenau, when I would walk up and down in front of the Thalhof with my flirtatious widow, the young wife of the owner of the hotel had sometimes joined us. Unlike her rather rustic husband, who was also still young, she flattered herself, justly, on being more worldly. For although, as the oldest daughter of the Stefanskeller and Südbahnhof Restaurant owner, who was quite famous in his own right, she was expert at running the kitchen, where steady visitors of the Thalhof

were occasionally permitted to visit and admire her working over
the shining stove—she could hold her own very well with the
majority of her female guests when it came to matters of taste,
general education, and especially in her appearance. She had
married when only sixteen and now, at the age of twenty-two,
was the mother of three sons. If she had ever loved her husband
(which nobody claimed she had), it was not noticeable, and at
times Frau Olga was perhaps overly clear in expressing the fact
that a deeper understanding no longer existed between the couple.

Since during that summer I had been absorbed by the flirtatious
widow, pretty much to the exclusion of everything else, I hadn't
paid much attention to the personality, reputation and fate of the
beautiful proprietress, however there had been a few points of
contact. For instance once, like Anni Holitscher, she had remarked
that my way of behaving reminded her of Richard Engländer,
who, with his family, stayed frequently at the Thalhof, as could be
read later in the beautiful books written by him as Peter Altenberg. Moreover, she could recall that the two of us had played
together, even fought each other as children in Vöslau, in the
Rademacher Villa (which later belonged to my Uncle Mandl),
incidents I had forgotten completely. In spite of such auspicious
associations, I had had the feeling during that previous summer
that I wasn't particularly sympathetic to her, and when I happened
to meet her half a year later on the streets of Meran, on the first
day of my stay there, both of us were satisfied to greet each other
politely from afar. Anyway, she was with friends.

It turned out that the hotel where I was staying didn't
please me; I therefore moved to another, the Tiroler Hof, where
I saw Frau Olga again, this time at the *table d'hôte*, and exchanged
a few casual words with her. After dinner I chatted with the
mother and sisters of my friend Nixl, who were also by chance
staying at the Tiroler Hof, and this is how things remained during
the days that followed. Nothing changed except for the fact that
the guests seated at table between Frau Olga and me left, one
after the other, as if on order, so that in the end the two of us
could smile at each other as dinner partners, so to speak. Even
though the gradual disappearance of the ladies and gentlemen
who had separated us had taken place in a very natural manner,
it pleased us to see our gradual nearing and meeting as desired

and favored by fate, and it came somewhat unexpectedly but not as a surprise when, during our first conversation at the table, she assured me of her confidence. "Funny that I should tell you that myself," she added, and I replied modestly, that I would have been even happier over her trust in me if I wasn't receiving it so-to-speak secondhand, for again she had mentioned my startling resemblance to Richard Engländer. In the course of this conversation we hit upon the subject of superstition. Although I considered myself fairly free of the foible, I had to admit that I did have a definite preference for numbers; for instance, for some time now, for the number twenty-six, and this for a very definite reason that was connected with my passion for the race track. My brother and I had been present, during some party or other, at the raffling off of a bouquet of flowers which had been won by the wife of conductor Robert Fuchs, not quite fairly, with the number twenty-six, whereupon we had decided to bet on a horse with the number twenty-six at the Derby, which was to be run the next day. As chance would have it, the favorite, Buzgo, wearing that number, came in first, and we won a not very substantial sum of money. I expressed my regret to Frau Olga that I wasn't occupying room twenty-six, but number five. "And you, *gnädige Frau?*" I asked. "Twenty-one," she replied. "Twenty-one and five make twenty-six," I declared, and fate had given us another sign. We looked deep into each other's eyes and all at once knew exactly where we stood.

Frau Olga introduced me to several of her friends, among them the manufacturer Salcher and family. He and his wife were a fat, quite ordinary couple with two just as undistinguished lean daughters, in whose company we now went for quite a few walks and outings. The first took us into the Naif Valley. Olga and I had little opportunity to talk to each other, but our silence was of the sort in which one tends to grow closer, the silence that rings on in one more miraculously and with a greater purity than words. On the following day the Salcher parents visited Bozen, the rest of us left the train in Sigmundskron, wandered around in the woods, stretched out on the gentle slope of a vineyard, climbed up to the castle on a narrow path across rocks and loose stones, a way which had been decided upon by Olga who was an expert mountain climber and huntress, and was quite proud of both accomplishments. She slipped, some stones rolled away beneath her; I grasped her hand, and half seriously she said, "What would it have mattered if I had gone down with them?" We descended into the valley and drove to Bozen in a carriage, where the older Salchers were waiting for us. Soon we were seated in a railway compartment again, Olga opposite me. We gazed into each other's eyes and I realized with a sense of painful shock that these moments would soon belong to the past. Again and again she turned to look back at Sigmundskron, which was sometimes visible, then again was gone, until finally it was lost from sight. Half an hour after our arrival in Meran, all of us were seated at the table, and Olga, while we were passing the platters, whispered to me, "I wish everything would sink into the ground and only you and I were left in the world." After dinner I did what I had done the night before, improvised on the piano in my dilettantish but pleasant enough style; the Salchers and a few other guests were dozing or chatting, but Olga sat facing me, a sweet sadness written on her features, and I knew the sadness was because of me, for the following day was to be my last in Meran.

The day dawned, cloudy and humid. We played croquet in the hotel garden, she and I and the two Miss Salchers. Whenever the clouds dispersed, the sun would shine hot and angry on the croquet field. We stopped playing and Olga asked me to go for a walk with her. We conversed haltingly; every now and then we were silent. At last, as if she had come to some sort of decision, she said, her eyes lowered, "One thing I want to beg of you, don't come to Reichenau before the autumn." And she went on to tell me about her husband's mistrust and jealousy, how he was so much in love with her and she not at all with him, of her father's severity, and she told me of something that had taken place in the second or third year of her marriage, almost five years ago therefore, between her and—as if I hadn't surmised something of the sort for some time—Richard, whom I allegedly resembled. It had been a completely innocent relationship which had burgeoned through the reading they had done together, and the most she had given in the way of tenderness, so she said, was to let him kiss her hand. But one day her husband had declared he would shoot the young man if he ever dared to show his face in the Thalhof again. She decided therefore to write Richard a farewell letter, and he was forced to leave Reichenau. From this day on she had been faithful to her husband, and was determined, as long as he could demand it of her, to remain faithful, and said finally in a sweet voice that trembled, "So I want to offer you my friendship since there is nothing I can be to you but a friend. I mean a metaphysical friendship. In every pain and joy I want you to think: there is someone who is happy with me or suffering with me. Will you accept such a friendship?" and she held out her cool white hand which I kissed passionately.

That afternoon we met, as had been arranged, in the library of the Kurhaus, and wandered off in the direction of Sankt Valentin. How could this have happened to us, we asked each other, and with childish pleasure, which actually was cruel so close to our separation, we recalled the few times we had experienced together, in which we had found each other. "Do you remember," she asked, "our outing into the Naif Valley six years ago?" And I replied, "Five years ago on the Sigmundskron, wasn't it even more splendid?" And we spoke of the past summer, which according to these calculations would have had to lie back a few thousand years, perhaps even farther, since at that time we had not yet loved each other. And we recalled the first, still half-alien meeting on the street in Meran, and the fateful disappearance of those seated between us at the *table d'hôte,* and the two Salcher girls, the pretty thirteen-year-old one and the boring seventeen-year-old one, and refined, polite Herr Basin, who was tubercular and had only two more years to live, and the dangerous path along the Sigmundskron wall, and of course the mysterious lucky number twenty-six, or rather twenty-one plus five, since the addition had never taken place. At Sankt Valentin we sat on the terrace, looked down into the valley and wished that the minutes would last forever. She was wearing a fur tippet with tassels, and—a habit of hers—was toying with them, letting them pass between her fingers, raising them to her lips. She tore one off and gave it to me. I kept it for years, like a treasure. At last we had to leave. On the way back she begged me not to play the piano that evening. "When you do, I feel as if you were speaking to me. You understand, don't you?"

We dined, as we always had done, all together at one table. After dinner Olga, I, and the refined Herr Basin, who was doomed to die—but wasn't this doom the highest refinement a human being could be allotted?—sat on in the dining room for quite some time, talking. At last everyone decided it was time to say good-night, and as if on purpose—for there are times when the coldest Philistine heart unconsciously feels respect for the sacredness of profound feelings—the others disappeared and I remained alone with Olga in the dimly lighted room. I kissed her hand in a last farewell, but then, suddenly, we were in each other's arms and we kissed passionately. She tore away from me and ran to her room, number twenty-one; I went to mine. The sum total was the only right thing about it.

The dawn brought a cold wind and rain that whipped against my face, yes it did, because first there was nature and only after that, the novella. I walked out of the Tiroler Hof for the last time, my cap pulled down over my forehead, my collar up—in those days, as a reserve officer, one traveled in uniform for economy reason (the fare on the train was half price),—and on the street, when I turned to take a last look, I saw Olga, standing on the balcony of her room (in the last analysis it might just as well have been number twenty-two), a shawl around her head and shoulders, nodding a sad, serious farewell. I hurried to the station, wept in the waiting room, and was still weeping in Franzensfeste, before lunch. While walking up and down the platform, I met a fleeting coffee-house acquaintance from Vienna, a harmless bank clerk called Kuranda. It did me good to exchange a few words with him. Since then over thirty years have passed. I see him oc-casionally, bent over his desk in the bank, and we greet each other in polite understanding without ever speaking to each other, but I still tell myself that he noticed at the time that I had been weeping, and that this meeting of ours in Franzensfeste has re-mained a romantic memory also for him; and for me he looks exactly as he did then, thirty years ago.

Book Six

❧❧❧❧❧❧❧❧

April 1886 to August 1887

THE SWELLING of my gland had receded considerably during my stay in Meran, but it had not disappeared; yet it seemed to mean a great deal to my father, who had been upset enough about my illness, to have me at home on the eleventh of April, his birthday; and his prognosis that the condition of the gland would continue to improve after my return to Vienna turned out to be correct. Still, a slight swelling remained noticeable to the touch for quite a few years, which continued to worry some of my colleagues but me not in the least.

Immediately upon my return I resumed my duties at the hospital, but went right on doing only what was absolutely essential as far as my medical work was concerned. All of a sudden I was overwhelmed by, for me, a most unusual longing for life in the country, for wandering where it was green. More than ever before I was strongly aware of the artist in me, and even if I still had to face the fact that frivolity, instability and a zest for life—which, however, I did not want to see condemned as banal hedonism—and above all the gift of being able to absorb deeply and with enthusiasm all that was art around me were far more strongly developed within me than any actual talent, still I was seized for a while by such a forceful sense of superiority toward my surroundings, and especially toward my efficient colleagues, that I was less affected than I would have been ordinarily by the repeated reprimands of my father who, not unjustifiably, reproached

me for my lack of scientific endeavor. I remained grateful to my
study of medicine for sharpening my vision and clarifying my
views, but I saw the fact that I had chosen medicine as my profession, especially with my tendency to hypochondria, as an act
of gross stupidity, which unfortunately could not be rectified.
However, I thought I was clear in my mind at last as to the direction of my personality. The aspirations which had touched my soul
already at the age of eighteen, now penetrated it more consciously
and decisively. Whereas my blonde Fännchen appeared in my
mind as a pallid symbol of my boyhood days, for the years of
my young manhood, I saw the marvelous woman with whom I
had walked arm in arm from Sankt Valentin to Meran on an
unforgettable evening in spring.

To see her again—this thought, this hope, kept alive at first
not by letters nor by any other form of communication but solely
by my faith in a fortunate chance meeting—became the content
of my life in the weeks that followed; and a spring festival in the
Prater, at the end of May, at last brought with it a first modest
fulfillment. With my mother, brother and sister, I participated in
the flower *cortège,* and among the many carriages, we passed one
in which Frau Olga was seated with her younger sister, Gabrielle.
She didn't notice me, but since flowers were being constantly
thrown back and forth from carriage to carriage, we too exchanged
a greeting; she unconsciously, I very consciously. After that I
couldn't stay with my family another minute, but got out and
walked against the stream of vehicles in the direction from which
her carriage would have to return. And there she was. I stopped
at the edge of the road and was seized suddenly by fear of this
first encounter after those heavenly days in Meran, and I looked
down. Gabrielle, however, drew Olga's attention to me. Olga
turned to look at me, blushed deeply and waved. I hurried closer,
and across a line of carriages that were separating us, threw a
flower into her lap, and from her hands a yellow rose fluttered to
my feet. Wordlessly we thanked each other. We didn't smile.
With the sacred earnestness of young love I followed the carriage
with my eyes until it had disappeared in the crowd. But the yellow
rose I kept, with her letters, until it became dust, a fate that was
to overcome her who had given it to me long before that.

Next day, as I had hoped and expected, I met her at the race track. Again she was with her sister, Gabrielle, who was now introduced to me, and we exchanged a few friendly words, rather self-consciously. Her father, stocky, martial, with his white moustache looking not at all like a *hotelier* but more like a retired general, came up to us. I was invited to join them in their box, sat down behind Olga and watched the races, probably for the first time without interest, and didn't say much, certainly nothing clever. Olga mentioned a few books I had recommended while in Meran, which she had read in the meantime. Suddenly, before I had become fully aware of a bliss which, as described in the blasé poems of my earlier days, "I could have felt"; the "magic" —one of her favorite words—was over. We left the box; I accompanied the father and his two daughters to their carriage, one of Vienna's finest equipages, and was able to exchange only a few fleeting words with Olga. "Again a new chapter: the races," she said in a continuation of the game we had played in Meran, where we had divided the beginnings of our relationship like a novel. And I: "And when do we go over it together?" She: "In Reichenau." And I: "So you withdraw your ban, *gnädige Frau?* I was not supposed to come until autumn." She nodded her agreement and pressed my hand fervently in farewell. The carriage drove off and I looked after it as long as I could, half-crazed with love.

A week later, on Whitsunday, I appeared at the Thalhof, and without registering, sat down in the dining room. Olga came in, wearing the same hat she had worn in Meran. She came up to my table; I rose. She said, "I knew you would come today." We exchanged a few casual words, then she had to greet some other guests, and I finished the meal with the famous torte which was now officially named after the flirtatious widow of the preceding year. In the afternoon I was permitted to visit Frau Olga in her home, where relatives of mine were also present. They were spending the holiday in Reichenau, and as good old friends of the proprietress were playing cards in her private salon: my Uncle Edmund, always ready for a game of chance, his fat, stupid wife, her quite pretty sister Dora, and her husband. Olga's husband, whom she called Charles, in a pretentious effort to elevate him to an aura of refinement, a name that had stuck to him even if people did occasionally make fun of it, did not appear; however, one not only felt his absence but also that he wouldn't have wanted to be there, since for various reasons he did not approve of his wife's social aspirations. Olga and I, therefore, since the others didn't let anything interrupt their game, were more or less on our own; yet we didn't feel quite right about it, nor any too secure. But when she picked out a picture that lay among others scattered around on plates, and handed it to me, and I recognized Sankt Valentin, then our eyes met and lighted up in a glow of remembrance.

After supper, in accordance with the house schedule, and just as we had done the summer before, we walked up and down in front of the veranda, I for the most part at Olga's side, but now her husband was present; or I should say he was sometimes there, then gone again, back to the dining room, the kitchen, the cellar, or perhaps only into the shadow of the trees; then he would turn up suddenly, let himself be drawn into a conversation for a few seconds or minutes, and be off again; all of which created a restless atmosphere. With only a few gestures in pantomime were Olga and I able to convey to each other that since Meran our feelings hadn't changed. I handed her the little fur tassel which she had given to me as a souvenir; she blessed it with another kiss and I pressed my lips to the spot where she had touched it with hers.

Next morning she remained invisible; after lunch she appeared briefly at the door of the dining room. We were not alone; a young girl called Clara, of whose existence I would know nothing today if her name were not inscribed in my diary, interrupted our conversation. She too had had a love adventure in Meran, and so our chatter was permeated by all sorts of allusions which everyone could interpret as they pleased. When Olga had disappeared again, I was joined by a young *studiosus medicinae*, Richard von Weiss, whom I had met the year before. Unsuspectingly, in the foolish and gossiping spirit of old and young, he began to talk about the fascinating proprietress, and to my torment had tales to tell about her, in the course of which he revealed the story of her youthful love for Richard Engländer. That was bearable, since I knew and had heard about it from Olga's lips. But now another figure rose out of her past, a much more questionable one than the neurotic poet who had tip-toed out of the life of his beloved after a platonic hand kiss (even if he had been received often enough in it after that, or at least at the Thalhof). This other figure was a man-of-the-world, a cavalry officer, a man constantly in debt, suave, and an expert fencer, although he had perhaps not yet fought a duel, a hunter who had hunted with Olga on the steep walls of the Schneeberg and Rax mountains, slim, elegant, fearless—a Jew, yet at the same time a striking replica of the Austrian aristocrat, differing from the latter only in that he was cleverer and more amusing, a young man I knew—in short: Rudi Pick, the youngest son of my mother's cousin, the famous Gustave. And, this dreadful Herr von Weiss went on, Olga had loved not only the poet, Richard Engländer, but also his exact opposite, the man of action, Rudi Pick; and her husband had forbidden this young man, too, to ever show his face at the Thalhof again, probably with more justification than the poet; but what was worst of all—Olga hadn't mentioned him to me, not a single word.

Was it not perhaps at this moment, when a too talkative medical student with whom I had never really conversed before, and was conversing now only to shorten the afternoon for himself and me, told me the story of the Thalhof proprietress' two love experiences, without any idea that I desired to be the third—no, the second—actually the first!—wasn't it then that a vision of Beatrice rose up in my mind, veiled in the shimmering mists of the future, for whose soul poet and duke fought a senseless battle over and over again and always in vain, but for whose beloved body their struggle was not so unsuccessful? And even if I had won out over the poet who was not yet famous, or I should say, had taken his place, was I not fated in the end to be overthrown by the "duke," who was bound to turn up again sooner or later in yet another form, even if for the moment he had been forced to retire in his incarnation as cavalry officer? Because I could have no illusions that Olga's inclinations fluctuated in a highly disturbing fashion between the spiritual and the sensual, between what was artistic and worldly, romantic and sport; that this fine, yes, almost noble woman had neither the strength nor the desire to resist the lure of snobbery; and even the fur tassel which she had just blessed again and which I was clutching in my hand, could not restore my serenity. In the evening, however, when I was sitting with Olga, Dora and Fräulein Clara, and the conversation brightened, became more meaningful and allusive, and the amorous solicitude with which all women coddle and swaddle every budding love relationship began to hover seductively also over ours, I began to feel better and, again, to hope. Anyway, right now I was the one who was there, nobody else. Olga was looking at me, and whatever memories or possibilities might have been lurking in the depths of those dark eyes, right now they were gazing into mine with an expression of utter devotion. That her husband was constantly milling around in no way intimidated but rather served to raise my spirits, and with satisfaction I decided that even if I hadn't had what could be called a happy evening, then certainly a good one. Suddenly, however, a servant appears. Charles asks his wife to come to him. She leaves. I see her go, and for the rest of the evening she does not reappear. The marital chains are rattling again, I tell myself. He *is* the stronger. And my good mood is gone.

Next day—I hadn't really expected anything else—Frau Olga was nowhere to be seen. She wasn't feeling well, was the story, and the consensus was that there had been another scene. I didn't leave the vicinity of the house so as not to miss the moment when she might put in an appearance, but only Charles remained in sight, almost uninterruptedly, as guardian of his house and honor. Every now and then he gave me a nasty look, and although there was plenty of opportunity for it, did not address me once. That afternoon, without having caught another glimpse of Olga in the kitchen, dining room or at a window, I left for Vienna, feeling deeply depressed.

Five weeks passed; not until the eighteenth of July did I visit the Thalhof again. In the few undisturbed minutes granted us with no one listening, Olga implored me to be careful; we were being watched from every side, and, she said, "Everybody knows about it." Her husband's gruff, frosty greeting didn't leave anything to the imagination, but it was Frau Dora Kohnberger who seemed to understand the situation better than anyone else. She greeted me with the words, "We have been expecting you." Then, as later, she knew no greater pleasure than to participate in a love affair, not in a gossiping or malicious way, but objectively and benevolently, to discuss it whenever possible and to encourage it. Sometimes one got the feeling that during such conversations, which she knew how to conduct with tact and humor, everything contained in her in the way of life and love was exhausted. Any-

way, there were many who believed that my Uncle Edmund, the
famous trial lawyer, had had more than the proper feelings of a
brother-in-law, during the time she had lived with them as a
young girl, toward this graceful, red-haired creature with the
very slight hare lip which somehow added to the piquancy of her
lively little face. She liked to talk about her virtue, not with pride
but with astonishment, because she never denied the fact that
she had no principles, and among the gentlemen with whom she
occasionally held highly equivocal conversations, there were
innumerable experienced heart-breakers and seducers who would
have known very well how to put a theoretical conversation about
love affairs and similar themes into practice at an appropriate
moment. At any rate, Frau Dora remained—if it ever got that
far—lover and beloved in a subsidiary capacity only, and according to her natural tendencies and inclinations was adviser and con-
fidante even for her humorous, phlegmatic husband, who was
distinguished by the unlikely and undeserved name of "Innocent,"
and whom she had once nursed—as she told me with satisfaction
—through an illness which husbands usually prefer to keep secret
from their wives.

In August, when I finally arrived in Reichenau for a longer stay,
which was to be interrupted only now and then for a few days
at a time, I found Dora no longer simply suspecting what was
going on, but thanks to Frau Olga, now fully informed. During
the first days, all I was able to find an opportunity for was to
whisper assurances of my love, and to hear Olga reassure me of
hers. The season was at its height and she was busy, not only as
proprietress but also as hostess, because there were always a
number of guests at the Thalhof who were friends of hers, or to
whom she was socially obligated. Moreover she had fresh reasons
for not noticing me in any way that could attract attention, of
which Dora informed me in more detail while I was walking up
and down in front of the hotel with her, arm in arm, in a somewhat feeble attempt, granted, to mislead Olga's husband. Olga,
it seemed, had been so foolish as to tell Charles about all the
people she had met in Meran without mentioning me, or if she
had done so, then only cursorily, just as she had failed to reveal
to me her relationship to Rudi Pick. It seemed that her husband
had found out from someone or other that, in Meran, Olga and I

had attended a concert of gypsy music, with others of course, but just the same—together (an event I can't find among my memories). He had written to her father, to whom he liked to appeal on the occasion of such marital differences; the stern gentleman had appeared at the Thalhof, there had been a terrible scene which had ended with a double threat: the husband's—that he would throw Olga out of the house; the father's—that in such case she would find no sanctuary in his. Naturally I was flattered to think that in spite of this, Olga had not forbidden me to visit the hotel any more, and it made her caution all the more excusable. My need for tenderness had to be satisfied when, later that evening, in the music room, we listened to the singing of a young lady, a cousin of Richard Engländer's, and Olga sat opposite me, looking at me quietly and unwaveringly. And we were even closer, and she seemed to sense that in this way I could communicate with her more passionately than with words, when I sat down at the piano and began to improvise in my more emotional than artful fashion, in front of everyone yet for her ears alone.

Next morning I had to leave for Vienna, for my official vacation had not yet begun, and on the first of July I had been made assistant *pro tem* in Dr. Standthartner's department. Just the same, that evening I paid a call in Baden, where the Adler family was spending the summer, and one of their twelve daughters, Gisela, with whom I had been very good friends for a long time, asked me why I had grown so cool toward her. On the dark paths of their garden I proved to her, with passionate kisses, that she was wrong. She kissed me and cried bitterly. The rest of that oppressive summer night was spent playing poker with the older ladies until the day dawned grayly and the birds were starting to twitter, and I lost, and deserved it.

The following evening I left for Reichenau again, by chance in the company of Frau Dora, who was now able to tell me at her leisure what had happened at the Thalhof during my absence. When Charles had found out that I had reserved a room for a longer stay, he had been furious, called me a creature who turned women's heads with his piano-playing, and had demanded that Olga wire me at once to stay away. Thereupon Olga had taken morphium, not so much however that the doctor, who had been called immediately, had not been able to revive her. At this point

Dora had interceded on Olga's behalf and had succeeded in calming her husband, or at least in talking some sense into him, something of which I could convince myself that evening, after my arrival, for while I was seated at dinner, he came over and greeted me politely, in fact in an almost friendly fashion.

The next day also began under the best auspices. Already in the morning, although only briefly, I spoke to my beloved—my restored beloved—who with her attempted suicide (whether she had meant it seriously or not), had for the time being gained the upper hand, and could therefore meet me with a gaiety that was genuine. In the afternoon we met on neutral ground, in Frau Dora's salon, and Olga presented me with a small locket with a four-leafed clover in it, which she had picked. Then we went for a little walk, I don't know where and probably didn't know where at the time. At an appropriate distance from us, Frau Dora strolled with Fräulein Mizi, the singer of the night before, who was called "the Wise Woman of Reichenau" because of her cleverness and reasonability, so that at last, at last, Olga and I could converse undisturbed and revel in memories of Meran and our love. She also spoke about morphium and the scene with her husband, but said nothing about the reconciliation which, judging by his reassuring behavior, had probably taken place. I don't know if such a reconciliation should have counted, or had to be counted, as a worse breach of faith than my kisses in the garden in Baden, be that as it may—I felt no scruples or jealousy over Olga's attitude toward her husband, which at this point was certainly not platonic. But my high spirits, in fact my entire feeling of bliss was soon terminated, when, on returning to the Thalhof, I caught sight of a new visitor—Rudi Pick, who had just arrived with his father. I was one of that breed, however, who do not betray their feelings and knew how to be just as politely cool and inscrutable as he; and I could even hold my own with him in the elegance of my appearance, albeit a rather different elegance, with a touch of the Bohemian in it; but admittedly it wasn't granted me to be as slim, gay and casual as he.

That same evening all of us accompanied Rudi's brother, assistant magistrate Alfred Pick, to the station. On the dark platform our group milled back and forth, and Olga was so bold as to walk up and down with me, arm in arm. "What a happy day this has

been, Arthur," she said, whereupon I immediately brought up the
question of Rudi. She shook her head, hurt, but not unkind. There
wasn't a word of truth in it. How could I possibly have thought
there was? Didn't I know she loved no one, never had loved anyone but me? "If only we could walk on like this forever," I said,
as we left the platform and strolled on beside the tracks into the
dark, without anyone paying attention to us, and she said, "Why
do you speak of a happiness that can never be ours?" Those were
the things we said as, behind us, the rest of our group waited on
the platform for the train that was to take Alfred from us. Rudi,
slim, a little hoarse, fair-haired and inscrutable, was chatting with
Frau Dora and Mizi, the Wise Woman of Reichenau, and Olga
was apparently completely indifferent to what he might be thinking of us. At this point—there could be no doubt about it—I had
won out over all of them. And when we drove back to the Thalhof
in the hotel carriage under the dark blue sky, Olga was at my side.
What a day! And now it was over.

On the following day all of us were assembled in Frau Olga's
salon: myself, Frau Dora, Pick-father, Pick-son, and the Wise
Woman of Reichenau, and there ensued a deep, intellectual conversation about love. I can't recall what the others had to say
about it, but Gustave Pick was the main speaker, and I do remember how he declared, in a solemn-sentimental tone that reminded
me of Sonnenthal, "If I had wanted it, I could have had more luck
with women than a hussar lieutenant," but he hadn't been interested in such "lieutenant conquests."

It was not a question of quantity but of quality. The soul was
the important thing. In short, he sang the praises of womanhood,
and the ladies were enchanted. At the time he was a tall, dis-
tinguished-looking man, in his fifties, with a fine gray beard, still
handsome, and with an aristocratic air about him in spite of a
touch of the Jewish patriarch. Although he was Jewish and a
businessman, albeit of some prominence, he was received and was
even popular in aristocratic circles. An especially good friend
of his was Count Wilczek; they almost looked like step-brothers.
Gustave Pick's wife had died when he was only thirty and since
then he had been living with his two sons, Rudi and Alfred, a
social, worldly man and amateur musician. In his earlier years, his
musical interests and the fact that he was my mother's cousin, had

often brought him to our house, until my father, who didn't like to see this glorifier of women playing duets with my mother, decided it would be best if the visits ceased, which Mama, who I am sure had never thought anything of them, frequently and proudly told us. Pick also wrote couplets in the Viennese tradition and composed pretty dance melodies to go with them. The most famous one was his "Fiacre Song," which Girardi introduced at some charity event or other. It made a lot of money for the smart publisher, none however for the poet-composer; something he liked to complain about, not unjustifiably, well into his eighties. Those who know my novel, *The Way Out into the Open*, will recognize in him the archetype of old man Eissler, and in young Willy, Gustave's son, Rudi.

At the time Gustave looked upon my boldness with more humor than most of his fellow-men, yet oh, how far away in the distant future lay "the way out into the open," together with a few other "ways," on that afternoon in August, in Frau Olga's genteel, bourgeois salon, as we spoke of love in general and of the love of the aging man in particular. Gustave told about a Frenchman to whom a young lady had said, "Why, you're in love just like a thirty-year-old!" To which the former had replied, "No, *gnädige Frau*, like a fifty-year-old, *et vous savez, Madame, c'est pire*," a sentence which since then has been quoted on every suitable and unsuitable occasion in our Reichenau circle.

I can recall little of what was said that afternoon, except these words, which have been borne across the decades by Pick's sonorous voice, and I can see the knowing look with which Frau Dora hung on the lips of this aging knight in shining armor, lapping up every word he said. But of what concern was the love of a fifty-year-old man to Olga and me, or what a fifty-year-old man might think of love? Hadn't she just given me a volume, bound in red, of Paul Heyse's *Meran Novellas*, in which several places had been underlined two or three times? And hadn't I read them at once? And weren't they passing painfully and blissfully through my mind during this theoretical conversation? "Oh, sister mine," it said in one of those underlined passages, "what wise things I told him, none of which I believed! What righteous platitudes! And all the while my poor tortured heart was moaning and screaming within me, giving the lie to my brave words." And another,

"He was so dear. Why may I not love him? So unhappy. Why may I not make him happy? And then I cooled my eyes, which burned from weeping, with the flowers that are the only thing of his that I may keep."

The novella was *The Good Comrades*, and the role of such a comrade, nothing more, was what Olga wanted to play in my life. Hadn't she already told me so in Meran, and had I not agreed? And had I not been satisfied to know, when we were far apart, that at least our eyes were meeting on the constellation Cassiopea?

Summer at the Thalhof became increasingly lively and reached its height with a ball. While I was dancing a quadrille with Olga, she said to me, "Only now do I begin to understand what jealousy is. Didn't you notice how I bit my lip the other day until it bled when there was mention of a young girl you were supposed to have been courting last winter?" Of course I had noticed. But weren't those little drops of blood I had seen glistening on her lips—oh, I knew better than to voice my doubts!—hadn't they been a little too violent a display of emotion when compared with what Olga was truly feeling? And it is quite possible that right here the vial of morphium came to my mind again. That evening I drank a little too much, which actually was a slight affectation on my part, and I was in poor shape next morning when Olga greeted me at the breakfast table, where Frau Dora was keeping me company. My behavior, which was new to her, seemed to displease her; she soon left, and that evening told me that to see me in such ill-humor had caused her the unhappiest hours of her life. On the following morning, as I was leaving Reichenau again for a few days to take my father's place at his office, Olga complained bitterly, "You can't possibly be going away again? I can't believe it!"

But even in those days, my soul was "a vast land," so that same evening I dashed off to Baden to exchange tendernesses with Gisela, and her even prettier sister, Emma, on the dark paths of their garden. That evening nobody wept. Next day I visited my family, who were spending the summer in Vöslau, and on the one after that I was in Reichenau once more. After supper we went for our usual walk, accompanied this time by Frau Dora, and among others—husband Charles. Olga and I were about to discuss a way of corresponding, when suddenly Charles was gone. Olga was quite unreasonably concerned by his disappearance, and when he didn't reappear, decided to go up to her room. She had just left, when her husband whizzed past me and followed her. Dora and I were disturbed, but in the end there was nothing left for us to do but retire to our rooms. Next morning we found out —Dora from Olga, I from Dora—that there had been another scene. Charles had declared that he had overheard me whispering to Dora about a divorce (of course between him and Olga), had implored his wife not to leave him and had collapsed as if dead, which didn't excite us to any great extent since it seemed quite evidently to have been an act, and wouldn't have moved us if it hadn't been. For in general, lovers are benevolent only where the object of their love is concerned; in respect to everything else, and especially toward those who may be expected to intrude upon their love, they can be hard to the point of cruelty.

On the following evening, without feeling any more concern for the poor actor than I would have felt if I had known him dead, we walked up and down again in the moonlight, Olga and I, but Dora and Mizi had been joined by a new arrival, beautiful Eveline Brandeis-Weikersheim, an Englishwoman who, like the others, was eager to shield my oh, not very sinful love for the beautiful Thalhof proprietress. But Dora was the most obliging one. Next day she left Olga and me, who—incredible as it may seem—both happened to call on her at the same time, alone, while she went into the next room to write a letter. Our kiss, which lasted for minutes, was all the more passionate because, on the following day, I was to leave for Ischl. "If I think I can control myself," she said, "I shall come down tomorrow." She came down, controlled herself, gave me a rose, her husband was standing at her side, and both of them accompanied me part of the way—an innocuous hotel guest was leaving and the owners of the hotel were being polite. The morphium hadn't killed her, he hadn't gone mad with jealousy, and the happy-unhappy lover hadn't come off as badly as had been expected.

From Ischl I wrote a humorous-sentimental letter to Frau Dora, in verse, which I insert here in its almost diary-like exactitude.

August 1886

Adored and worthy friend,
Most precious *gnädige Frau,*
Behold me alone in Ischl,
Dreaming of Reichenau.

The rushing Traun received me
On a humid Sunday eve,
While the mist was rising slowly,
Over the greening lea.

The first to come and greet me,
As I sat in a café,
Was a man with a beard that was false—
Alfred Pick, to my dismay!

Today for his prank he atones
And does what he doesn't like:
In Wolfgang play the violins
While he—sits in Bayreuth!

On the terrace of the casino
The fiddles laugh and croon,
The cymbals clash *fortissimo,*
As the gypsies strike up a tune.

I sit, my wine before me,
A Somlauer it is not,
And listen as I let my hands
Hide my eyes—ah, my sorry lot!

The cymbals and the violins,
A story is in their song,
I listen to the bitter end,
With which the eve is gone.

And next day—'tis a Monday,
Ne'er one so blue did I see,
So to hear a glee of men singing
I proceed to Ebensee,

With two quite pleasant companions
I listen to the song,
And drink a dreadful brew
Till again the day is done.

Monday is followed by Tuesday,
How trivial are the weeks!
With mother and sister in Kammer
A change this poet seeks.

Aunts appear, and uncles,
And cousins of sexes each,
Naught to be seen but family
As far as the eye can reach.

The ladies were playing whist
As the piano was tried by me.
A lot of the keys were out of tune,
Just a few were left for me.

Now these too have been shattered,
Oh, magnificent summer places!
And you, my blissful Kammer
A silent keyboard graces.

Then came the Emperor's birthday,
Which in Gmunden I passed,
Where I saw some lovely women
And pretty maids, too, alas. . . .

That evening, at the water's edge
I stood and saw glide by
Many a festive lighted boat,
Red shimmering 'neath the sky.

And rockets shot into the air,
Popping, sparkling, dying,
As they cut into the fog so thick,
Like man's happiness and sighing.

They sparkled, oh so merrily,
Their popping a jubilate,
But in the end they scattered and fell,
In the water to sink was their fate.

As I sank into sadness,
Like a man of fifty-year,
But no, more like a youth,
(*Vous savez, Madame, c'est pire!*)

Lamenting, while in Reichenau
A bevy of women fair
Are dressing for a ball, I'll vow.
Alas, I can't be there.

But e'en if this dreamer can't join them,
He'll come later, that I swear,
And climb to Schneedörfl with them.
On Tuesday he'll be there.

Ah, life is like a crusade
Into the promised land.
Therefore, until I see it again
Take these greetings in thy hand:

To you, my enchanting Dora,
The loveliest *gnädige Frau;*
To little Minnie and Mitzka,
The Wise Woman of Reichenau;

To beautiful Frau Evelina,
My reverences as well;
And I kiss the hands of Frau Olga,
Which I beg you to her tell.

My best to the landlord, Herr Charles,
Which includes Herr Rettinger too,
From one who in boring Ischl,
For his sins must penance do.

And so I bring this to a close,
For I shall return, please be sure,
To kneel at your feet in person—
Your faithful friend, Arthur.

Herr Rettinger, whose name appears for the first time in this
letter, deserves a word or two. He was bookkeeper, business manager and assistant director of the Thalhof, a short, fat, agile little
man in his thirties, dressed for the most part in a citified fashion
or in a green huntsman's coat, but always without collar or tie. He
had a droll, rapid way of talking, was factotum, confidant and
more or less the husband's spy, which did not prevent him or
perhaps even encouraged him to be on friendly terms with Frau
Olga, who didn't trust him for a moment, but on the other hand
was quite fond of him. He was an indispensable member of the

household; in his office all threads ran together, business and private. He attended to the correspondence, assigned the rooms, made out the bills, was busy every minute of the day and was there for any of the hotel's regular guests, always obliging, always in good spirits. Nor was he more insincere than was unavoidable under the complicated conditions that prevailed in this strange hotel where the proprietress was at the same time housekeeper, cook, and woman-of-the-world, and the owner was in a way squire, *hotelier*, peasant and jealous husband. However uniform Rettinger's behavior may have been toward the Thalhof guests, there was no misunderstanding where his sympathies lay and where he felt it necessary to draw the line, and actually I couldn't resent the fact that he valued witty, ever-amiable trial lawyer Alfred Pick more highly than me, who was somehow or other a disturbing element, especially since he never really let me feel it. At the time he didn't seem to give a thought to any material advantages for himself, only later, especially at the height of the season, when rooms were scarce, did it become customary to get on his good side with small presents of money or more substantial tips.

Little Fräulein Minnie, to whom I send greetings in the same letter, was the youngest daughter of Frau Marianne Benedict. At the time she was a very pretty, dark-eyed girl, fifteen years old, who looked like a dainty gypsy. She was quite precocious, and witty far beyond her years, and was certainly more attractive than her older sister, who wasn't bad-looking but was slightly deformed. When I want to recall my first vision of Minnie, I see her on the tennis court behind the Thalhof, in the sunshine, trying to teach me the rudiments of the game, which she didn't play too well. Her pretty Mama, still quite young but with prematurely gray hair, looked to me, at twenty-four, like a matron, and is sitting there, relaxed, watching us. But in the background, in the direction of the Schneeberg, dark fir trees cover the slope.

So I had to miss the ball for which they had been expecting me, and eight days passed before I at last—no, I didn't climb to Schneedörfl as described in the poem—but drove in the elegant Reichenau manner, in a spanking *fiacre*, from the Payerbach Station to the Thalhof, where, after the intoxication of all past festivities, everything was back to normal, and I was welcomed from

every side with a greater or lesser degree of sincerity. The first
thing Frau Dora had to tell me was that Olga, after receiving the
news that I couldn't be there for the dance, had broken a plate
in her fury. Only a plate, but even if it had been a whole set of
china, then, logically speaking, a certain morphium solution
should have been stronger. But with Olga apparently so happy to
have me back, as if she had smashed at least a soup tureen in anger
over my non-appearance, I couldn't really complain. Her husband's distrust, however, had evidently increased during my
absence, and since I found it increasingly difficult to hide my
feelings, and Olga also at times lacked the necessary vigilance
and dissimulation—although she frequently whispered to me in
English, "Take care," if she thought we were in danger—the
atmosphere became more and more oppressive and threatening;
and when her husband and I would meet and silently take each
other's measure, I was beset by a vision that was probably exaggerated, of two tigers face to face, ready to spring.

Our circle of acquaintances, friends and guests grew ever wider,
and soon Olga and I didn't have a moment to be truly alone together. We therefore had to take advantage of every opportunity,
sometimes under not very favorable circumstances, to at least be
close, even if in the company of a lot of indifferent and boring
people. Thus we would let a good-natured dilettante like Baron
Erlanger read a foolish novel aloud to us, or encourage a stupid
little lieutenant to play to us on the piano, if by that an hour was
gained during which we could communicate silently with a look
or a smile. New guests kept arriving, some more interesting and
important than others, among them Olga's youngest sister, Fanny,
a nice, friendly, bourgeois girl, not very attractive, one of those
women who seem destined to be old maids and sometimes marry
between thirty and forty, as she finally did. She was followed by
the middle one, Gabrielle, who was not as beautiful as Olga but
more stylish, and with it all lively, forceful, arrogant and determined to marry nothing less than a count, who promptly turned
up a few years later, as ordered, in the person of a Prussian, dyed-
in-the-wool conservative, six-foot-tall Junker.

So now we went for walks, five, six, eight of us, and if we were
lucky, Olga and I might stand for a few seconds, separate from
the others, on a gentle mountain slope with a view toward the

twilit valley. Olga would draw a line across the sky with the point of her parasol, as if she were explaining the region to me, and would whisper, "Tell me once more that you love me. I can hear it a thousand times. If only you knew how I worship you." Was it the Rax or the Schneeberg towering in front of me into the reddening sky? I didn't know at the time, didn't know for years, and was constantly getting them mixed up, and I scarcely ever went more than a quarter of an hour's walk away from the house because my adored love might appear at any moment on the veranda, in the courtyard or garden. Rax, Schneeberg, paths in the woods, the meadow and the sky above—scarcely any of it was landscape for me in those days; all was wings and backdrop; and instead of taking my agonized longing out for a walk in the fresh air, I would sometimes lie on my bed for hours, my head throbbing with despair because that morning, even if perhaps of necessity, my beloved had spoken coolly to me, or in a pitiful state of tension because of possible inimical action on the part of her husband, unnerved by the constant farce we had to play, for which I wasn't clever enough, and sometimes too broken and weary even to weep.

One day Olga and I hit upon the idea—I can't remember how it came about—of playing chess together. Now we sat every afternoon at five, in the courtyard, which was open on one side, at a small table beside the rear entrance of the hotel. Here there was uninterrupted but not too lively traffic—carriages drove in and out; guests came and went, employees of the hotel, busy Herr Rettinger, also Charles's taciturn father, old Waissnix, with his white Emperor's beard and a scornful expression playing about his lips; and of course Charles himself, on his way to and from the utility buildings or stables, was visible every now and then for minutes at a time. Frau Dora, Fräulein Mitzka, little Minnie, Lieutenant Latinovics, Baron Erlanger, and whoever felt so inclined, would remain standing beside our small table for a longer or shorter while and would cast a casual glance, sometimes with a gentle smile, at our chess board, on which the figures, after short or longer pauses, actually did move back and forth according to the rules. Could there be anything more harmless than such a game, played in the open, in a courtyard, next to a hotel entrance, so to speak in the face of the whole wide world? And if, while

moving the figures, the fingers of the two players touched fleetingly, could anyone possibly have found it shocking? And when
a trembling ran through our bodies and our cheeks reddened and
our eyes glittered, couldn't that be explained away by the tensions
of the game? And if someone, from afar, from one of the windows
on the first or second floor, for instance, could see that our lips
were moving, just a little, could any benevolent person guess that
this trembling of our lips did not mean "Checkmate," but possibly,
"A moment at your side, Arthur, makes up for all the pain I suffer
for you"; not *"Gardez!"* but, "I wish I could sink at your feet, Olga,
and weep." No. No one thought anything of the kind, for all of
them were guileless . . . busy Herr Rettinger, obliging Dora,
scornful old Waissnix, and "Uncle Minnie," which was our nickname for the little gypsy girl, for no reason I can recall. And as
far as Charles was concerned, he could hardly stop his wife, after
the day's hard work, from playing a game of chess for everyone to
see, with a young gentleman of good family who was residing at
the hotel and paid his bills promptly.

One day, in the middle of a game, I was talking—not about the
present but about the past; not mine, of course, but hers; not
about neurotic Richard Engländer, who was over and done with,
but about cavalry lieutenant Rudi Pick, when, as happened frequently, an open *fiacre* rolled into the courtyard, and who should
get out of it, genial and as inscrutable as ever, but the man I had
just been talking about, none too happily and confidently—Rudi
Pick! He wore the most elegant summer suit imaginable.

Right away he sat down beside us, was amusing, irresistible, fair-
haired, slim, and a little hoarse, and although he spoke of quite
different things and deigned to cast only the briefest glance at the
chess board, I knew that he didn't believe for a moment in the
seriousness of the game we were playing, nor in the faithfulness
of women, and certainly not that Olga loved me truly, much less
loved me more than she had loved him when they had gone
chamois hunting together. And hunting chamois in the lonely
mountains—the thought lay close at the moment, for me as well
as for him—had all sorts of advantages which chess, played in an
open courtyard, surrounded by windows, couldn't possibly have.
But we were men-of-the-world, both of us, and neither of us let
the other know what was on his mind; and Olga was not only a

woman-of-the-world but a woman of heart, and during the miserable two days Rudi spent at the Thalhof, did her best to reassure me and keep me calm. The way she looked at me promised more than ever; her words were pitched high emotionally, and since her husband, during just these two days, seemed to be less worried, was, in fact, in much better spirits, as if he didn't begrudge me Rudi's presence for a moment, she didn't have to be as cautious as usual, nor whisper her warning "Take care" so frequently, which always erased the most passionate words from my lips. "I could weep when I see you so sad," she said. "Have you any idea how madly I love you? Every minute of my life, my every thought is yours alone." But Rudi also seemed to be in the best of spirits during those two days and was certainly the most amusing person around of all the parties concerned and unconcerned. He told anecdotes and recited some monologues he had written, for instance, a Jewish version of *Wilhelm Tell*, (of which I can recall only the indignant protestations of Landvogt Gessler, "So I'm a knight, maybe?") and was also the wittiest participant when we played games, for instance "Secretary," which was a popular pastime after meals.

To play this game, a person wrote somebody's name, preferably the name of someone present, on a piece of paper, and folded it; the next person, without knowing what name had been written, added an attribute, the next one the name of a woman who was to be tied in with the first unknown; the next—the nature of the connection; the next—world opinion on the subject, followed by various other rubrics, without anyone getting to see anything but what he had written. In the end the paper was unrolled; the whole thing was read aloud, resulting in quite a few funny, ambiguous or pertinent "warrants" and suspicious data. "I can very well imagine," Rudi Pick commented once gloomily, in his hoarse voice, at the end of a game, "that one could leave a game like this with a few challenges to a duel." Hm, I thought, a few? Wasn't he exaggerating? But that's what he said. A duel wouldn't have meant anything to him. Not that he had ever fought one, but he would have been ready, naturally, and willing to fight one at any time. Who could have doubted it? And how the women adored him!

There, for instance, was beautiful Frau Eveline, his aunt, rather too young for an aunt, and an Englishwoman to boot, with whom

he sat on a bench on one of those two evenings, scarcely a hundred paces from the hotel. But the bench stood at the edge of the
woods and merged into the darkness. Eveline's husband had been
a lieutenant in a dragoon regiment, perhaps only in the reserves,
just the same—a dragoon lieutenant, but was now a tall, fat man.
He may have had a profession, but one didn't notice it. Anyway,
he was considered an idler and a gambler. His favorite partner
was a cousin of our friend Charles, the most notorious scoundrel
in Reichenau, a handsome fellow, who looked rather as one felt
a poacher should look, which he may well have been once, among
other things. His name was Romanus; he had served for three
years in the army, then driven a *fiacre*. I can recall a game of
poker that lasted until late into the night, in Rettinger's office, in
which Eveline's husband, Innocent, Romanus and I took part—in
short, a dandy little group; and it will astonish no one to hear that
I was not one of the winners. But on this particular evening, on
which the bench with Eveline and Rudi dissolved in the dark, I
was sitting with her husband, Herr Weikersheim, in front of the
hotel. He was smoking a big cigar and had stretched out his leg on
a chair. He had broken it recently, and it was still stiff. Heaven
knows what we were talking about when he asked suddenly, "By
the way, where is my wife?"

Politely, and with no bad intentions, I replied that she was over
there, sitting on a bench with Rudi. Over there? Yes. I pointed. I
must say one couldn't see very much.

Herr Weikersheim went on talking as if this didn't bother him
especially, but a few minutes later he said casually, "Well, let's
join them," and accompanied by me and supported by his cane,
he walked stiffly to where his wife was chatting with her nephew.
She came forward out of the darkness and greeted us with a
smile, after which a quite general, natural and totally harmless
conversation took place. The story, unfortunately, or thank God,
lacks a point, except in my sympathetic heart. Yet even if my
heart had trembled in accordance with the age-old laws of love
and jealousy, my face had betrayed nothing, all of which comes
under the heading of elegance.

Rudi Pick didn't have a profession either. He was an amateur
artist and only made a name for himself much later as a painter of
sports subjects and with his caricatures. At the time he was toying

with the idea of an army career. On one of those days—what didn't all happen in those twice twenty-four hours—so much that was completely unimportant and no concern of mine, yet how it has remained with me! On one of these days, the son of old Baron Erlanger, a lieutenant in a Uhlan regiment, arrived for a stay at the Thalhof. He was a baptized Jew, smart, inclined to impertinence, with a long saber scar on his forehead. Rudi asked this expert, in my presence, for his advice as to whether he should become a career officer. The Baron looked thoughtful and shook his head. The thing wasn't all that simple. As an officer, especially in a cavalry regiment, Rudi would find it difficult as a Jew, even as a baptized Jew—because not baptized he didn't have a chance —to avoid conflicts with his comrades. Unfortunately he himself had more than once had the opportunity . . . he really didn't have to say any more. The scar on his forehead was still blood red and strong enough testimony.

Rudi nodded. He could have been just as dashing as the next man, and would probably have been perfectly willing to change his faith; the only thing he lacked in order to hold his own as a baptized Jew among his cavalry comrades was the advantage Baron Erlanger had over him—wealth. So he decided to remain a civilian and probably never regretted it, since he soon found himself accepted for other attributes, gradually also because of his success as an artist, in those aristocratic and sporting circles to which he had been drawn since his youth. He was invited to the castles of business magnates, traveled to Africa with a prince to hunt lions, and made fun of princes, lions, horses, jockeys, in short, the whole world he loved so much, a little also of himself, in amusing and stylish *aquarelles*.

One evening, after Rudi's departure, Olga's friends were unable to catch even a glimpse of her, neither in the dining room nor on the veranda nor anywhere outside, and were told that she wasn't feeling well. Next day she appeared, looking pale, beckoned to me to come closer and whispered, "Come to my salon in five minutes," and left.

I felt dizzy. What did it mean? Something bad? Something good? When the five minutes had passed, I followed her. She was leaning against the piano, looking even paler than before. I rushed over to her; she sank into my arms and we kissed passionately.

"You must leave," she said. "He is going to kill you. Last night, when you followed my chambermaid [whom I had asked where I could find her mistress], he was ready to go down and kill you. I told him, 'Rather kill me.' "

I fell on my knees. I couldn't make up my mind to leave her, much less to flee. With quite conscious grandeur I declared that I would consider it a supreme joy to die for her, but by all means let us think of a better solution. In a hasty conversation, interrupted constantly by passionate kisses, I developed a plan of which she approved and which I proceeded at once to carry out. I asked to speak to Herr Charles and demanded to know why he insisted on torturing his wife with groundless jealousy, and disrupt and embitter her innocent pleasures with his distrust. I begged him not to insist, also for his sake, because it would be embarrassing and only attract attention, that I leave earlier than intended, since my planned departure, as he must know, was to take place in a few days anyway.

He replied quite calmly, and only his tortured features, his hollow cheeks and red-rimmed eyes with the drooping lids, like a hound dog's—later a friend of mine liked to call such faces, distorted by jealousy, "hound-dog faces"—betrayed his agony, which I could contemplate with indifference and even found ridiculous. Nothing was further from his mind, he said, than to seriously suspect his wife. As for her flirtation with me, I was not to think that was anything new. "She carried on in just the same way with Richard Engländer and Rudi Pick," he went on, in a well-aimed second line, and quite possibly my face now began to show signs of hound-dog features. "But," he continued, "I have no intention of putting up with it. It doesn't suit me to know people are talking about it. They did it then and they're doing it again."

Just the same, our conversation now took on a lighter character, in fact became almost cordial. By his remark about his wife's earlier admirers he had so to speak made me a fellow sufferer. One thing was clear—he had no intention of killing me, if anybody then preferably Rudi Pick; and it wasn't necessary for me to leave a day earlier than planned. He also had nothing against any decent orderly conversation between his wife and myself as long as there were others present. In short, I had achieved practically everything I wanted; yet I couldn't say that I felt exactly victorious, not as I said goodbye to him with a cordial handshake nor even that evening, during an impromptu little dance in the lounge, when Olga's cheek touched mine and she whispered words of love in my ear. I made her feel it next day, while we were playing chess, when I tortured her with her husband's spiteful remarks, in which she insisted on seeing nothing but his vengefulness.

Since my letter from Ischl had established me as a talented poet, I was given the honorable assignment of writing a little piece for the birthday of Frau Eveline, Rudi's beautiful English aunt. I was all the more delighted to do so when Olga declared she was willing to play a part in it, namely that of the Spirit of the Thalhof, which under other circumstances I would not have included. Little Minnie was eminently cut out to play the Spirit of Beauty; I can't remember who played England, it may have been Minnie's older sister, Emmi; to myself, the only male in the cast, I assigned the role of the Spirit of Vienna. Naturally all these spirits were vying for their right to Eveline, and it goes without saying that in the end Beauty triumphed.

The first rehearsal took place the day before the performance, which was when I finally managed to finish the piece; another on the following morning, and that afternoon, in the office, I transcribed the verses neatly for the prompter. This otherwise tedious job was made sweet by the fact that Olga came in every now and then, leaned over my work and I kissed her hands. That evening, at last, and with only relatives present, the performance took place. We didn't look at all bad; the ladies were prettily costumed, and I made up for what I lacked as a thespian by speaking in an exaggeratedly Viennese dialect and dressing up like a ragamuffin, of course with the obligatory "Virginia straw" behind one ear. Olga, in her dark voice and without much talent, recited her verses like a lady, but I can still remember fifteen-year-old Minnie's words: "I come from far-off regions / To look at my dear child. / Be not afraid, I ask for naught, / Not we, this earth needs joy," spoken in her consciously childish, pleasing voice.

The play was followed by a birthday dinner and at last, after that, dancing. Again and again I took refuge from the agony of my desires in the contents of my wine glass because this evening . . . this evening was to be my last in Reichenau, the end of those wonderful, bittersweet summer days that had been saturated with longing and passion, during which, even if my ultimate and most fervent wishes had not been granted, I still had progressed in love experience and knowledge of the soul of man and woman, but above all in knowledge of myself, far more than at any other period in my life. And although I realized that things were by no means over between Olga and me, and that we would see each other again, soon and often; even if the boldest hopes for the future were alive in me and remained alive for a long time, the recognition that the most beautiful aspect of our relationship—in a profound sense beautiful—that which could never happen again, the aspects of it that were unique, were over and done with, cast a gloomier shadow over my soul than any banal farewell scene might have done, and on this last night at the Thalhof I shed tears that may be counted as the bitterest and most desperate of my youth.

And next morning, I left for Vienna. Olga was with me, which didn't attract unusual attention since she often visited her father, the owner of the Südbahn Restaurant, and stayed with him for a few days. Besides, Innocent was traveling with us, in the same compartment, and demonstrated his understanding and good nature in that, from Gloggnitz on, he pretended to be asleep. Since there was no one else in the compartment and one didn't have to fear that someone who was pretending to be asleep might wake up, our journey as far as Meidling was nothing but one long, passionate kiss. At this station Innocent opened his eyes as loudly as he could and without batting an eyelash apologized for his rude behavior.

Next Sunday I was back in Reichenau, but I wasn't very lucky. Dora received me with the news that Olga was ill and was in her room, weeping. Without having seen her, I returned to Vienna that evening, leaving a note for her with despairing, perhaps even bitter content, because Rudi Pick had also been at the Thalhof but had not left with me. In Vienna I again saw Lolotte, whom I had met fleetingly the summer before, and my hour of love with her cost me nothing but a pearl which, I am sure through no fault of hers, must have fallen out of the setting of the only ring I ever wore, and disappeared, never to be seen again, in the joints of a creaky hotel bed. Only a few weeks before, in connection with all sorts of Lolotte possibilities, Olga had sighed, "What rights does a woman like me have?" So she probably would not have resented the little episode, but I am sure she would have been pleased over the loss of the pearl.

On the following Saturday I left again for Reichenau, this time with my brother, to visit our mother who was spending a few days at the Thalhof, perhaps in part at my instigation. My parents were of course not unaware of what was taking me back constantly to Reichenau and had kept me there for such a long time during the summer just past, and through my father's half-veiled intimations I was able to gather that, because of the well-known brutality of the husband, they were worried about my physical rather than my spiritual welfare. During this stay, however, nothing happened that could possibly have attracted my mother's attention or worried her. Frau Olga, who had attended a wedding in Vienna, didn't appear until our party had retired to the music room after dinner, and I had only one chance to catch her for a moment when no one was looking, and ask her if she loved me. "You know I do," she replied, but it sounded a little sharp; then she said she wasn't feeling well and retired. Next day Dora told me that the week before, Olga's father had been there again and there had been another scene over me, but what made me feel even worse than this bit of news was what Dora told me as a result of her observations, namely that Olga was lacking in temperament, that she loved me probably as much as she could love anyone, but that she was not capable of a grand passion. I tried to console myself with the thought that surely Olga had not told her friend Dora everything that had taken place between us, and that evening, while we were playing games, I took the opportunity to pass Olga a mad love-letter. On the following morning, before my departure, she appeared at a window, a white lace scarf around her head, just as she had done on the morning she had waved farewell in Meran. She gazed at me for a long time; her look was veiled, she passed the lace scarf across her tear-swept eyes and disappeared.

And now our correspondence started. "I shall not be visiting Vienna often in October," she wrote in her first letter, "and therefore won't have the pleasure of seeing you. Frau Kohnberger is going to be so kind as to give you all my news. Please, Herr Doktor, preserve your friendly feelings for me and accept my heartfelt gratitude for many a pleasurable hour granted me during the summer, thanks to your dear company. I hope we shall meet again in the winter, as good friends. Please grant me one more request: don't torture yourself and others with unnecessary and untrue notions. I know only too well that so many aspects of life are ugly, and that that which is considered the greatest happiness means nothing but a long series of torments. But I have always considered the greatest triumph to be the ability to manage oneself. I hope you will still want to discuss this or that with me, and that you are not angry with me. I am not going to say goodbye, but *Auf Wiedersehen*. Cordially, Olga Waissnix. I would be very happy if you would occasionally give me a sign of life, in writing. [The words 'in writing' had been added.] May I beg you to do so?"

A farewell, I thought, and deeply disturbed, hurried to see Dora, who at first tried to assure me that in my excitement I had misunderstood Olga's letter, but otherwise had little of a consoling nature to say. Olga would never be anything but a friend to me; if her father—there was less talk of her husband—were to demand categorically that she break off all ties with me, or if he had already done so, there was nothing I could do but accept it. I left Dora in even greater despair than I had felt on going to see her, and my efforts to recall all Olga's intimate and passionate words, the promising looks and kisses, were not much help in restoring my faith in her love, nor in filling me with felicitous hopes. I answered her letter with the necessary reserve and caution, since I had to reckon with the fact that unauthorized eyes might get to see it; just the same, I let shine through the thought that I didn't consider her virtuous resolutions irrevocable.

Her next letter was written in a lighter, warmer tone and wasn't sparing with intimations that I could interpret to my advantage, especially a quote from the aforementioned Heyse novella *The Good Comrades:* "If I could do what I wanted to do." She wrote of lonely walks and hunting parties, about her children, whom I had hardly ever seen while at the Thalhof. She was evidently very much occupied at this point with their upbringing and education. Arabesques of pressed autumn flowers, which she had picked herself, decorated the pages for which I was waiting longingly and which I received with such delight. My replies were composed in a sentimental-humorous vein. I told, not with absolute honesty, about the monotony of my life within and outside the walls of the hospital, described the room in the Allgemeine Krankenhaus into which I had moved on the first of November, as assistant doctor now in the psychiatric clinic, and didn't omit a few ironic remarks about her well-known predilection for the Jockey Club and all the elegance that went with it. But although she came often to Vienna, where she shopped and paid calls and stayed at her father's apartment, in the room she had occupied as a girl, our intercourse remained strictly limited to written correspondence, and at best I would find again, in Frau Dora's salon (with a bit of imagination on my part), faint traces of the perfume Olga had used on her last visit there. But the consolation of this scent was dimmed considerably as Dora continued cruelly to dash my hopes, and finally, as if it had been a message for me, repeated Olga's dreadful words, to the effect that she never wanted to see me again, her only goal being to remain a respectable woman. "And since she is heartless," Dora went on, "she should not find this particularly difficult." But then, at the beginning of December, I received the following telegram: WEDNESDAY, SMALL SLEIGHING PARTY. LEAVE VIENNA EARLY WEDNESDAY SEVEN O'CLOCK, POSSIBLY TUESDAY AFTERNOON. WOULD BE PLEASED IF YOU CAME. PLEASE REPLY. WAISSNIX. (No first name.) My reply was in the affirmative.

I arrived in Reichenau on a beautiful moonlit evening and drove along the white wintery road to the Thalhof. The couple greeted me amiably. We repaired to the well-heated office where I was welcomed by Rettinger, whom I sometimes remember as "the funny man" in an old-Vienna farce; but soon I was alone with Olga. She was sitting, hands folded, on a hassock at my feet, and of course all I wanted to do was tell her about the agony of mind I had suffered, which had been kept alive in me, or I should say had been aroused in me by the things Dora had said. She was astonished. How could I have believed Dora? Of course she didn't tell her and Eveline everything; on the contrary, she felt it was important to mislead people and was glad to hear that the act she was putting on for others was such a success, with her husband too, it seemed, because the meal all of us partook of together in the otherwise empty dining room couldn't have been gayer or more harmless.

On the following day a sleigh took us through the pure, white,

icy winter landscape to the Höllen Valley. I sat in the carriage of
the vehicle with Olga, like prince and princess, while her husband
sat on the box with the driver, like a lackey. We didn't say very
much, in fact scarcely looked at each other, since Charles, sitting
alertly upright, evidently had no intention of letting a word
escape him, and turned every now and then to make an obvious
remark about the weather or the scenery. We stopped to rest for
a while at an inn near the valley entrance, then drove homeward
through the gleaming snow with the twilight settling upon us. For
supper I was their guest, in their apartment. My hostess received
me in the salon and at first, for a while, we were alone. I played
the piano, or rather a few notes and chords; she stood facing me;
we spoke very little, but at last, with no one to hear or watch—
or so we thought—were able to express with our eyes the words
we had longed to speak and hear the other say in the long months
of our separation.

Then came supper, which was exceptionally good. A Fräulein
Hann joined us, a pleasant, rather limited woman, governess, companion, friend, one of those creatures doomed to be an aging factotum, who knows how to make her admiration for another
woman, more favored by fate, the focal point of her life, and frequently lives a happier because more modest life, with less responsibilities, than the friend whom she admires or secretly envies. An
English teacher, who lived in during the winter, also joined us for
the meal, which was scarcely over when host and hostess abruptly
and unexpectedly left the room. With my good spirits considerably
dashed, I tried to keep up a conversation with the two ladies left
me, until at last, ten minutes or so later, Olga reappeared, with
no response to my questioning glance. In a puzzling mood of
despair and resignation, and quite evidently driven to it, she
poured herself one glass of wine after the other and drank them.
Charles, too, returned and sat down again at the table with the
unmistakable hound-dog expression on his face. The conversation
became forced, frequently died down altogether, and was difficult
to resume. Suddenly Charles got up, just as unexpectedly as
before, and left the room. Fräulein Hann and the Englishwoman
followed him; Olga whispered, "He heard everything. *Il sait
que je vous aime.* Now it is all over." Before she could say any-

thing more, he came back, sat down between us and offered me a cigar, just as if all he had done was go and fetch them from the next room, chatted and was peculiarly friendly, an attitude which I had every reason to question.

The sleigh was waiting; it was high time for me to leave. Olga's silence, the rigidity with which she leaned in a corner of the sofa, almost in a reclining position, Charles's insidious attentiveness and the murkiness of the whole situation were so oppressive, so unbearable, that in order to put an end to our misery one way or another, I asked him, with an embarrassed, and I am sure very clumsy, comment on his suspicious nature, to accompany me to the station. He refused, politely. Finally, after being prodded to some extent by his wife, he asked me coolly but amiably enough, to come again, and the next thing I knew, I was alone in the sleigh, like someone who has been fopped, like someone whom a man bent on revenge first likes to play an insulting trick on, driving through the cold, white, starry night to the station.

On the following day I was on duty at the admission room of the hospital, and while I was occupied with the reception of the sick, preliminary examinations and the assignment of patients to the various sections, I was constantly expecting the wronged husband to turn up, or his second, but I waited in vain. The day passed, so did the one following it, without any such incident or other tidings from the Thalhof, until at last, on the third day, a letter from Olga arrived in which she explained that she had not been well but hoped to meet me one evening, as had been arranged previously, at the Benedicts', who had extended invitations to both of us some time ago.

And this is what now took place. We had plenty of time to talk things over, and she told me that her husband had had to admit that he hadn't heard a word we had spoken that evening, but had watched us in the lighted room from a roof opposite, something he had probably done before, more often than we realized, and had observed our lively gestures. Since these gestures, taken all in all, had been relatively harmless, his wife had been able to calm him down, and she was even willing to take the risk and grant me a few brief meetings during the winter of the sort which could take place anyway. I was allowed to take a fifteen-minute walk with her on the Ring, or to accompany her after a Philharmonic concert, through the Heugasse, to the vicinity of her father's apartment in the Südbahnhof building.

On the evening of my return from the Reichenau sleighing party, my father left for a medical consultation on the Riviera, and I was to look after his patients, as usual. During his office hours I made the acquaintance of a Hungarian Jewish girl who had come to Vienna with her mother to study singing, and had stayed on in Vienna after her mother had left. She seemed to prefer to be treated by me rather than by my father, and after he had returned and taken over his practice again, I continued to look after her in my pleasant, secluded hospital quarters and also sometimes visited her in the little room she occupied in the apartment of some nondescript people, something I am in a position to recall only from her letters. She was fairly pretty, flirtatious, hysterical, affected, untruthful, but quite good-natured, and she threw herself at me as she would have done at any young man under similar circumstances—a lawyer or a theologian—and delighted me one day with the announcement that she was pregnant. Her brother, allegedly a lieutenant but quite probably nothing better than a clerk in a department store, would surely kill her—so she said—and with a tragi-comic effect that was helped by her Hungarian accent, she kept repeating over and over again, "A duel is inevitable."

I had already treated her badly enough, since basically I couldn't stand her. I had insulted her; rejected her. She had written me innumerable farewell notes, and in them expressed the hope that she would find consolation for her faithless lover in her profession, but she had always returned to kneel imploringly at my feet, eyes cast adoringly heavenward. However, her latest lies and threats, both probably only half-conscious and not badly intended, made it seem advisable to definitely terminate our relationship. This didn't happen at once, although she did return to Budapest that spring and wrote to me from that city, also from Gödöllö, where she was to spend the summer—desperate, passionate, resigned and yearning letters, which I rarely answered; but six weeks after her departure she turned up suddenly in my room at the hospital. I received her so rudely that I was sure I had finally got rid of her; however, at midnight of that same day, as I was walking through the hospital garden in the direction of my room, the night-watchman called out to inform me that a young lady had been waiting for me for two hours, and there was Helen, sitting on a ledge of the wall under my window. She rose to meet me and was so gentle and lost in her unhappiness that I simply didn't have the heart to send her out into the night, but instead took her up to my room with me. Not until the following morning did we say farewell, forever, as usual. Next day she implored my friend, Fritz Kapper, to intercede for her. On the following morning—I was still in bed—she turned up again, showed me reports from her singing teachers, which were intended for her relatives, who were to bear the cost of her training, flung herself on my bed and implored me to be "merciful," which at the moment was not directed solely at the meager charity of my caresses.

That morning I saw her for the last time for some time to come, and also didn't hear from her again. Six years later, in 1893, I met her uncle (how did I happen to know him?) in a Prater restaurant, and heard from him that his niece had gone mad and died five years before. I therefore had every reason to be astonished when I received a letter from her, two years later, in which she asked me to put in a word for her with Jauner, the director of the Carltheater. Soon after that she turned up personally, poor, faded, and still looking in vain for a part. And she got in touch with me again several years later, allegedly on behalf of a Budapest publishing house, in connection with a manuscript they wished to obtain from me, and closed with the words, "We people of Budapest are faithful admirers of yours, and of your inestimable works. . . ."

The smile of memory never dies on a woman's lips. Women are on the whole more vindictive but also more grateful than men. They take revenge sometimes for the tenderness and sacrifices made on their behalf and even after decades are grateful for the disappointments and insults suffered.

If the above thoughts are also to be found in *Anatol*, this may be justified by the fact that this account covers a period in my life from which that in many ways characteristic, even if at times perhaps embarrassing cycle emerged, and it would be surprising if in the later recounting some of the atmosphere of those bygone days were not evident. I realize that this atmosphere was neither too pure nor uplifting, not so much from individual experiences nor from my way of life as a whole, but much more out of the tenor of my diary entries in those days, which were by no means free from affectation nor even of a certain foppishness. Today I consider the worst entry to be the one where I fleetingly consider "my sister's boring infatuation with a young doctor" as a partial reason for the bad atmosphere in our home, which was actually caused much more by my father's dissatisfaction with me than by anything else, and by his justified vexation over the way his fraudulent and bankrupt relatives made financial demands on him, which he invariably had to fulfill.

I find the brightest spots in my letters to Olga, also in hers to me. This is not to say that I put on an act for her, although to some extent my behavior toward her was a pose, but because, according to the laws inherent in such a relationship, there was nothing I could do but guide my true nature along its innate way, albeit uplifted to a nobler and loftier element.

In the spring I found more frequent opportunities to see Olga, but rarely for more than a quarter of an hour at a time, on the Ring, or at exhibits, where we again assured each other of our love and addressed each other—at least when we said goodbye—with the intimate "Du." At the beginning of the summer I was even granted a chance meeting with her in a railway compartment. Between Baden and Vienna we were alone, and in her kisses I could again imagine that we belonged together forever. But I could not get her to agree to a real tryst, which I was demanding with increasing vehemence. "I am afraid of you, and of me," she said, and left me—knowing very well all about them yet evidently not letting it worry her—to the Helenes, Malvinas, Lolottes, and some who were nameless, with whom I amused myself or was bored, more or less platonically. Not one of them had so far imperiled my heart, and this includes the young society ladies, a few of whom were friendlier than ever as I became increasingly eligible as a husband. Helene Herz, virginal and sharp-witted, was still my favorite. A lively friendship developed also with Fräulein Rosa Sternlicht, who was my partner in an amateur theatrical that winter. The play was of course by Emil Limé-Brüll, and was titled *The Growling Lion*. The actors appeared as court players, and I excelled with my famous Hartmann impersonation. Fräulein Rosa was a nice, not exactly stupid, moderately pretty and affected little creature, who wasted half her pocket money on sweets, as she confessed later, which she offered me when I visited her, to put me in a good mood. In spite of which our friendship prospered no further than an outing to the Kahlenberg, accompanied by her family, with nature enthusiasm, supper *al fresco*, snapshots, and clandestinely, during a dance, a fleeting kiss, which both of us pretended not to have noticed.

I valued the Benedict household more than any other because of the possibility of meeting Olga there, however rare the occasions, but also because I liked the two daughters—Emmy, who was supposed to be the clever one but was actually only precocious and forward, and especially Minnie, to whom I had dedicated a mazurka entitled "Uncle Minnie," whereas my "Reichenau Waltz" needed no dedication to indicate to whom it belonged.

Meanwhile I had reached the age of twenty-five, a point in my life which was an inducement to look back and forward. "Oh, the things with which, at eighteen, I deluded myself would have been achieved at this age," I wrote in my diary, and proceeded to balance the record superficially: "The reputation of a clever but arrogant man with those who know me little; a man-of-the-world for a few, which annoys Papa; and for my friends a witty, highly talented person who can't seem to pull himself together to get anything done. And still," I concluded, "it is only my imagination that may help me eventually to achieve anything at all. Certainly not the practice of medicine, although right now, in some strange way, I am getting used to it."

Was I really? I had spent six months in the so-called "observation room" in Professor Meynert's psychiatric department, but hadn't been more active there than the position demanded, although every now and then there were patients who interested me. I wrote my case histories properly, participated in the doctors' rounds of visits, read all sorts of literature on the subject, but did no serious scientific work to speak of. From my chief, Professor Meynert, I received little inspiration, which was perhaps not entirely my fault. He was a great scholar, an excellent diagnostician, but as doctor in a more immediate sense, that is to say in his personal intercourse with patients, at least at the clinic—I never had an opportunity to observe his private practice—I could not admire him. However competent his attitude toward the illness itself may have been, when faced with the sick person, his behavior seemed too aloof and unsure, almost apprehensive, and his procedure antagonized me most of all when he sometimes tried to talk an incurable patient out of an *idée fixe* with arguments of a sensible nature. Today, however, I ask myself if a green young man like me, with his cheap skepticism, shouldn't rather have been deeply moved to see an old, world-famous psychiatrist again and again and with such tenacity take up the struggle which had been proved vain a thousand times, against a streak of madness, as if physical law would in the end have to bow before the power of the human will.

In Dr. von Pfungen the psychiatric clinic had an efficient, kindly but not outstanding assistant who, like many doctors, was the victim of slight, in this case innocent, therapeutic monomania, something about which I had occasion to comment a while back. At the time it was the problem of peristalsis which absorbed Dr. von Pfungen; later he believed that he had found the true cause of bronchial catarrh in the ordinary habit of washing one's back, and went so far as to declare seriously that he found the right side less frequently affected than the left, which was because the left hand, being weaker and less nimble, could not wash the right half of the back so vigorously as was the case on the left side, which was cleansed by the stronger right hand.

From the Meynert clinic I was moved, on April 1, 1887, to the department for skin diseases and syphilis. It was under the direction of Professor Isidor Neumann, who had no great scientific achievements to his credit but as practitioner, and especially as diagnostician, enjoyed a well-deserved reputation. Nobody tried to deny the fact that one or the other of his pupils was responsible for a greater part of some of his later works, published under his name. He looked less like a scholar than a stock exchange man, the type comic magazines with anti-Semitic tendencies like to portray, and with his jargon, personality and behavior displayed more traits of this particular group of human beings than was fitting for a doctor, much less a clinical professor; yet he was jovial, obliging, one could even say good–natured, whenever his feeling of insecurity and lack of courage permitted, also whenever profession, reputation or chance personal sympathies played a part.

But he was relentlessly egotistic and possessed of a boundless indifference toward the fate of his patients.

In his department, fortunately for his patients, his admirable assistant, Ehrmann, and other departmental doctors, exercised a surveillance of sorts over him, but even in front of them he frequently let himself go, and a passing success with his students, whether through a minor operation or a bad joke, was more important to him than the well-being of those under his care. His examinations were superficial, and to me he always seemed much more worried about infecting himself than about carrying infection from patient to patient. One heard the most unbelievable stories about his private practice, not gossip, but proven, among which his operative treatment over a period of months of a Balkan prince for gummatous (syphilitic) swellings of the skin, deserves to go down in history. At the same time he was a splendid husband and father.

All in all he belonged to that category of Jews who, according to a superficially typical expression, "make anti-Semitism comprehensible," and his portrait would not be complete if it hadn't been he who had always declared that he had never noticed any anti-Semitism, much less directed against himself, and as proof of how respected he was in Catholic circles, would cite the fact that members of the aristocracy liked to invite him to hunt with them. He was especially friendly toward me, as the son of a professor who was a friend of his, without however taking any serious interest in helping me as a doctor, or with the research which I intended to pursue more purposefully in his department than I had done heretofore.

At my father's suggestion I concentrated on syphilitic involvement of the throat and larynx, and for a time examined all our patients with the laryngoscope. But here also my interest was too short-lived to produce any results, not even of statistical value. For an atlas on diseases of the nose, throat and larynx, on which my father was working, I was to write the chapter on syphilis. It was to the advantage of the work that the final draft, also of this chapter, was taken over by the co-publicist, my brother-in-law Hajek, beside whose name stands mine, highly unmerited, as equal to his on the title page.

Since January 1, 1887, I was also an editor of the *Internationale Klinische Rundschau*, which had been founded by my father after he had had to give up the editorship of the *Medizinische Presse* for perfectly ridiculous reasons. The publishers of the latter journal, Urban and Schwarzenberg, had not been seated at the head table at the banquet celebrating my father's jubilee on January 6, 1886, but at one of the large tables nearby, which naturally had not been intended to slight them in any way, but that was evidently how it was interpreted by them, especially by Herr Schwarzenberg, who was vain and extremely sensitive. They retaliated by not renewing my father's contract, which had just expired, and hiring another editor instead. My father's contract stipulated that he receive severance pay and in turn was obligated not to edit any other medical journal for several years. However, he had no intention of giving up his journalistic activities nor the influence that went with them, which he needed less for himself than for the Polyclinic, and managed to get around the clause by creating a new journal, the *Internationale Klinische Rundschau*, and inducing me, or I should say compelling me, and a good but totally ineffectual Dr. Bela Weiss, a general practitioner from Mariahilf who looked like a gypsy baron, to co-sign as editors. Everybody knew that Bela Weiss and I were nothing but straw men, and that the new publication was to be directed and for the most part created in the spirit of my father.

I was pleased to some extent that Herr Schwarzenberg's malicious revenge had been thwarted, all the more so since, among the reasons for the publishers' dissatisfaction with my father's management of the editorial office, there had been mention of the fact that he had let a *Gymnasium* student work for the paper (namely me, who had written an article eight years before on the medical convention in Amsterdam), still I couldn't quite reconcile myself to my father's action because, although within the limits of legality, it was ethically not beyond reproach. I didn't try to hide my opinion from him, which upset him terribly, and he let it pass only as evidence of my lack of courage. Granted that the public attacks which I was expecting did not materialize, yet in certain circles in which my father had anyway not been popular, there were some who didn't hesitate to draw vexatious parallels between my father's behavior and that of the political journalist

Szeps, who in an analogous move had founded the *Wiener Tag-blatt* as a rival paper to the *Neue Wiener Tagblatt*. I was even less pleased with my role in the entire affair, because the little everyday medical-journalistic assignments, of which there were now a great many more than heretofore, did not particularly interest me. My main work was compilation. I edited excerpts of articles which had appeared in other trade papers, reported on conventions at home and abroad, read proof, now and then wrote a short or somewhat longer article, for which I occasionally heard a word of praise from my father, but on the whole didn't distinguish myself in the field of medical journalism more than in any other trodden by me so far, and was more than ever condemned to lead this earthly life as "my father's son."

Just the same I did manage during this time to take a fresh step publicly also in a belletristic capacity. Toward the end of the year 1886, the *Deutsche Wochenschrift* printed a few aphorisms of mine, also a sketch, *He Is Waiting for A God Off-Duty* (*Er wartet auf den vazierenden Gott*). The editor, Dr. Neisser, asked me to come and see him and expressed his hopes for a future development of my connection with his paper, which however ended with the aforementioned contributions, irrevocably, since the *Deutsche Wochenschrift* soon ceased publication.

But with my more serious works I still couldn't seem to make headway. I could see *The Mystery of Marriage* (*Das Mysterium der Ehe*), a comedy on which I had worked for six years, in a new light; still it didn't progress beyond a sketchy first act and the start of the second. *Gabriella's Remorse* (*Gabriellens Reue*), or *The Remorse of Innocence* (*Reue der Unschuld*), was the title of a novella in which I let a young woman atone in the arms of her lover for years lived virtuously; but I was even less adroit in the art of storytelling than I was with dialogue, so the result was again a sentimental, in spots mildly witty product, certainly completely amateurish in spite of the vivid experience which had inspired it, a piece of work therefore which I found repulsive.

During this time and after a long interval, Fritz Kapper was again my confidant in all things pertaining to poetry and the heart. I found in him a warm, sensitive human being, in speech and mood pleasingly exaggerated, and I tended to overvalue his intelligence as happens to one occasionally with glib talkers, and as happened to me in those days also with others, for instance Adolf Weizmann, who had just turned up and was around for a while. On beautiful summer evenings, since my father was on vacation and his carriage was at my disposal, I sometimes took Fritz out into the country with me, and we would end our ride preferably at the Rohrerhütte, with breaded veal cutlet and cucumber salad. Fritz was trying to liquidate his affair with Fräulein Amy, and I kept him company dialectically, rather as he had done for me in the case of Helene Kanitz. Amy was very much in love with him and swore she would kill herself if he left her, in spite of which he did. Two years later I came across a picture of her at the house of a good friend, an amateur photographer, in which she actually did seem to have thrown off all earthly vanities but otherwise looked almost as cheerful as the lieutenant in whose company she had let herself be photographed.

Among the others, Richard Tausenau was still my closest friend, and the strangest one, because of his personality and experiences. A short while before, one of his loves had died, the mistress of a Polish diplomat with whom he had almost fought a duel over the woman, or, as he expressed it elegantly and nonchalantly— "a shooting match." From the funeral he came straight to the Arkadencafe, sat down with us at the gaming table and joined us in a game of poker without further ado, which we let happen respectfully yet not without a shiver of disapproval. Incidentally, he was a highly unwelcome partner for reasons mentioned earlier, and indulged in all sorts of slightly unscrupulous and shady actions, for instance when he jokingly pocketed and kept bank notes that weren't his, or borrowed patent leather shoes which he also never returned, without it ever occurring to any of the injured parties to stop seeing him. He was about to take his last oral examination, which he had put off again and again after two reprobations, had quarreled with his parents, was living in some so-called student quarters or rooming house in the Wickenburggasse and receiving a hundred gulden monthly from Louis Friedmann, which of course didn't begin to meet all his needs.

Louis Friedmann had introduced Richard, and shortly after that me, to a young couple who were happily married and had two children. Herr Kniep, who was an executive in a big manufacturing company, was a good-looking, quite elegant gentleman with social and business aspirations that were not entirely free from snobbery. His wife was a pretty, pleasant woman, quite clever and rather reserved. They were very sociable and liked to entertain guests from big business circles, preferably Gentiles, and there could be little doubt about their anti-Semitism, which was tempered to some extent by business and social considerations. With the Friedmann brothers and their friends, a free, worldly bachelordom had moved in on them, one might say broken in on them, which soon began to undermine a famliy life that until then had been sedately bourgeois. It was of course Richard Tausenau who began to take an interest in the young wife, who seemed to be in love with her husband; certainly she had no compelling reason to deceive him, but since the laws of gravity are valid not only in physics but also in human relationships, we did not have to wait long for the logical finale between the young man and the young woman, as their friendship became increasingly intimate.

Richard's friends watched the gradual development of the affair with all due excitement and pleasure, and as Richard came closer to the goal of his desires, were his faithful allies and collaborators. On a brief trip in which I did not participate, it so happened that the young couple and the merry bachelors who were with them, spent the night in a hotel at the foot of a mountain, which it was their intention to climb on the following day. The husband, with two of the gentlemen who had apparently aroused mountain climbing ambitions in him, beside other sporting interests, set out early in the morning; his wife and two other gentlemen remained in the valley below. One of the latter accompanied the mountaineers part way through the summer dawn, then stayed behind and watched them proceed on ahead without him, and when there seemed to be no possibility of anyone turning back, gave the two who had been left behind—it was Richard who was watching from a window—the signal that had been agreed upon, and he immediately left his room for that of the young wife, who had not locked her door after her husband's departure. This little story may give some idea, not only of the frivolity and indiscretion but also of the laxness with which such escapades were treated and judged in our circle, and if one takes into consideration that such an honorable and serious man as our good geologist Geyer took part in such intrigues, and that a young woman who until then had been the soul of virtue was not only acquiescent but knew that all of us were aware of what was going on, then one may estimate what irresistible power the specific atmosphere of a social group represents and exercises, quite independently of the caliber of its members.

This atmosphere—one may call it immoral, unencumbered, or quite simply, true—is the ambiance in which my tragi-comedy *The Vast Land* is played out, in which some of the members of this group have been transformed, perhaps also enhanced, and a few of the situations resulting from the interplay of these persons turn up, changed to some extent and stylized. A few of the remarks that I put in the mouth of the hero, Friedrich Hofreiter, I heard at various times, practically verbatim, from the lips of his prototype, and when Hofreiter watches his wife's lover hurrying across a meadow to the garden of his villa, and through their bedroom window sees him disappear, then I was thinking of Richard, who when the Knieps were staying in the country in the summer, found his way to his beloved in a similar fashion. However, it was not this indiscretion, nor a few others that took place when the husband was present, which together with Richard's carelessness, the collusion of so many non-participants and the gradual development of the husband's jealousy, precipitated the inevitable discovery; this happened because Herr Kniep, whose suspicions were being steadily nourished, broke open his wife's writing desk and found their love-letters.

It was on an autumn day, during the same year—I was still in bed—when Richard, or Kuwazl, as we used to call him, burst into my room at the hospital, and with his short ironic laugh, which by now I knew only too well, informed me that he had just received the unwelcome visit of the cuckolded husband. For the time being he had got off fairly easily. Herr Kniep had not assaulted him physically nor demanded satisfaction, but he had insisted—with highly defamatory abuse, to be sure—that Richard give him his word of honor never to go near his faithless wife again, because, in consideration of their children, Herr Kniep had decided not to throw her out of the house, but as far as the outside world was concerned, would continue to live with her as man and wife.

It was easier for him to carry out this decision than it was for my friend Richard to keep his word. Already a few weeks after the discovery, the affair between Richard and Frau Kniep was in full swing again, and continued for some time. It was not the beautiful wife's last affair, perhaps also not the last affair which her husband was to discover; just the same, he resigned himself quite decently to what was going on and was satisfied to take his own form of revenge. To all outward appearances it remained a good bourgeois marriage, and in the course of the years, as all passion was gradually spent, who knows—it may actually have developed into one. Their house was run in a praiseworthy fashion, their children were brought up admirably, Herr Kniep's career was highly successful, in due course he even became titled, and Frau Kniep, after dismissing her last lover, distinguished herself not only by an exemplary way of life but also by a visible religious ardor, which was not entirely free of political considerations. Louis Friedmann, who was her second lover, told me once, in reference to her, "I consider it biased to judge women only from an erotic viewpoint. We constantly forget that in the life of a woman, even if she has a lover, there are many hours during which she has other things to think of beside love. She reads books, she makes music, she forms charity organizations, she cooks, she brings up her children, she can also be a very good mother, even an excellent wife, and a hundred times more valuable than the so-called virtuous woman."

They are the words spoken by Friedrich Hofreiter in Act IV of *The Vast Land*, which doesn't prevent him from shooting his wife's lover in Act V, so as not to be "a sucker," as he says. A contradiction? Not at all! Feelings and understanding may sleep under the same roof, but they run their own completely separate households in the human soul.

Although I was frequently a guest at the Kniep home, I remained relatively an outsider, and various other friendships entered into that summer, especially during my brief holiday in Ischl, and kept up in the city following it, were just as superficial and transient. I was very well received by the Cohn family, to whom my friend Fritz, who was engaged to the pretty oldest daughter, Adele, had introduced me. Her father, still a young man, a Don Juan type, was married to a rather stupid, unattractive woman. He was a dashing fellow who felt and behaved like a bachelor, and in Ischl I occasionally accompanied him on "deer stalking expeditions," which for me more often than not ended harmlessly and without results, except for one half-hour during which I enjoyed letting a pretty little thing pass herself off as an actress, as if with such artifice the dangers which I was prone to fear in such contacts would be considerably lessened. But for the most part I found myself in the more respectable company that was grouped around the couple in close or wider circles. There was, for instance, a Frau Koritchoner and her three pretty daughters—the oldest one, Frau Glogau, had already been married for two years; attractive Lili, and pert young Leonore, still in her teens. A few young doctors, as for instance Otto Zuckerkandl and Oscar Krauss, participated in our outings and walks, and we did not pass up an occasional poker game which, as in the Szeps home, sometimes lasted until morning. A charming young Frau Hirsch floats around in my mind, with her laughing face and her black but not at all somber bathing dress. A Hungarian painter, Vilma Parlaghy, was considered unapproachable in spite of her beauty and the fact that she was an artist. I was attracted by her piquant, almost enigmatic personality, and had the feeling that her virtue wasn't to be taken all too seriously, but with me she remained aloof. Yet sometimes I saw a gentle scorn play about her lips, which may have been directed at my inept shyness.

Because of her accent, her moods and her coquettishness, I was drawn to a young American girl, Cora Cahn, who was only sixteen years old and was staying in Ischl with relatives. In a tunnel between Gmunden and Ebensee, things almost became critical, but tunnels are short and a stay in Ischl not much longer, especially when so much has to be crammed into it, so this little adventure also came to naught. But the most impressive personality was Fräulein Nelly, who, as everybody knew, was in the habit of deceiving her unattractive little husband with elegant aristocrats. On a beautiful summer afternoon we went for a walk along the Nussensee in the company of quite a few others. Nelly and I walked on ahead, kissed whenever we could get out of sight; she talked about all sorts of things which young ladies don't usually talk about—of her beautiful skin, her nightgowns—our kisses became increasingly passionate, hundreds of them, and grateful as psychiatrists tend to be, I prophesied for this distractive rather than attractive female a great career as a *cocotte*, which flattered her. I never saw Nelly again after that summer, probably not after that day, but found out years later that my prophecy had been gloriously fulfilled. Under the name Judith, Nelly's double flits through one of my plays which, as of this writing, is not yet completed.

Dora Kohnberger, who was staying in Ischl that summer, kept me company on a rather embarrassing mission to the Hotel Bauer, where we had to plead with a good friend on behalf of my Uncle Edmund Markbreiter, Dora's brother-in-law, who was again on the verge of ruination, perhaps even about to come into conflict with the law. It was a question of a few thousand gulden, which we were trying to collect, mainly from relatives, those who were not yet weary of helping the incorrigible spendthrift and stock exchange gambler, who also happened to be a famous lawyer but personally had lost all the credit he had ever had. After a lengthy discussion, which by him was not exactly pursued with tact but which Dora handled with dignity while I kept quiet, Herr Cz., a wealthy art dealer, bachelor, friend of the family and, without success of course, a great admirer of Aunt Dora, decided to contribute five hundred gulden. I have no idea whether this was the sum that saved my uncle for the time being; at any rate, the catastrophe was temporarily averted.

And did no mighty light ever fall on the hundredfold scattered existence of this young doctor, poet and man-of-the-world, who in his worst hours bungled medicine, poetry and life and in his better moments was a dilettante; whose true nature was recognized by no one and scarcely sensed by himself; who was surrounded by dozens of friends to none of whom he was dedicated wholly; and who stood between many girls and women, none of whom belonged to him utterly; who, without doubt discontented yet not without his moments of self-gratification, was occupied prac-

tically to the exclusion of everything else with himself? Did a
strong glow from outside never fall onto this unsurely lit existence,
in which so many minor lights fluttered, a glow under which those
little lights would not have been momentarily extinguished? Was
he never touched by the vast, eternal questions? And if there was
no God in whose hands he could be calmed and feel secure, did he
not have a homeland from which to draw strength and life, a
fatherland of which he was a citizen, with or without pride?
Wasn't there history, world history, which never stood still and
which blew around one's ears as one raced through time? Of
course there was. But homeland was a place to cavort in, wings
and backdrop for one's private fate; fatherland was a creation
of chance, a totally indifferent administrative affair; and the weav-
ing and working of history penetrated one's ears, as happens most
frequently to those experiencing it, only in the cacophony of
politics, to which one didn't like to listen unless one happened
to be one of those who professionally, or because of business interests, was attracted to the political event. And yet, if I am correct,
it was just during those summer days of 1887 that the question of
whether we young men were going to be drawn into the whirlpool
of politics and history hung by a hair. There was imminent danger of war with Russia; rumors of mobilization filled the air; there
were a few days when, as a reserve officer, one could expect to
be called up with only twenty-four hours' notice. Today, when
we know once more what war can mean, it seems incomprehensible that at the time we were not in the least excited by such
possibilities, in fact scarcely gave them a thought. However, all
reserve officers received hectographed letters in which they were
advised and urged to purchase a certain kind of knapsack which
was considered highly appropriate for field purposes, and to put
in their order with the district recruiting officer in good time.
I, for my part, did so on a piece of paper, without using the form,
whereupon I was ordered to appear at barracks, received a friendly
reprimand from the officer on duty and at the same time the
unofficial advice not to purchase the aforementioned piece of
equipment because it was neither reasonable nor practical, but a
different kind which could be purchased at such and such a place.
I thanked him (*gehorsamst*), and thought what one so often had
to think, gayly or sadly, on trivial and important occasions, in this,

our beautiful fatherland—oh, my poor dear Austria! At any rate, I decided to postpone buying my luggage until war had been declared, which as is well-known, took a while, but when it came, then all the more thoroughly.

Book Seven

September 1887 to June 1889

ON AN EVENING in September, in the year 1887, I was standing with my friend Kuwazl on the platform of a horse-drawn streetcar which was about to turn from the Ring into the Universitätsstrasse, when we noticed, among the throng crossing the tracks, a pretty young lady, to all appearances a better-class shop girl or model, who responded to our gallant, admiring glances with a smile that was not unfriendly. Since the two of us didn't have anything better to do—which sometimes happened—we jumped off the car and politely offered to accompany the young lady. She didn't object; the three of us walked on together, and in the short distance from the Schottentor to the hospital, our acquaintance had made such rapid progress that the young lady, who evidently also didn't have anything more important to do, accepted our—or I should say my invitation to come up to my hospital quarters with the two of us, where there was always a bottle of cognac or something sweet to eat, for expected and unexpected guests. Moreover, the apartment had other attractions for creating the right mood, such as a piano, a bedspread with two children playing embroidered on it, a red-green chandelier hanging down from the ceiling, and on the window ledge, the *pièce de résistance*, from my parental home—a slightly damaged alabaster vase with a Makart bouquet of dried flowers.

We ate and drank a little, conversed merrily but perfectly respectably, and finally the three of us left together, but it was

I who had the honor of accompanying the Fräulein to her home on the Zimmermanngasse, and when we said goodbye she was so kind as to promise to visit me the day after tomorrow.

I waited for her in a pleasant state of excitement, improvising on the piano until she arrived with promising punctuality, and settled down at my feet, which interfered to some extent with my use of the pedals; but since I was very soon fingering my visitor's golden hair rather than the piano keys, which were slightly out of tune, this little prelude was soon over. On that evening neither of us had any idea what a serious turn the events that lay in store for us were to take.

Jeanette visited me in the evening two or three times a week. Sometimes we would first dine together in some restaurant or other, in the beginning at the Römische Kaiser or the Riedhof, or on beautiful autumn evenings in the Prater garden restaurants, after which she would spend the night with me and didn't even wake up when I had to report for duty in my department, and it was a delight to return to my room at noon and find my sweet girl all ready to be loved again, still lying on rumpled pillows. It was in recollection of such a morning that I wrote this endearing appellation, "sweet girl," in my diary for the first time, with no idea that it was fated to go down, so to speak, in literary history; and in those days I imagine it must have suited Jeanette very well, at least according to my sentiments.

A short separation during the first weeks of our bliss only served to fan the flames of our love. I accompanied my father, who never missed an opportunity to include me in any business of a medical nature, to a naturalists' convention in Wiesbaden. He had to return to Vienna before me; I spent a day alone in Rüdesheim, and in the garden of an inn on the banks of the Rhine, wrote letters, not only to Jeanette but also to Olga, to the latter of course a much more eloquent one, and these are the only moments of the entire trip that I can recall vividly today. On the return journey I stopped in Frankfurt, where it pleased me to play a few Viennese waltzes on Goethe's spinnet; and in Munich, without however taking home with me any strong impressions of the paintings I saw there or the theaters I visited. Not only longing but restlessness drove me home. I had had to resign myself to the fact that Jeanette, at twenty-two, had not preserved her virtue to the day when she had met me. She had admitted to having had six or seven lovers before me, but I have completely forgotten what else she told me, or any of the details of her love life, probably not much and not entirely true.

She lived with three sisters and a brother in a modest apartment on the Zimmermanngasse. Her oldest sister, who at the time certainly couldn't have been more than twenty-five or -six years old, yet was already unattractive and faded, kept house for them, and probably earned a little money on the side as seamstress. My Jeanette, the second girl, did needlework for the better shops (I still have some examples of her skill), and did most of her work at home. The third girl, Tini, barely twenty, was sometimes nursemaid, then again salesgirl, and didn't look like anything better. The fourth girl, Ritschi, I can't remember at all; the same applies to her brother, Theobald, who soon moved out of the apartment. My only lively memory of him is in connection with a pawned watch and ten gulden that were owing him. I have also forgotten the story of Jeanette's childhood which, according to an entry in my diary, seems to have included much that was appealing and moving. From those letters of hers which I have kept, it is evident that there was a father, living somewhere in the provinces, but he was never mentioned; also that there existed a sum of four-thousand gulden, left by an uncle, a treasury official (unless this sum had been the settlement of one of her six lovers), which, together with what the girls earned, helped to run the household. Be that as it may, during the first months Jeanette not only made no financial demands on me but would refuse to discuss such matters, and it is quite possible that during this first winter of our love she was not only unselfish, but in the conventional sense of the word, also faithful. Even when I came home from a party or from the theater, to which I went frequently, sometimes with friends but never with Jeanette, she would be waiting for me in my hospital room and would stay with me until dawn, or until my good old servant, Frau Ettel, would come in, while it was still dark outside, and prepare our breakfast. It was going to be something beautiful to remember; that was how I saw it at the time, and it might have been just that if I had known how to end it in good time. But I became more and more attached to Jeanette, and was increasingly and foolishly tortured by jealousy of her past, while the thought of ever parting from her became more and more inconceivable.

We were not always alone together. For obvious reasons I did not ask Richard to join us for any more of our little dinner outings. At first Fritz occasionally came with us, but he had broken off his affair with Amy, and as happy fiancé rarely had time for us. In his stead an old acquaintance sometimes came along, a school-mate of my brother's, who had of late shown a greater friendliness toward me. I don't know why anymore.

Rudolf Spitzer was the only son of a wealthy merchant who had been widowed early in life and had spoiled his son from childhood, and in a way raised him to be a poet. The fact that he once gave his son, for his birthday, a printed copy of all his German compositions, may pass as an example of this. Rudolf Spitzer, who for his literary career had chosen the name Lothar, which sounded better, had advanced beyond these German com-positions long ago and was now writing poetry, novellas, novels, plays, reviews and essays, all of them with the same extraordinary superficiality which he managed to preserve to a ripe old age and —if one may put it that way—knew how to develop in depth. For his basic characteristic was a superficiality which was already expressed in his manner of speaking, and by the speed with which he expressed ten, a hundred, a thousand ideas, news items, half-truths and untruths, which he happened to believe at the time, also by the frequent bursts of laughter with which he liked to interrupt himself, making what he had to say almost incompre-hensible. His *bonhomie,* about which there could be no disagree-ment, came not so much from the purity of his childlike soul— although he was basically naive and almost totally lacking in envy —but rather out of just this superficiality. The same applies to his complaisance, for which I often had to be grateful and which was rooted in his bustling activity and pomposity rather than in kind-ness or altruism.

At the time he was living in his father's elegant apartment in the Asperngasse, where he liked to receive friends who nurtured the same ambitions as his, or those who had already gone further —journalists, writers like Ludassy (who meanwhile, in December of the year 1887, had married my cousin, Olga Mandl), also Fuchs-Talab and J. J. David, all of whom I now met for the first time. In those days Lothar had his connection with the *"Presse,"* (an editor-in-chief was distantly related to his father), and the determination to exploit it, which seemed perfectly harmless and at times even quite funny. I find in my diary that he once read a play of his aloud to me and Richard Tausenau, about which I have nothing more to say than that the title was *The Sorcerer's Apprentice (Der Zauberlehrling)*. On the other hand, the beautiful winter day has remained unforgettable on which Lothar, his ambitious father, and I made an excursion to Baden to attend the première of his social drama, *The Tantalides*. He saw to its success in his fashion, and asked his father, in my presence, for a small sum of money to buy seats for the *clacque*. He was called out many times, enthusiastically, and with him the actor who had played the lead, a certain Herr von Varndal, who walked up to the footlights and delivered a short, powerful speech against the capitalists in the orchestra seats, without however in any way endangering those who happened to reside in the Asperngasse. Much more gifted than the play was the report Lothar composed himself, about its enthusiastic reception, which he had inserted in various Viennese newspapers, with which the theatrical career of *The Tantalides* came to an end.

This pleasant, gay, bustling young man, whose actual capabilities I couldn't value very highly, even during the brief blossoming of our friendship, was determined to be my literary manager. In this he was concerned less with my personal success than with the pleasure of management itself. Recently I had again been satisfied with functioning as a poet in only a very narrow circle. I had sent my two novellas, *Human Love (Menschenliebe)* and *Gabriella's Remorse*, to Olga Waissnix in Reichenau, and had been rewarded with friendly, one might even say glowing praise. I had also read the second novella aloud to Dora Kohnberger, but had undertaken nothing further for either work because of my firmly established mistrust of their value. In the meantime I had written a few novelistic sketches, *Heritage (Erbschaft)*, *The Madness of My Friend Y (Der Wahnsinn meines Freundes Y)*, and a one-act play, *The Adventure of His Life (Das Abenteuer Seines Lebens)*. Here, briefly, its content: A young man has a mistress, a seamstress, something of the kind, and at the same time worships a young woman whom he considers the great adventure of his life. One day she appears unexpectedly at his student quarters, but finds only his mistress present. He has just gone out for a moment to bring in something to eat, and soon reappears. Needless to say, not long after that a "friend" turns up, and an embarrassing supper for four takes place, at the end of which the dilettante lover is abandoned by both women and ridiculed mildly by his friend, and decides to seek a replacement for those who have abandoned him, or, as he cries out in the end to make his point—*two* replacements.

Out of this not wholly fruitless idea, the source of which doesn't have to be sought far afield, I hadn't succeeded in making anything much more than an empty, not very humorous farce. The dialogue sounds rather like an awkward translation from the French. To be sure, hero and confidant are already called Anatol and Max, but little is discernible of the pleasantly effective spirit and modest lyricism displayed occasionally by both figures in later one-act plays, even if Max is introduced as a poet, and there is no lack of aphorisms which now and then seem to be mocking their own obliqueness. Lothar however felt that the moment had come to do something for me. He gave the little piece to the theater agent, O. F. Eirich, who was already quite notorious; he accepted it in return for payment of the printing costs, and the publication of this comedy in one act as a drama script constituted, as far as I was concerned, a much more decisive step in my literary life than some more important ones experienced later. With a little self-irony, as if I didn't want to tempt fate too much, I wrote in my diary on the occasion of this first printing, "In the end I may yet be produced!" How this actually did come about a few years later with just this *Adventure of His Life,* without my having anything to do with it, at any rate with no credit due to me, will be told later.

My father remained unsympathetic toward my literary efforts (not that he got to see all of them), and in consideration of my medical reputation, which for good reason didn't seem to want to establish itself, he was against my appearing publicly as a writer under my own name. He really cannot be reproached for not being too happy about my activities—literary or medical— nor about my way of life. My relationship to the opposite sex especially, of which he was of course only vaguely informed, filled him with growing anxiety. At this time, or perhaps a little later, it so happened that I was in a restaurant with him after the theater, and we were conversing more confidentially than was our wont. In the course of the conversation, a question welled up in my mind, and I asked him how a young person was to go about not coming into conflict with the demands of propriety, society or hygiene. Seduction and adultery were forbidden and dangerous, intimate relationships with *cocottes* and actresses were questionable and costly, and then there were the so-called respectable girls who might already have strayed from the paths of virtue but with whom one "got stuck," according to an expression of my father's, just as much as with a girl one had seduced. Nothing seemed left therefore but the prostitute, who, however well one knew how to protect oneself, remained a rather repulsive love object; and I suggested that my father give me some advice on the subject.

He chose not to go in for any discussion of the matter, but with a gesture of finality said simply, and in a rather somber tone, "One disposes of it," which was no great help; and he must have been aware of the fact that I wasn't cut out to dispose of anything, in this or any other respect. I imagine that what my father would have preferred to see, would have been for me to marry a well-to-do girl of good family; but for that it was a little too early, and he knew, even if not too precisely, that I was much too deeply involved in an affair with a woman of a class lower than mine, therefore not open to practical considerations under present circumstances. He had been embarrassed one evening, when he had wanted to visit me in my room at the hospital and I had met him at the door and told him he couldn't come in, and this may have been the moment when he came to a decision which he had been considering for some time— to send me abroad for a while for further medical study, and specifically for specialization in the field of laryngology.

On January 1, 1888, I had been moved to the surgical department of Professor Weinlechner, where I felt even less at home and was even less active than I had been in earlier assistant positions. I kept as far away as possible from actual surgery, and can recall only one operation in which I removed a fatty tumor from somebody's arm, and another time when I had to put several stitches into the upper lip of a drunkard who had been injured in a brawl (to my astonishment it healed without a scar). I also pulled some teeth when it was my turn to be in charge of the out-patient unit, and had every reason on such occasions to be astounded over the long-suffering attitude of my patients. I was frequently late for morning rounds, and mostly only half-awake, which caused my chief to consider me an alcoholic, and I dutifully wrote my case histories, which however did not meet with the approval of Professor Weinlechner, who once upbraided me quite violently about my "miserable handwriting." I told him emphatically that I had no intention of putting up with his tone, after which he chose to ignore me completely. In consideration of my feelings for him personally and for surgery in general, this suited me fine. He was—no doubt about it—an excellent practitioner, but in character and behavior more like a barber-surgeon than a doctor. His manner toward his patients just before a major operation, which may have been nothing but the result of impatience, but was certainly to all appearances heartless, remains in my mind, an embarrassing memory. Under these circumstances I could only feel relieved to leave his department; moreover, Berlin, Paris and London held many attractions for me, even if the thought of leaving Jeanette for six months in the dangerous city of Vienna caused me considerable anxiety.

My departure was set for the beginning of April. In the early morning hours Jeanette and Lothar accompanied me to the North Station. To my displeasure my parents also turned up before the train left, contrary to their promise. My father now saw Jeanette for the first time and was not favorably impressed; so I sent her home with Lothar. As I boarded the train, I got into an altercation with a Berliner; however, in the course of the journey he turned out to be a quite affable fellow, albeit a rather too heavy drinker. On arriving in Berlin I went directly to the Hotel Continental which had just opened, where for the first time in my life I enjoyed a room with electric lighting, which in the year 1888 was quite an innovation for Central Europeans.

On the following day I at once set about looking for living quarters, and soon found two attractive rooms at No. 60 Dorotheenstrasse; dutifully left my card at the houses of several professors of the medical faculty—with Senator, Lazarus, Fränkel, and Tobold, the so-called father of laryngology; signed up for a course in laryngology with Fränkel, the only one I was to attend with comparative regularity but without profit; took a look at various departments of the Charité and Friedrichshauser Hospitals, and even participated in a meeting of the Society for Internal Medicine, with which I felt I had done my bit as far as my duties toward study and father were concerned.

I went to the theater almost every night. Performances at the Deutsches Theater by Kainz, Siegwart Friedmann, Somerstorff, and by Agnes Sorma and Theresina Gessner, made the strongest impression on me. I had introductions to several members of the literary and theatrical world, so every now and then could be found visiting Julius Rodenberg, Karl Emil Franzos or Siegwart Friedmann, also the comedian Tewele, whom I knew from Vienna and at whose home I met Josef Kainz for the first, and for some time to come, last time. He was then at the start of his famous career, but could recall twenty years later how a young compatriot had stirred his Viennese heart after lunch one day by playing some waltzes, yet had forgotten completely that I had been this young man from Vienna. I made a few timid efforts to gain recognition for *The Adventure of His Life*. First I sent it to Siegwart Friedmann, who ignored it, then to Tewele, who as a friend of the family at least felt he had to say a few friendly words about it. Director Lautenburg had already had a copy of the script sent to him from Vienna by Eirich. I had heard nothing from him, but when Lothar arrived from Vienna, a meeting was arranged with Lautenburg at the famous Viennese restaurant Krziwanek, and Lothar soon found a way to direct the conversation tactfully to my comedy. At first Lautenburg didn't seem to remember it. I helped recall it to his mind. Suddenly he knew what we were talking about, gave me a polite, pitying look, shook his head and said just one word, "Terrible." A few minutes later, as if to console me, he added, "Your first effort, I presume." Since I couldn't even offer him this as an excuse, he apparently gave me up as literarily hopeless and we talked of other things.

The mood in the capital was darkened during those weeks by Kaiser Friedrich's fatal illness. A famous English doctor, MacKenzie, had been called in for consultation and had taken over the case, much to the jealous but certainly understandable vexaation of the German doctors. They reproached MacKenzie for desisting from or even preventing a radical operation on the larynx, which was where the cancer was located, at a time when it might still have been possible to save the patient. That political considerations influenced therapeutical opinions on the subject to some extent was fairly clear, and some very unpleasant polemicizing in various articles dimmed the last days of the noble and patient sufferer. Not only medical journals but the daily papers as well took sides, and MacKenzie was surrounded by an "official staff," so to speak, of journalists, who were called "press reptiles" by the opposition.

One day Ernst von Rosenberg arrived in Berlin, an acquaintance of my younger days and the oldest son of a recently deceased patient of my father's. He was a foolish, dandified fellow and already at that age, quite deaf. As co-publisher of a French journal in Vienna, he wanted to interview MacKenzie for his paper. He had asked my father, as a Viennese colleague of MacKenzie's, for an introduction, which was to make it possible for him to see the famous English doctor. I was to accompany him. As soon as MacKenzie had agreed to the interview, Ernst rented a magnificent private equipage, lined with blue silk, and on April 24, 1888, the two of us drove up in front of the gates of the Charlottenburg Palace, where, after producing all the necessary identification, we were given permission to see the Kaiser's doctor.

MacKenzie received us in a large twilit room and told us to be seated. Ernst drew a deep breath and launched into his well-rehearsed speech, in which he deemed it necessary to stress the importance of his paper, and rocking back and forth on his chair, began several sentences, one after the other, with the words, "The *Correspondance de l'Est* is a paper that . . ." "The *Correspondance de l'Est* considers it its duty . . ." "The *Correspondance de l'Est* would consider it an honor if . . ." while MacKenzie showed obvious signs of impatience which only increased as he realized that the publisher of the *Correspondance de l'Est,* partly because of his deafness but also because of his poor command of the English language, wasn't able to follow the very diplomatically formulated information he was being given. Finally MacKenzie begged me, since he couldn't speak louder or speak German, or didn't feel so inclined, to translate what he said to his interviewer,

which I did as best I could, but had to relate most of it in the
blue silk lined equipage which took us back to the city fifteen
minutes after our arrival at the Palace. I don't know if Rosenberg's
official account turned out as MacKenzie would have wanted it
to; be that as it may, a few days later not only he, but I with him,
were being cited in the nationalist papers which were inimical to
the English doctor as members of the "reptile press." In the name
of my companion and myself I demanded a retraction, and that
was that.

Ernst von Rosenberg was not only *doctor juris,* journalist and
publisher of the *Correspondance de l'Est,* he was also a man-of-
the-world, and we spent quite a few evenings in various places
of amusement, rarely without female companionship. Among the
friendly ladies who helped to shorten our evenings, I like to
recall a very young thing who was standing on the threshold of her
career. We confided the stories of our hearts to each other. She
told me about a *medicinae studiosus,* Rudolf Gottlieb from Vienna,
by chance a young man I knew well, with whom she had lived and
loved the past winter through and whom, she assured me, she
would never forget. A few months later, when I brought him
greetings from her—he was a good, diligent mother's boy—he pretended not to know what I was talking about and changed the
subject. I in turn talked to Lizzi about my dearly beloved whom
I had left behind in Vienna, and I can still hear the passionate tone
of her voice as she faced me, almost threateningly, on the first and
at the same time last night we were to spend together, with the
words, "You're thinking of her!" Probably she was right, because
scarcely an hour passed without my thinking of Jeanette. Every
morning I waited with longing and in a state of excitement for
her letters in which, beside her love and constancy, she had a
great deal to say about all sorts of physical ailments such as palpi-
tation, headaches, blood in her sputum, toothache, erysipelas, as
well as innumerable vexations of a household or business nature.
In my letters I tortured her incessantly with my mistrust, thoughts
which she called "witches," and tried to dispel by repeated assurances of her everlasting love.

There were moments when I managed somehow to believe in
her faithfulness, even though I, for my part, was completely incapable, nor did I make the slightest effort to remain faithful, in

spite of my love for her. Fräulein Lizzi, my Berlin "sweet girl," was by no means the first or only girl in whose arms I thought of Jeanette. Before Lizzi, on one of my first evenings in Berlin, I had met, on a suburban street not far from a theater, a very pretty, elegant young lady. Although she came with me to my quarters without any further ado, I realized on the following day, when I saw her apartment, that although there could be little doubt as to her profession, she was of better stock than I had at first taken for granted, and I was quite flattered when a carriage drew up while I was enjoying afternoon coffee with her, I could see two highly elegant gentlemen get out of it and had to disappear via the back stairs like a true *amant de coeur*. A few days later, when I told a friend of mine who lived in Berlin about the incident, I found out that the young lady, whose name he took right out of my mouth after I had told him her address, was one of the "best kept" *cocotte*'s of the day, and that she was notorious in Berlin fast society. She promised me one more tryst, and was waiting for me at the Brandenburger Tor in a second-rate cab. We dined in a *cabinet particulier*, but this time she remained cool, told me to consider what we had experienced the previous time as invalid, and we never saw each other again.

One day Herr Cohn, the future father-in-law of my friend Fritz, turned up in Berlin, and I also spent a few evenings with him which might be termed amusing. For instance, one night we dined with three Jewish *chanson* singers, the Neumann sisters, together with their patriarchal parents. In the Flower Rooms of a notorious dance hall we were on the look-out for pretty girls. Herr Cohn, with his blazing eyes and bold, black upturned moustache, looking rather like a *rastacouère*, waltzed tirelessly through the hall with an exceptionally pretty creature, and finally disappeared with her. I was mildly astonished by his rashness, although during this period I too was prone frequently to cast caution to the winds. However, the behavior of this forty-five-year-old married man became clear to me when I found out, a few years later, that in those Berlin days he was suffering from an advanced case of syphilis, which he had contracted recently, and was therefore not threatened by the danger that spoiled such fleeting little adventures for me and often induced me to deny myself in this respect. Nothing much more could happen to this enviable man; at best he could develop softening of the brain, a fate that actually did overtake him a few years later.

But on those evenings in Berlin, Herr Cohn was not only my comrade but also my adviser and friend. That I was so ridiculously seriously in love with Jeanette seemed to worry him. The fact that she was a woman who could not be expected to share the life of a sensible young man of good family was made clear to him, not so much by me, as by his future son-in-law Fritz. On his return to Vienna therefore he at once wrote me a letter with warnings that were well-meant, but that made me feel even more desperate.

It so happened that around the middle of May, my Uncle Felix was expected in Vienna, from London. Contrary therefore to my father's original plans, it was decided that I should leave Berlin and first go home, then travel to England with Uncle Felix. A few days before leaving Berlin I tried, in my usual fashion, to balance my spiritual and physical life to date, again with miserable results, an effort in which I personally came off very badly. I was as restless as ever and fully conscious of the fact that this was only because of my distracting yearning for Jeanette, and had to admit that I should have broken off our affair before my departure. I had met a lot of people in Berlin, superficially, but none of these encounters had borne fruit, and I couldn't say that any person or event had made a lasting impression on me. The main reason however for my ill humor, aside from a precocious ennui which I realized I only talked myself into, was undoubtedly my profession, or rather my conviction that I had neither the sincere wish nor the actual talent to practice it. Moreover, burdened as I was with the impressions of my medical work, I felt I lacked the vigor to create for myself the necessary atmosphere of freedom in which to indulge in my literary activities; and since I considered myself a hypochondriac and hyper-sensitive human being, who clung ridiculously to his habits, great and small, without possessing a spark of true vitality, I was ready, in spite of a slightly comforting feeling that there might after all be some good in me, to mourn as totally unsuccessful a life in which I could see no possibilities of development spiritually nor progress materially, and to resign myself to being a hopeless case.

On the twelfth of May I traveled to Dresden, visited the art gallery, dined on the Brühl Terrace, went on an outing to Blasewitz and to the theater, where they were playing Moser's *Bureaucrat*. After supper (or the day wouldn't have been complete), I made the acquaintance of two young ladies and was just talking to a cab driver who was to take us I can't remember where, when I happened to turn around and to my annoyance and astonishment saw that the two ladies had managed in those few seconds to vanish from the big square, which was practically empty, without leaving a trace. To understand a cliché one has to experience it. On that evening in Dresden I became convinced that the earth could open up and swallow people. Still I considered it possible that the two mysterious ladies had simply driven off in another cab while I was talking to the driver. More modestly than the hero of my play, *The Adventure of His Life,* I tried to console myself with one girl, whose name happened to be Elvira. She was the first and last female I ever came across who bore this name, and I don't doubt but that she was originally given a quite different one.

On the following evening I arrived in Vienna. Jeanette met me at the station, pale and a little woebegone. We spent the night in her shabby little room, the only window of which looked out onto a courtyard. Next evening I was a guest of the Cohn family, and could participate in the joy of my affianced friend Fritz; on the evening after that I celebrated my twenty-sixth birthday at home, and on the sixteenth I was off to Reichenau. Olga received me tenderly, assured me of her love but declared that she would never be mine, and prophesied that I would marry Minnie Benedict. In Vienna, Jeanette again met me at the station, and knew, or at least sensed that I had just visited "the four-leafed clover lady," which was what she called my mysterious friend in Reichenau, after the little locket I wore attached to my watch chain, a precious gift. The following evening—I was treated like an honored guest passing through—I spent with my parents in the Prater, but soon stole away to meet Jeanette again on the Hauptallee, near the third coffee-house, and to go home with her.

One celebration after the other! On the evening of the nineteenth, my entire family assembled at the home of my uncle Edmund Markbreiter, this time in honor of Uncle Felix and Aunt Julie. The drink, food and cigars were excellent, paid for of course with the money of Uncle Edmund's creditors. The following evening was spent in the Prater, in the same company, until I again fled into Jeanette's arms, something I did repeatedly in the course of this week, for a few rushed hours, sometimes more than once a day. On the next day, at last—and in the pain of parting I couldn't help but breathe a sigh of relief—I was off, with aunt and uncle, in the Paris express.

We arrived toward evening on May twenty-first. One evening, one night and a day for the miracle city—it wasn't much. I can't recall where we stayed. I can remember a little more clearly yet still as if in a dream, how all of us—Felix, Julie, my Paris relatives, Sandor and Mathilda Rosenberg (a name which here was given its French pronunciation), and the black sheep of the family, ugly, foppish little Szigo Jellinek, wandered from one amusement area to the other along the Champs Elysées, dined *al fresco* at the Ambassadeurs, and finally strolled home in the early morning hours along the brightly lit boulevards.

On the following day I saw what was possible to see in such a hurry, without any idea that I was to have so much more time for it all a few years hence—the Panthéon, the Louvre, the Bastille, and that evening we took off for London where, after a pleasant Channel and railway trip with my English relatives, we arrived on the twenty-third.

We left the train at Herne Hill because my uncle's villa, where I was to stay for the first few days, was in the country, in Honor Oak Park, not far from the Crystal Palace. It was a pretty, nicely furnished house in which there was plenty of room for the couple and their two small children, and for their nephew, Edmund Markbreiter's son Otto; there was moreover a comfortable guest room for me. The house had a view on all sides, across villas into the green countryside beyond. The garden, which was not too well cared for, rose gently and bordered on fields and meadowland. On this first morning I didn't take time for anything more than getting cleaned up after the long journey, then we left— Uncle Felix, Otto and I—for London. We got off at London Bridge, and moments later were engulfed by the throng crossing this gigantic structure into the city. I accompanied my relatives to their office, a branch of the Paris banking house Dreyfus. Felix was their London manager. For a while I wandered around the streets alone, or with Otto, and took in as many of the characteristic sights of the city as could be expected in those first hours—the traffic, the noise, the buses, the huge buildings and the "bobbies," without really taking any great pleasure in them, and at once reported my impressions in a letter to Jeanette. We lunched in an unprepossessing, dim but lively restaurant, surrounded by businessmen and stock exchange employees. My uncle ordered porter-beer. It was served in goblets which I seem to recall were silver. "How do you like it?" Uncle Felix asked with a wry smile. I shook myself. I found the sweet prickly taste horrible. Uncle Felix laughed. "Go on, try some more. You'll see, it'll go down all right." With the next swallow I caught on. It wasn't porter-beer, it was champagne! Since that day I have often found an opportunity to tell this little story, which I found highly instructive, rather like a fable.

Right after lunch—I was wound up tight as a clock-spring—I proceeded to visit the man my father had insisted I look up, Felix Semon, a doctor, born and educated in Germany, who was at the time one of the best known laryngologists in London. With his thick mane of dark hair, his bushy moustache and black eyes, he looked more like a Spaniard than the German Jew he was. He received me with great friendliness but did not try to hide his disapproval of the *Internationale Klinische Rundschau,* which even if it had not taken sides against the German doctors had also not come out decisively against MacKenzie, and Semon wasn't at all pleased that I had visited the English doctor in Charlottenburg. He spoke derogatorily, not of MacKenzie's standing as a physician but of his treatment in this particular case. It wasn't difficult to see that his attitude was not wholly free of jealousy, even if he may well have been right, and that he was honestly convinced that MacKenzie's erroneous wait-and-see rather than operative treatment of the Kaiser was influenced by political rather than medical motives. Semon didn't seem to have a much better opinion of his London colleagues and expressed himself unsparingly about some of them, especially Lennox

Browne. He told me quite a bit about the conditions for English
medical students, declared himself ready, at any time, to provide
me with information or references, if I needed any, and invited
me to have breakfast with him on the following day, after which
he would take me with him to his hospital.

As far as I knew, he was happily married to a beautiful German
woman who had been a concert singer. She was not present when
we sat down to lunch, and a servant announced that she was
going to eat in the city. The calm with which Semon received the
message that his wife was dining where she saw fit, not at home
with him but in town, made a great impression on me. How could
he trust her so blindly, I wondered, and was positive that at this
very moment she was keeping a tryst with her lover. Not that I
imagined for a moment that a certain Fräulein Jeanette, needlewoman, with a fairly lively past to her credit, temperamental and
without a very secure income, was being faithful to her lover in
a far-off land. Still I was far from visualizing with absolute certainty that Fräulein Jeanette was at this very moment enjoying
lunch with a lover, while I was partaking of the same meal with
Felix Semon, hundreds of English miles away, and would certainly have been ready and willing to be unfaithful to her within
the very next hour.

St. Thomas's Hospital, where Felix was specialist for laryngological diseases, was divided into five impressive pavilions and
was situated magnificently in a park beside the Thames. Semon
led me through various rooms and introduced me to one of his
patients, who, like the Kaiser, was suffering from cancer of the
larynx and was fated to follow the gruesome course that illness
was to take with the monarch. Semon was therefore able to
demonstrate, in the case of this patient, that he was correct in his
theory that perichondritis and the rejection of necrosed cartilage
also took place with carcinoma, and that MacKenzie, who believed the opposite, was wrong.

I continued to visit Semon frequently and was occasionally
present at his consultations, but I saw very little more of his hospital patients. This time it was not indifference that induced me
to give up my hospital visits, not only in Semon's department but
also in those supervised by Lennox Browne and Butlin, but the
fact that, unlike in Germany and especially Vienna, English

patients did not care to serve as object lessons for medical students or doctors, nor were they in a position to do so, with the result that I was given very little opportunity to use my laryngoscope but had to be satisfied with a glimpse of the larynx caught in the mirror of the head surgeon, while standing behind him. There were no courses at the time in London, certainly not of the type to which I was accustomed. At last I understood why English and American doctors came to Berlin and Vienna, in fact had to do so in order to study laryngoscopy and other branches of medicine, which could be learned only by contact with the invalid himself, and this not always without a certain amount of discomfort to the patient. I had often marveled at the good-naturedness and long-suffering of our Viennese patients, some of whom had even accepted with pride the fact that they were "interesting cases," or that they were simply good patients, or that their vocal cords were exceptionally well visible. I couldn't find a trace of any such "ambitions" in the patients I saw in London.

Semon was the only doctor with whom I kept up what might be termed friendly intercourse. It was with him that I made the acquaintance, briefly, of the painter Alma-Tadema, who was so famous at the time. He improvised a little sketch on my menu, which unfortunately I have lost. From Semon I gathered some of the material for the three London letters which my father had authorized me to write for the *Internationale Klinische Rundschau*. The first contained a short summary of the courses of medical study available in England, but apparently included quite a few errors which justifiably displeased Semon. I submitted the next two to him in manuscript. The last one he liked, especially the conclusion, in which I praised fortunate England, "where dozens of private hospitals are flourishing side by side without the interference of power politics or professional animosities, proof of a liberal tendency for which it would be futile to presently try to arouse any understanding in authoritative Viennese circles," an observation for which my father was willing to forgive me quite a few of my sins.

I stayed at my uncle's house only during my first weeks in London, after which I moved to a boarding house in South Kensington, at 18 Cromwell Place, where I rented a pleasant room on one of the top floors, and was awakened every morning by the same tunes being played on a hurdy-gurdy. As I write these reminiscences, I can still hear one of them, from the operetta *Dorothy*, which was popular at the time. In the morning, at any rate at first, I tried to do my duty to my profession in the fashion already described, or I visited museums and galleries—the British Museum, the National Gallery, most often the South Kensington Museum, which was nearby. I ate my lunch at the pension, unless I happened to prefer to eat alone or with friends in a restaurant in the City, or regularly on Sundays, to dine at Honor Oak. I participated as well as my English permitted in the dinner conversation, which was led by my friendly hostess with the customary phraseology and was seconded by a few other guests, most of them middle-aged ladies, and one retired German captain who spoke very loudly in English that was worse than mine. At the beginning of my stay I spent most of my afternoons in my pleasant room with its view across roof-tops into the distance, continued reading French novels and dialogues, an occupation begun at Honor Oak, where I had found little else to read, wrote letters and a one-act play, the short piece that was later to become *Anatol's Wedding Morning* (*Anatols Hochzeitsmorgen*) although in this first concept the protagonist's name was Richard, and he represented nothing more than the eternally fateful hero of countless old French farces. The influence of Halévy's dialogue, *Monsieur et Madame Cardinal*, with which I had just become acquainted, is easily discernible, but not strong enough yet to make an acceptable comedy, at any rate not of *Wedding Morning*. I was so strongly aware of this that I wouldn't let the play be produced for a long time, not even after the success of *Liebelei*. Strangely enough it was produced in Paris before Germany.

I usually dined at my boarding house, and right after the meal went to the theater, a music hall, or one of the three exhibitions that were open at the time—the Danish, Italian and Irish Expositions, either with my aunt and uncle or with acquaintances. I didn't pay much attention to more serious forms of entertainment. A concert at the Albert Hall, where with Woods conducting, I heard Tchaikovsky's "Symphonie Pathétique" for the first time, a Hans Richter concert, and a comprehensive Händel Festival at the Crystal Palace, with an ensemble of two thousand, may be

counted as more enduring artistic impressions. Most frequently
though, sometimes in the early afternoon or often after dinner,
especially on oppressive summer evenings, I would visit my relatives in Honor Oak, where I was always welcome and felt most
at home. Felix was a rather nervous, slightly smug but clever and
amiable host; his wife, Julie, mentioned in earlier chapters,
reigned quietly and with womanly serenity over kitchen, house
and garden, and took a familial interest in me when I had
shopping to do in the city. Their nephew Otto, a meager soul
and intellectually quite limited, was bearable because he was
young, physically attractive, and his manners were passable, so
that a rather trivial affectation of his had a humorous rather than
a foolish effect: he was interested, or let us say he pretended to
be interested in "strategic problems," and would fail to hear the
gong that announced dinner because he was lost in some sort of
"tactical experiment."

That a handsome, young, single man was living in the house
without the slightest hint of an amorous relationship between
him and his young aunt was something which my easily roused
rather than depraved imagination had first to get used to. For
my distrust of all things connected with love was universal. Faithfulness between two lovers or between man and wife was something I saw, at best, as a happy coincidence, a state of affairs
which I liked to think it would be my good fortune to enjoy
some day, even if this was most unlikely. And yet, if ever there
was a home predestined for marital bliss, it was Woodville Hall
in Honor Oak. Here the thoroughly bourgeois and above
all completely unerotic atmosphere was also not disturbed by
any elements of restlessness because music was practiced dili-
gently in the home, sometimes very good music. For the most
part we were dilettantes, enjoying the chamber music we were
playing and giving pleasure to our benevolent audience of
friends; but sometimes professional musicians joined us, not only
as visitors but as players. My uncle, although his taste ran for
the most part along classical lines, was not averse to modern
music and took some pride in the fact that he wasn't. Just as he
had been an unconditional Wagnerian in his early youth, he was
now constantly on the look-out for fresh musical talent, which in
those days, especially in England, was not easy to find. But also

without music and quite apart from it, Woodville Hall was the scene of much pleasant sociability. Thus I spent many hours with various members of the Ölsner and Cronbach families, was a guest at their homes, went for walks and on outings with them, yet can't recall anything more about them today than that they were nice, friendly people.

The faintness of my memory may be due to the fact that all these persons merged into the atmosphere of the Markbreiter home and now, in retrospect, are still to some extent absorbed by it, whereas I can recall much more clearly a few other persons, young people, whom I met on a more bachelor-style level, first and foremost, a German cavalry officer called Wien, a fair-haired, slender young man in a gray drill suit, with whom I went riding several times. Once, as we were passing some railroad tracks, with the trains rushing by, my tame riding academy horse seemed about to shy, which however did not result in an accident. Herr Wien was also my companion on a few outings that took us into the farthest outskirts of the city, after I had enjoyed shorter walks to Greenwich, in the environs of the Crystal Palace, and above all in the wonderful parks of London itself. A few days after my arrival, as an old racing fan, I had driven out to Epsom in a rented cab, together with half a dozen unknowns, to see the Derby, and had come home after the exertions of the day with nothing but a headache. Wien and I visited Richmond, Kew Gardens and Hampton Court, in the company of a blonde Miss Florence; from there to Brighton, where I had a brief conversation with Theodore Herzl, and finally via Portsmouth to the Isle of Wight, where on a stormy evening we went for a short sail along the coast— I, in the firm conviction which I was to cling to for years, that one got seasick only on big ships, felt perfectly well in the little boat.

Isn't it strange that I can see the small fair features of this slim creature, Florence, so much more clearly today than the face of pretty Claire, who one might say was my sweetheart in London? She was nothing better than the maid, and in a fashion housekeeper and secretary of the boarding house where I was staying, and paid me tender visits nightly in my room, but since she was constantly worried by the fact that somebody might hear her going up and down the stairs, we moved our meetings to a miserable little hotel, which Claire seemed to know from previous occasions. But for the fact that I find "Portland Street," where this hotel was situated, jotted down in my diary half a dozen times, I would have sworn that we hadn't visited it more than once. I also took her to the Italian Exposition and to music halls, because she was attractive, looked perfectly respectable and behaved very well. We had little to say to each other. Here my scant knowledge of English was at fault, and I imagine she was just as bored with me as I was with her. Since nothing of a serious nature was ever discussed between us, I couldn't help but be surprised when one day I found a letter from her in my room, in which she expressed some gentle hints concerning the future, and was worried about "getting into trouble." Although I didn't know the expression, I immediately understood what it meant, and promptly became even cooler toward her than I had been previously. She disappeared from the boarding house before I left London, after a stay there of two months. At the end of July I traveled via Dover to Ostend. It had been agreed that I remain in Ostend for a few weeks, then return to Vienna with my family, who were expecting to arrive in Ostend the middle of August.

In spite of my yearning for Jeanette and the restlessness I suffered because of her and her letters, which, although they were quite beautiful and loving, gave me some cause to be nervous, this recreational pause between London and Vienna in a lively, fashionable resort by the sea suited me quite well. I took up residence near the casino in an elegant hotel where I was given a large room on the fourth floor, with two windows and a view of the sea, for which, surprisingly, I had to pay only four francs. I went bathing daily, walked on the beach, occasionally played billiards at the casino, a game called "baraque," was proud of my white flannel suit which my uncle in London had frowned on as highly unsuitable for a young doctor, and on the very first day struck up an acquaintance with two rather dubious females. One of them, tall and blonde, was from Berlin; the other, Frau Lösch, was a short, dark, Polish-Rumanian Jewess. A rather boring, sober-sided gentleman from Vienna, Heinrich Knepler, was my rival for the favors of the latter. One evening, while I was accompanying her home, this gloomy fellow joined us, unin-

vited. I was unable to hide my impatience, with the result that
he asked ironically, "Am I disturbing?" "Yes," I replied rudely,
whereupon he disappeared. But he didn't shoot himself until
seven years later, and I, the victor, accompanied the lady to her
apartment for the first and last time. There she read aloud to me
a letter, just arrived, from her husband, that indicated some
financial failure or other which I chose to ignore, especially
since I had already overstepped my budget and had no idea how
I was going to make ends meet until the arrival of my parents.
But Frau Lösch wanted only one thing, and that not until the
following day, so until then I could imagine that I was being loved
for myself alone. What she wanted was a pair of ankle-boots, a
certain very pretty, very elegant pair of ankle-boots, which she
pointed out to me in a shop window, and I must say I was cha-
grined that it was impossible for me to fulfill her wish. Frau
Lösch didn't insist in the matter, but I had to listen to bitter
reproaches about my miserliness from her blonde friend, who
was the mistress of a rich Berlin Jew and was altogether a much
more practical girl.

Although with this my relationship to the two ladies ended,
I was still to experience a minor shock that was connected with
them. A few days later, an elderly gentleman who had occasionally been a member of our bathing party, said, as Frau Lösch
passed us with a curt greeting, "I've heard pretty bad things
about her." It isn't difficult to guess what bad things flashed
through my mind, and I drew a deep breath of relief when the
old gentleman added, "She's a thief." I thanked him for the warning, but with my finances in the condition they were in, didn't
have to look in my wallet to see if anything was missing. Ten
years later I met Frau Lösch again in the foyer of a Berlin vaude-
ville theater. She greeted me like a dear old friend, told me she
was divorced, and asked me please to visit her. She would be
delighted to introduce me to a few very pretty girls from the
best Berlin families, who were frequent visitors at her home.

On August thirteenth, my parents, brother and sister arrived
in Ostend. I hadn't seen them for almost three months. Now, for
a while, I led the life of a dutiful son. We went for outings together to Blankenberghe and Bruges, the latter in the company

of a wealthy Viennese financier, whose oldest daughter, in my
father's never voiced but obvious opinion, would have been a
fine match for his oldest son. Altogether it was his very understandable wish to see me put the innumerable perils of bachelordom behind me in exchange for a solid bourgeois marriage; my
partiality for writing for an orderly medical career; and my
financially insecure position for more well-to-do, or even wealthy
prospects. However, I didn't give my family all my Ostend time.
Before their arrival I had met a young lady who enjoyed a deserved reputation among Vienna's ball and fashion beauties. Her
figure was flawless, an attribute she knew how to exploit in a
bathing dress, and the smile that played enigmatically about her
all too red lips was just as studied as everything else about her:
her way of looking at you, which would flash, then soften as if
veiled, and her voice, which was sometimes passionate only to
die down again, dark and soft. She talked about nothing but love,
above all, "the grand passion," the thought of which seemed to
intoxicate her, and all this without any exceptionally clever or
original word on this or any other subject ever crossing her
half-open, shiny-wet lips, and she had nothing on her mind but
to please. After we had spent days on the beach and on walks,
conversing in a banal, witty and hypocritical fashion, which
seems obligatory for two people of the opposite sex as introduction to a minor love adventure or tragedy on a grand scale, she
demanded, without however being prepared to involve herself
in any way, that I give her an official avowal of my love, which
I refused to do. She was staying in Ostend with her husband,
and a young man who was presumed to be her lover. Her husband was a businessman, tall, sloppily dressed, slightly stooped;
his behavior was peevish and ironic, as befits husbands who are
jealous and don't want anyone to notice it, who despise their
wives but can't leave them. The lover, or beloved, was a rich
Viennese manufacturer with a Hungarian aristocratic name. He
had the forced elegance of a rather obese Don Juan and looked
after his adored one with big calf eyes when she was swimming
out to sea, devotedly, correctly, and on very good terms with her
husband, who also seemed to feel great sympathy for him, as if
he had settled finally for this one man and had weighted him

down with all the responsibilities, misery and unpleasantness which, according to the laws of God and man, he, the husband, should have been carrying.

On August twenty-first I bade this demonic woman farewell, for the present, with the pleasant prospect of seeing her again in Vienna, although or because she felt it would be wise for us not to commit ourselves in any way, and set out for home with my parents, a journey that was to be interrupted several times. As far as I was concerned, I would have preferred to proceed straight to Vienna, because my longing for Jeanette, in spite of or perhaps because of all these distractions of a more or less harmless nature, which hadn't really given me much pleasure, had grown more and more troubled and violent during these last days, and even if her letters did seem to be calling me back to Vienna with a yearning that was equal to mine, the "witches" had grown increasingly powerful within me during the last three months. In the meantime Jeanette had begun to admit that she was in financial difficulties and had not refused to accept from me the very small sums of money I had occasionally been able to send her from London. Her needlework brought in practically nothing. She had soon had to give up her job in the needlework salon where she was earning twenty gulden a month for fatiguing work from eight to one and three to seven, because of heart symptoms, blood in her sputum, headaches and backaches, a move to which I couldn't object because it meant that she didn't have to travel every evening from the city out to Hernals, a route that was doubly, six times, a hundred times risky because of her doubtful virtue. Now she was embroidering and crocheting at home and selling her work to various shops, but was finding it very difficult to get the money coming to her, and sometimes never did get it.

If I was to believe her letters, she spent most of the day at home, sometimes went for a walk with her quarrelsome sister, Emma, and it was an occasion when her sister's lover, an ungainly little clerk, in his joy over an infinitesimal raise, invited both ladies to dine with him in the Prater. But there were also some rather strange goings-on, for instance, one day a Herr Julius Herz from Prossnitz turned up at her apartment, a bookkeeper, employed at Heberfellner's on the Burggasse, and without further ado asked her to marry him. She explained to him—so she told me—that she had a friend, and turned down the flattering offer, which induced me to write to her that I didn't want to interfere with any good fortune that might come her way, especially since I had made up my mind never to marry her, whereupon she replied with assurances of her eternal love and faithfulness. Furthermore, there was an encounter with Richard Tausenau, who in his frivolous way had asked her just how faithful she felt she had to be to me, which irritated me profoundly. And finally there were visits to a doctor on the Rennweg—quite a distance for an ailing young lady to travel to her doctor—who had laughed at her because she believed I was being faithful to her, with which he was trying to dispel her faith in me to his advantage—something I grasped right away—probably not without success. There were, in all probability, quite a few other experiences which she didn't mention, just as I made no mention of mine, which I am sure did not prevent her from being passionately in love with me nor from feeling that I might quite possibly be faithful to her, just as my negligible little adventures did nothing to disturb my love for her, nor prevent me from believing, sometimes, that perhaps she was not deceiving me.

My father did not want me to return home alone, since he was fully aware of why I was in such a hurry and was repulsed by the very idea. I therefore spent two days with my family in Brussels, two more in Baden-Baden, then, in the railway compartment, shortly before our arrival in Vienna, I had to listen to my father explain what an unreliable impression the young lady who had accompanied me to the station before my departure for Berlin had made on him, and not until the evening of August twenty-fifth was I able to fervently embrace my Jeanette, who received me, all tenderness and passion.

Now we were together evening after evening, yet somehow couldn't be happy. I tormented her incessantly with my jealousy, strangely enough not in connection with the months just gone by but with the more distant past. She wept, kissed my hands humbly, yet couldn't assuage me. Sometimes, and not under the influence of some groundless hypochondriac mood or other, I felt that I was on the verge of utter despair and was filled with dread as I realized the futility and irrevocable passing of the years. Gone were the days in which a talented young man had deceived himself and others with trivialities, the time for achievements had come, yet I was still unable or not in a position to distinguish myself in any such fashion. My father, sometimes bitter, frequently hurt, watched me, unable to find my way in life, in my profession or in the arts, and between my efficient and incredibly diligent brother and my excellent future brother-in-law, both doctors like myself and disapproving strongly of me, I played a truly pitiable role. While I gave vent in my diary to all the ambivalence and misery within me, I was quite ready, as usual, to accuse myself of affectation, felt I was somehow or other pleased with the struggle going on inside me as I wrote about it, and thus could somehow be compared to the poet in *Beatrice,* who was to cry out years later: "And if out of this folly there should rise / Just once, a song, then shall it be the prize / Giv'n me by life, to mitigate the infamy / That I'm too weak to live it splendidly."

As autumn passed, Jeanette and I became closer again and experienced better days, which however were not destined to last. Sometimes Lothar supped with us, either in Jeanette's apartment or in a restaurant. In spite of the fact that my opinion of him hadn't changed, he was still my closest friend. Although I had been made assistant in my father's department soon after my return, and had moved into a small apartment in the same house as he, on the same floor, and had begun to practice modestly on my own, and to seriously study neuroses involving the larynx and experiment with hypnosis, still Lothar didn't hesitate to prophesy that before long I would turn my back on medicine, and with that to some extent took upon himself the responsibility of looking after my literary efforts.

Actually I hadn't been entirely idle in this respect during the autumn. I had perfected *Wedding Morning* and given it a different ending, and written a new one-act play, *Episode,* the first play in which Anatol, however high or low one cares to evaluate him from a human-artistic viewpoint, and the specific aura of the Anatol scenes, whether pleasing or not, make their presence felt clearly. I had reworked a dialogue, which a few years before, with Sonnenthal and Wolters in mind, I had titled *Remembrances* (*Erinnerungen*)—only decades later did I know how to use its basic theme poetically in *Hour of Recognition* (*Stunde des Er-*

kennens)—and the idea was going around in my mind of publishing four one-act plays: *The Adventure of His Life, Wedding Morning, Episode* and *Remembrances,* under one title: *Faithfulness (Treue).* I enquired of S. Fischer in Berlin, who had distinguished himself with the publication of the first Hauptmann dramas and other modern works, if he would be interested in my book; without showing any desire to know more about it, he turned it down with the explanation that he didn't see any commercial possibilities in dramatizing small talk. Lothar now advised me to send my story, *The Madness of My Friend Y* to the *Schöne blaue Donau,* the literary supplement of the *Presse,* where there was an interest in modern literature, and when I couldn't seem to make up my mind, he not only dictated to me the letter to the editor, Fedor Mamroth, but took the manuscript to the post office himself. A few days later my father brought me a letter to the Polyclinic, which bore the return address of the editorial offices of the *Schöne blaue Donau.* I was in the process of making a laryngological examination, my mirror strapped to my forehead. After opening the letter I had the satisfaction, not only of telling my father that my story had been accepted, but was also able to show him a few friendly lines inviting me to visit the editorial offices. And so I began to feel much happier and more hopeful about that which interested me above everything else, but also much better in every respect, and less hypochondriac. My relationship to Jeanette was not so tempestuous and therefore less tortured than in the months gone by, and now became healthier also for practical reasons, due to the fact that she had moved to the Pelikangasse, into a quite pretty room with two windows and a nice view; and of course I suffered no lack of female inspiration from other, stronger, even if less satisfactory quarters.

At the beginning of October, on a day that had been arranged in Ostend, I had called on Frau Adele, and from then on had spent many an afternoon in her small salon, which was arranged obviously to create a sensuous atmosphere, as was her whole appearance and personality. We played the little game of being in love without ever convincing each other. She was tender without heart, demonic without soul, lascivious without passion, and devoted to the point where, in her opinion, adultery actually began, as if it were only a case of not committing perjury in front of her husband or lover.

I also met Gisela Adler quite often in those days, but always when others were present, most frequently in subterranean nine-pins alleys, where with a pressure of the hand and a glowing look we became aware all over again of how tender were our feelings for each other. My reunion with former Gisela Freistadt, now wife of the wine dealer in Leoben, as mentioned in an earlier chapter, falls into this period, and on the same date on which I entered this banal experience in my diary, December 10, 1888, I find the names of other females, for instance "Fännchen," who married Herr Simon Lawner that autumn; and Fräulein Rosa Sternlicht, who in the meantime had married a general practitioner, and finally beautiful, virginal Helene Herz. The latter I met again and again and probably still preferred her to all the others, and one evening, touching her champagne glass to mine, she toasted me half sadly, half compassionately, with the words, "To your aims in life . . . that they should become clearer. In every respect."

Occasionally I wrote such diary entries in Jeanette's humble room while she sat opposite me, sewing busily, sometimes looking up at me, with no idea of what I was writing, especially not of how many different names of girls and women I was scribbling down on the loose pages. And yet, with all my presentiments and knowledge, I was not much less ignorant than she, who I am sure didn't remember all the names that made up her past and, beside mine, also her present.

The new year opened gayly with a wedding party at our house. My sister's marriage to my colleague, Marcus Hajek, was about to take place after years of quasi-secret engagement which had been followed, during the preceding October, after parental opposition which had been very difficult to overcome, by an official engagement. Although my father admired the young doctor for his diligence and ability, he had resented the fact that the Hungarian Jew-boy, who had been accepted at our house more or less as a charity guest at meals, had dared to raise his eyes to the daughter of the professor and privy councillor, not only at a time when other fathers might have done so, but he never quite forgave him for it even later, when as son-in-law and assistant doctor he was well on his way to prosperity and fame, and there could no longer be any question of a *mésalliance*. My father's thinking was so strongly concentrated on show, and he had so completely forgotten his youth and early career, that he would have preferred to give his daughter in marriage to an unloved but wealthy man of our own or preferably better circles, than let her marry this excellent albeit not apparently brilliant suitor whom she happened to love. My mother, in spite of all reasonability, never had an opinion contrary to that of her husband, and we two brothers, in spite of our sympathy and respect for Hajek, had never shown any great enthusiasm for the match either. The marriage took place on the sixteenth of January and was followed by a simple dinner for a small group of friends. My father couldn't make up his mind to address his son-in-law with the intimate "Du," not on this occasion nor later, although he thought well of him. Frankly, Hajek's manners did leave something to be desired and occasionally got on my father's nerves. Others, including us two brothers-in-law, were at times similarly affected.

At this pre-nuptial party and at the wedding that followed it, Helene Herz was the person to whom I paid the most attention, and she was constantly waiting for me to speak the words that I could never make up my mind to utter. Now that the carnival season had opened, dances and balls were added to the innumerable forms of evening amusement which included theaters, concerts, card games and parties, loud or dignified. This year the party held by the Polyclinic deserves special mention, not for any exceptional splendor but because, as a member of the committee in charge of the affair, I became involved in a rather foolish piece of business which however was characteristic because it mirrored the general political atmosphere of the times.

As was customary, the event was announced in the liberal Viennese papers, but there was also an advertisement, contrary to committee decision, in the *Christian-Socialist Deutsche Volksblatt*, which could be traced back to the arbitrary behavior of one of the committee members who belonged to the anti-Semitic wing of the Polyclinic. At our next meeting I brought up the subject and made no bones about my distaste for the political trend and the ignoble tone of the paper in question, of which our colleague, by his action, had proved himself to be a devotee, and

I demanded a vote of no-confidence against him which was accepted unanimously. A few days after the ball, when we were assembled for a final meeting in an inn called the Tabakspfeife, my opponent, after all business had been dealt with, asked for the floor, something for which I had been confidentially prepared, in order to bring the following charges against me: contrary to the dance program, yes, even over the protests of another committee member, I had told the conductor, who was about to announce a quadrille, to repeat a waltz, which had just been loudly applauded (or perhaps—here my memory may not be absolutely correct—a polka rather than a waltz). I had to confess, with a smile, that I had proceeded in such an arbitrary fashion, but excused myself on the grounds that there hadn't been time to call a meeting of the committee to discuss the matter, and that moreover my action had not disturbed the mood of the dancers, on the contrary, had tended to heighten it, and could scarcely be said to have harmed the success of the ball in any respect. I may have expressed myself a little too sarcastically, considering the childishness of the revenge that was being planned; be that as it may, my opponent declared he was not satisfied with my excuse and became increasingly sharp and rude in his attacks on me, and finally demanded that I and I quote him literally "eat humble pie"; in other words, I was to apologize formally to the committee for my arbitrary behavior. This I rejected categorically, whereupon there was nothing my opponent could do but propose a vote of no-confidence against me. Five of the gentlemen were for, five against me. The chairman of the committee was an opportunist and cast his vote for me, probably because my father was vice-president of the Polyclinic. My opponent, with his followers, left the meeting room, and I finally got around to eating my supper, which had meanwhile grown cold.

Two of my colleagues who had remained behind with me— one of them was my friend Louis Mandl—seemed pretty sure that the affair was by no means settled. "Eat humble pie," my otherwise so gentle friend Louis kept repeating. "I don't want to agitate against him, but I wouldn't put up with it." I, however, chose to "put up with it," and did not call my opponent to account. But our foolish reserve officer and chivalry concepts had by now so thoroughly confused us, that in many cases we did what was sensible not because it was sensible but simply out of cowardice, and in spite of my conviction that it would have been the most wretched idiocy to risk life, health, or even the nail of one's little finger for such a triviality, for a long time I couldn't rid myself of the feeling that I really should have behaved with more verve, and that my friend Kuwazl especially was not very pleased with my behavior; and before an officer's council of honor I would probably have lost my commission a few years before it was my fate to do so.

At about the same time, on the thirteenth of March—and here it is possible to sense a deeper connection—the best fencer among us, Max Friedmann, had had the misfortune, during practice with a friend, to pierce the latter's mask with his foil. The weapon had passed into the eye and killed the man on the spot. At the time Max and I were seeing quite a lot of each other and often visited places of amusement and masked balls together (this year the latter were my preference). I therefore considered it my duty to visit him the day after the accident, to commiserate with him. I was strangely affected by the fact that, not only in his conversation with me but also with others, Max dealt hardly at all with his unfortunate victim but seemed occupied solely with the question of whether or not the courts would find him in any way delinquent. We felt we could reassure him on this point, and actually the investigation was terminated a few days later because of a lack of incriminating evidence; and sooner than any of us would have thought possible, friend Max was back in the fencing arena.

At the masked balls, on the whole, I was bored. Perhaps I went to them because I had an insuperable aversion to going home early. A fancy dress ball at which I arrived late after an evening scene with Jeanette and a brief stop at some small gathering or other, seemed to start off on a better note. The moment I entered the dance hall, at about two-thirty A.M., I saw, to my pleasant surprise, a young, perfectly beautiful creature floating past me, whom a few months before I had accosted on the street but never seen again. That she happened to be dancing by in the arms of my friend Kuwazl dampened my delight to some extent, just the same, I was the one, who after a gay hour spent by the three of us in a coffee-house, took her home in a *fiacre*, and from her tenderly kissing lips heard the promise, "I'll come to see you on Tuesday."

She didn't come, but we met several times after that, probably not entirely by chance. Her lover, the youngest son of a rich manufacturer, lived in the same house as I did, yet he wasn't really her lover—said she—because he had missed the right moment when he might have become just that. Still he seemed to feel it was his responsibility to support her in style, which was noticeable in the way she dressed, not only smartly but in good taste, as befitted a simple, middle-class girl from Vienna's suburbs, but also betrayed the fancier demands of a young lady studying for the theater. Her blonde little head was just a trifle too small for her slender, not too well-developed figure, but her pale face, with its *retroussé* nose, her full, pouting red lips, her big gray restless eyes and her fair curls tumbling over her forehead were so sensually attractive that one could have only one wish—to see it on a white lace pillow which was where it belonged.

One afternoon in March I found Kuwazl in my waiting room when I came home. He was in the habit of visiting me during my office hours, when he could be fairly sure of finding me alone. He was conversing animatedly with Fräulein Mizi Rosner, who had come to see me, not to keep her promise made at the ball but to have her sore throat (really a sore throat, albeit a fairly light case of inflammation), treated by me. After that she came again often, always at the same time and long after her throat was well, and took great pleasure, in just those moments when she seemed about to forget her duty to her lover who wasn't her lover, in reminding me of my mistress, and assuring me that she would never, never be mine. When I tried to make love to her she would seem to acquiesce; when I became more passionate, she rejected me angrily, and the closer I had come to my goal a while before, the more furious was her farewell. For this sweet blonde girl the main attraction of our meetings may have been that they took place in the same house in which her lover—whether he was her lover or not—lived, that he knew she was visiting the young doctor and was consumed with jealousy. No. Too much psychology here. Let us say simply: he was a fool, she was a little beast, and I was awkward.

Just like Fräulein Mizi, but expressing herself more grandiloquently, as was correct for a demonic woman, Frau Adele also resisted my not so stormy advances. For some time now, ever since I had come into conflict with her husband—I can't recall what excuse he had found for his jealousy—we had met for the most part for afternoon walks, and on other occasions also under not very favorable circumstances, yet every now and then our tryst took place in a romantic setting, as for instance one evening in spring, when after a few sweetly relaxing hours with Fräulein Mizi, I waited patiently in a remote suburban street, in a closed *fiacre*, until the door was opened and a veiled lady got in with me; the carriage drove us to a dark Prater *Allee* and we delighted each other behind the drawn curtains with the most audacious caresses. And from this beautiful woman, who thought she was as demonic as she was actually foolish and ordinary, off I went to the only one who was mine in the superficial sense of the word, but to whom I actually hadn't belonged anymore for some time.

Compassion, convenience, habit, but not love were what still bound me to Jeanette. Occasionally we enjoyed hours during which we found our way back to each other with the passion of memory, yet both of us realized that the affair was drawing to a close; and as was befitting for a doctor, I wrote in my diary, "The final agony has begun." Her stupid questions, which once had seemed to me the happiest proof of her love; her voice, which had once been capable of exciting me physically; her touch which had ravished me, all had only one effect and influence over me now—to enervate me. She became jealous, or behaved as if she were; there was scene after scene. She had pains in her chest. I realized that I should have been devastated, but all I could feel was torture. Then she would kiss my hand, beg for forgiveness, we would rest side by side, and I was consumed by boredom. I ate oranges and was annoyed by the thought that I would have to get up in the middle of the night and go home. And as I held her in my arms, I was thinking of any other woman, longing for any other woman, a prostitute for all I cared, if only I could have kissed other lips, heard other sighs than Jeanette's.

A little story by Catulle Mendès came to my mind, *Le Troisième Oreiller*, a sentimental causerie by the third pillow that lies, invisibly, beside the two pillows of every loving couple, but I hesitated to dream the story further and include a fourth pillow, on which Jeanette might have been conjuring up the head of another lover, if that were necessary only in her dreams. And so

I lay there until the gray dawn of the next spring day, got up at last, looked out the window at the garden of the insane asylum which lay in the gray light opposite, kissed my sleeping girl farewell, hurried down the four flights, walked home, met other early risers of mood or on business bent—laborers, bakers, servants, butchers, waitresses, gentlemen in evening dress, their collars turned up, and when I got home had just enough time to change my clothes, eat my breakfast and hurry off to the Polyclinic, where my patients and probably also my father were waiting for me to appear, whereupon the daily grind began.

Yet it was no longer quite the same daily grind. Signs pointed to the fact that I was gradually, very gradually, progressing, sometimes in one direction, then again in another. I had begun to practice hypnotism, an interest which had been aroused in me above all by the research of Charcot and Bernheim, and had succeeded in treating successfully several cases of aphonia, that is to say, the loss of voice without any organic change in the vocal cords, by hypnotizing the patient, or simply by the power of suggestion, and had published some case histories in the *Internationale Klinische Rundschau.* Since I had found several excellent mediums, I did not limit myself to this form of therapy in the field of laryngology only, but in emulation of the famous hypnotists, tried all sorts of psychological experiments, which although not uninteresting, did not result in any new information. I jotted them down but never worked them out scientifically. Certainly my happiest achievement from a medical viewpoint was when I was able to induce a partial anesthesia without putting the medium to sleep, simply by power of suggestion, so that it was possible to perform painlessly a minor operation on the larynx, and in one case even a tooth extraction. More stimulating but of little importance medically was when I had my medium experience under hypnosis all sorts of situations and sensations, whatever I felt inclined to invent; or when from one day to the next I arranged for a murder attempt against myself, which I was able to parry successfully because I was prepared for it, and the patient chose to use a dull letter-opener instead of a dagger. Not only my colleagues in the department, but various doctors from the Polyclinic and other hospitals sometimes came to watch my experiments. Those who came most frequently spread the word, spitefully, that I was "putting on shows" at the Polyclinic, which led to my stopping outsiders from watching what I was doing, although for a while I continued to let my closer associates be present as observers. But here again I failed to proceed and draw the consequences of the way I had chosen, and when I began to notice that my most interesting mediums seemed to suffer a loss of will and a certain damage to their health by the repeated experiments, I desisted from any further experimentation of a purely psychological nature, and used hypnosis only in certain cases and for strictly defined healing purposes.

Meanwhile my latest venture out into the open in a literary capacity, however timid, had been more successful than any attempted before. I had accepted Dr. Mamroth's invitation and visited his editorial office, and on this occasion had made the acquaintance of his representative and nephew, the writer of the friendly letter of acceptance, Herr Doktor Paul Goldmann, a twenty-four-year-old, pleasant young man, dressed in a loden jacket and a sports shirt with an open neck and braided cord with tassels for a tie. He was a squat fellow, heavy-set, with a slightly humped back, curly hair and beautiful, light blue eyes. We got along marvelously from the start, shared the same views on most things pertaining to life and art, and Fedor Mamroth treated me almost as warmly. He was a clever, amiable, well-informed man and a journalist of the highest caliber, whose life had been marred by an unhappy marriage and other worries, but who—although he was a critic—never made anyone, not even those writers who had been more fortunate than he, suffer for his personal misfortune, nor for his meager success, which was by no means proportionate to his talents and achievements. The difference of age and circumstances—although I occasionally met with his family in my capacity as doctor—made it impossible for me to be as intimate with him as with his nephew, with whom I enjoyed for years one of the best relationships of my life, and about whom, should this story ever be continued, there will be frequent mention.

The Madness of My Friend Y appeared in the *Schöne blaue Donau* on May fifteenth, and on June first, another contribution, *America*, the only one of my works which I could have dedicated to Jeanette. Both were still pretty amateurish, with sentimental overtones, but not without a certain individuality. *Episode* also soon appeared in the same supplement; but before that I had submitted the manuscript to Sonnenthal, who at the time was provisional director of the Burgtheater. He gave me a highly favorable reading of the piece, but found the ending not sufficiently dramatic for a German audience. The little piece was also applauded at occasional readings, as for instance at Louis Friedmann's home; but more flattering for me than any other success was the fact that Olga, to whom I had sent the manuscript, just as I had done with earlier efforts of mine, spent a whole night copying it in her beautiful handwriting, and made me a present of the transcript.

Lately our correspondence had been conducted with week long pauses between letters, but in mine I still adhered allusively to a tone that seemed to convey that the only true and strong emotion in my heart remained my love for her; and in her letters I could read, now as then, that in her heart also nothing had changed, in spite of the increased number of aristocratic visitors, especially during the hunting season, whom she always mentioned with a self-irony that was not altogether convincing. After almost a year had passed since my last Reichenau visit between Berlin and London, she wrote to me in the spring of 1889 that she hoped to see me at the Derby. But we were not to meet again under favorable circumstances. Her father was present, we exchanged a few words after which she dismissed me with a cool, *"Auf Wiedersehen,"* and I was laid on ice for the rest of the afternoon, except for a trace of warmth which was granted me from another quarter. However, it did not come from Adele, who between husband and lover (who presumably was not her lover), came walking across the grass, a type rather than a living human being, whom I was only permitted to greet in passing; it came from Helene Herz, who was walking at my side, virginal and lovely, just as Adele responded to my greeting, her eyes brimming with emotion. "Is she your friend?" Helene asked gently. "What do you mean?" I replied, as if I didn't know exactly what a lovely young girl like herself might be implying with such a question. "You understood me very well," she said, looking straight ahead between her dark lashes.

I said nothing. All my practical friends were urging me to marry her, most pressing among them her best friend, my cousin Elsa, daughter of my Uncle Edmund, a clever, sarcastic little thing who rather liked me yet at the same time despised me a little. And I had to admit that of all the possibilities for the future, a marriage to Helene was more to my liking than any other solution. So why didn't I make up my mind and ask for her hand in marriage? Certainly not because of Jeanette, although she had sworn only a short while ago that the day I married would be her last on earth; even less because of any of the others, all those whose favors I sought without any true elan, whom I desired without true passion; not Olga, "the adventure" of my life, which by now had paled considerably; not Adele, that demonic goose; not Mizi Rosner, that lasciviously playful, stubborn sweet girl; and certainly not Malvine, who keeps turning up in the pages of my diary, sometimes coming to get a free ticket for a Polyclinic dance and reciprocating for it by little tendernesses during the dance, then again as singer, participating in a concert which I presume I attended, but who has as completely disappeared from my mind as if I had never known her—none of these. And least of all did I hesitate for the reason I imagined to be the true one, that Helene wasn't wealthy enough for me, and that I had to marry a richer woman. The true reason was that the time hadn't yet come for me to marry, that I still had to experience a great many things as bachelor in order to become that which I was to become, however much or little it was in the end.

This sounds like fatalism, but it is nothing of the sort. I don't believe in a predestination that concerns itself with individual fates, but I am convinced that there are "individuals" who *know* what is right for them, even if at best they only *sense* it; who make their decisions of their own free will, even when they believe they are being driven by a coincidence of events and mood; who are always on the right path, even when they are reproaching themselves for having strayed or missed something. With all of which I don't mean to say that only I have the right to count myself among these individuals; but how could one possibly live, create and occasionally enjoy life if one did not imagine that one was a member of this select company?

Appendices

❀❀❀❀❀❀❀❀

I. Brief Biography and Main Works

1862—May 15: Arthur Schnitzler born in Vienna

1865—July 13: Birth of his brother Julius

1867—Dec. 20: Birth of his sister Gisela

1871–1879: Attended the *Akademische Gymnasium* (secondary or high school) in Vienna

1879—July 8: Passes his final examinations with honors

Autumn: Registers in the medical faculty of the University of Vienna

1880—November 13: The poem, *Liebeslied der Ballerine* (*Love Song of a Ballerina*), appears in the magazine, *Der Freie Landesbote,* in Munich

November 15: Essay, *Ueber den Patriotismus* (*On Patriotism*) appears in the same journal

1882—October 1: Is inducted for one-year army service at the Garnisonsspital No. 1 in Vienna

1885—May 30: Receives his medical degree

1885–1888: Intern and assistant doctor at the Vienna Allgemeine Krankenhaus (University Clinic)

1886–1888: Publishes poems and aphorisms in the journals *Deutsche Wochenschrift,* and *An der schönen blauen Donau,* also medical articles in the *Wiener Medizinische Presse* and the *Internationale Klinische Rundschau*

1888—April 5 to May 13: In Berlin for purposes of study

May 23 to July 31: In London for purposes of study

O.F. Eirich, Vienna, publishes *Das Abenteur seines Lebens* (*The Adventure of His Life*), a comedy in one act, as a play script

1888–1893: Assistant to his father at the Allgemeine Wiener Poliklinik

1890: *Alkandi's Lied* (*Alkandi's Song*), a drama in verse is published in the magazine, *An der schönen blauen Donau*, Vol. V., nos. 17, 18

1893—May 2: Death of Arthur Schnitzler's father; departure from the Polyclinic; A.S. opens his own private practice

July 14: Première of the one-act play, *Abschiedssouper* (*Farewell Supper*) from the *Anatol Cycle*, at the Stadttheater in Bad Ischl

December 1: Première of the drama, *Das Märchen* (*The Fairy Tale*), at the Deutsche Volkstheater, Vienna

1894—July 12: First meeting with Marie Reinhard who was to play a decisive role in Arthur Schnitzler's life until his death

October–December: *Sterben* (*Dying*), a novella, appears in the *Neue Rundschau*, Vol. V., nos. 10–12

1895—October 9: Première of the drama *Liebelei*, at the Burgtheater in Vienna, together with the one-act play, *Rechte der Seele*, by Guiseppe Giacosa

1896—January 26: Première of the one-act play, *Die Frage an das Schicksal* (*A Question Put to Fate*), from the *Anatol Cycle*, at the Carola Theater, Leipzig

July 8 to Aug. 25: North Sea voyage; visits Ibsen

November 1: Première of the drama *Freiwild* (*Fair Game*), at the Deutsche Theater, Berlin

1898—Jan. 13: Première of the one-act play, *Weihnachtseinkäufe* (*Christmas Shopping*), from the *Anatol Cycle* at the Sofiensäle, Vienna

June 26: Première of the one-act play, *Episode*, from the *Anatol Cycle*, at the Ibsen Theater, Leipzig

October 8: Première of the drama, *Das Vermächtnis* (*The Legacy*), at the Deutsche Theater, Berlin

S. Fischer, Berlin, publishes *Collected Novellas;* title: *Die Frau des Weisen* (*The Wife of the Wise Man*), including: *Blumen* (*Flowers*); *Ein Abschied* (*A Farewell*); *Die Frau des Weisen* (*The Wife of the Wise Man*); *Der Ehrentag* (*Commemoration Day*); *Die Toten schweigen* (*The Dead Are Silent*)

1899—March 1: At the Burgtheater, Vienna, première of the drama in one act, *Der Grüne Kakadu* (*The Green Cockatoo*), together with *Paracelsus,* a one-act play in verse, and the one-act drama, *Die Gefährtin* (*The Companion*)

March 18: Marie Reinhard dies after an illness of only two days, of septic poisoning following a ruptured appendix

March 27: A.S. receives the Bauernfeld Prize for "his novellas and dramatic works"

1900: A.S. has two hundred copies of *Reigen* (*La Ronde* or *Roundelay*) printed at his own expense and distributed among his friends, under the heading: "Printed as an unmarketable manuscript"

Dec. 1: Première of the drama *Der Schleier der Beatrice* (*The Veil of Beatrice*), at the Lobe-Theater, Breslau

Dec. 25: The novella, *Leutnant Gustl* (*Lieutenant Gustl*), appears in the Christmas number of the *Neue Freie Presse,* Vienna

1901—January to March: The story of *Frau Berta Garlan* appears in the *Neue Deutsche Rundschau,* Vol. XXI, nos. 1 to 3

June 14: A.S. loses his commission as army doctor because of the publication of *Leutnant Gustl,* since in his presentation of the lieutenant he "tarnished the image of the Austro-Hungarian army"

Oct. 13: Première of the one-act play, *Anatol's Hochzeitsmorgen* (*Anatol's Wedding Morning*), from the *Anatol Cycle,* at a literary evening of the social-scientific society, Herold, at the Langenbeck Haus, Berlin

1902—Jan. 4: Première of a cycle of one-act plays, titled: *Lebendige Stunden* (*Living Hours*), and including: *Die Frau mit dem Dolche* (*The Woman with the Dagger*); *Die letzten Masken* (*The Last Masks*); and *Literatur* (*Literature*) at the Deutsche Theater, Berlin

Aug. 9: Birth of A.S.'s son Heinrich

1903—March 17: A.S. rceives the Bauernfeld Prize for the cycle, *Lebendige Stunden* (*Living Hours*)

April: The first trade edition of *Reigen* (*La Ronde*) is published by the Wiener Verlag

Aug. 26: A.S. marries the mother of his son, Olga Gussmann

Sept. 12: Première of a sketch in one act, *Der Puppenspieler* (*The Puppeteer*) from the cycle, *Marionetten*, at the Deutsche Theater, Berlin

1904—Feb. 13: Première of the drama, *Der einsame Weg* (*The Lonely Way*), at the Deutsche Theater, Berlin

March 16: The Berlin district attorney bans the book, *Reigen*, in Germany

November 22: Première of the puppet play in one act: *Der tapfere Cassian* (*Courageous Cassian*), from the cycle *Marionetten*, at the Kleine Theater, Berlin, together with the one-act play, *Der grüne Kakadu* (*The Green Cockatoo*); another one-act play, *Haus Delorme*, which was to be presented for the first time on the same evening, was forbidden by the censors a few days before the opening

1905: S. Fischer, Berlin, publishes *Collected Novellas*, titled: *Die griechische Tänzerin* (*The Greek Dancing Girl*), and including: *Der blinde Geronimo und sein Bruder* (*Blind Geronimo and his Brother*); *Andreas Thameyer's letzter Brief* (*Andreas Thameyer's Last Letter*); *Exzentrik;* and *Die griechische Tanzerin* (*The Greek Dancing Girl*)

Oct. 2: Première of the comedy, *Zwischenspiel* (*Intermezzo*), at the Burgtheater, Vienna

1906—April 24: Première of the drama, *Der Ruf des Lebens* (*The Summons of Life*), at the Lessing Theater, Berlin

March 16: Première of the one-act farce *Zum grossen Wurstel* (*The Big Side-Show*), from the cycle *Marionetten*, at the Lustspieltheater, Vienna

1907: *Collected Novellas*, published by S. Fischer, Berlin. Titled: *Dämmerseelen* (*Souls in Twilight*), and including: *Das Schicksal des Freiherrn von Leisenbohg* (*The Fate of Baron von Leisenbohg*); *Die Weissagung* (*The Prophecy*); *Das neue Lied* (*The New Song*); *Die Fremde* (*The Strange Woman*); and *Andreas Thameyer's Letzter Brief* (*Andreas Thameyer's Last Letter*)

1908—Jan. 15: A.S. receives the Grillparzer Prize for his comedy *Zwischenspiel* (*Intermezzo*)

Jan. to June: The novel, *Der Weg ins Freie* (*The Way Out into the Open*), appears in the *Neue Rundschau,* Vol. XIX, nos. 1–6

1909—Jan. 5: Première of the one-act comedy, *Contesse Mizzi oder der Familientag* (*Countess Mizzi or Family Day*), at the Deutsche Volkstheater, Vienna

Sept. 13: Birth of A.S.'s daughter Lili

Oct. 30: Première of the musical play, *Der Tapfere Cassian* (*Courageous Cassian*), music by Oscar Straus, at the Neue Stadttheater, Leipzig

1910—Jan. 22: Première of the pantomime, *Der Schleier der Pierette* (*The Veil of Pierette*), music by Ernst von Dohnanyi, at the Royal Opera House, Dresden

Summer: A.S. purchases a house—Sternwartestrasse 71, Vienna XVIII, where he resides until his death

Sept. 18: Première of the opera, *Liebelei,* music by Franz Neumann, Frankfurt am Main

Nov. 24: Première of the historical drama, *Der Junge Medardus* (*Young Medardus*) at the Burgtheater, Vienna

Dec. 3: Première of the *Anatol Cycle,* not including *Denksteine* (*Memorial Stones*), and *Agonie* (*Agony*), at the Lessing Theater, Berlin, and at the Deutsche Volkstheater, Vienna

1911—Sept. 9: Death of A.S.'s mother

Oct. 14: Première of the tragi-comedy *Das Weite Land* (*The Vast Land* or *The Vast Domain*), at the Lessing Theater, Berlin; Lobe Theater, Breslau; Residenztheater, Munich; Deutsches Schauspielhaus, Hamburg; Deutsches Landestheater Prague; Altes Stadttheater, Leipzig; Schauburg, Hannover; Stadttheater, Bochum; Burgtheater, Vienna

1912: In celebration of A.S.'s fiftieth birthday, S. Fischer, Berlin, publishes his *Collected Works in Two Parts: Die erzählenden Schriften* (*Prose Works*) in three volumes; *Die Theaterstücke* (*The Plays*), in four volumes; also a collection of novellas, title: *Masken und Wunder* (*Masks and Miracles*), including: *Die Hirtenflöte* (*The Shepherd's Flute*); *Der Tod des Junggesellen* (*Death of a Bachelor*); *Der Mörder* (*The Murderer*); *Der Tote Gabriel* (*Dead Gabriel*); *Das Tagebuch der Redegonda* (*Redegonda's Diary*); *Die Dreifache Warnung* (*The Threefold Warning*)

Nov. 28: Première of the comedy, *Professor Bernhardi,* at the Kleine Theater, Berlin; the play was banned in Austria and could not be produced until the downfall of the Habsburg monarchy

Oct. 13: Première of *Reigen* in Hungarian, in Budapest, Hungary

1913—Feb. to April: The novella, *Frau Beate und ihr Sohn* (*Frau Beate and her Son*), appears in the *Neue Rundschau,* Vol. XXIV, nos. 2–4

1914—Jan. 22: Première of the first motion picture (*Liebelei-Elskousleg*), based on a script by A.S., in Copenhagen

March 27: A.S. receives the Raimund Prize for *Der junge Medardus* (*Young Medardus*)

May 13–23: Mediterranean cruise with Olga Schnitzler

1915—Oct. 12: Première of a cycle of one-act plays entitled *Komödie der Worte* (*Comedy of Words*), and including: *Stunde des Erkennens* (*Hour of Recognition*); *Grosse Szene* (*The Big Scene*); *Das Bacchusfest* (*The Feast of Bacchus*); at the Burgtheater, Vienna; the Hoftheater, Darmstadt; the Neue Theater, Frankfurt am Main

1916—May 15: Première of the one-act play, *Denksteine* (*Memorial Stones*), from the *Anatol Cycle,* at the Volksbildungshaus Wiener Urania, a war relief charity performance

1917—March 10–17: The novella, *Doktor Gräsler, Badearzt* (*Dr. Gräsler, Spa Doctor*), appears in the *Berliner Tagblatt*

Nov. 14: Première of the comedy, *Fink und Fliederbusch* (*Mr. Finch and Mr. Lilac bush*), at the Deutsche Volkstheater, Vienna

1918—July to Sept.: The novella, *Casanovas Heimfahrt* (*Casanova's Homecoming*), appears in the *Neue Rundschau,* Vol. XXIX, nos. 7 to 9

1920—March 26: Première of a comedy in verse, *Die Schwestern oder Casanova in Spa* (*The Sisters, or Casanova in Spa*), at the Burgtheater, Vienna

Oct. 8: A.S. receives the Volkstheater Prize for *Professor Bernhardi*

Dec. 23: Première of *Reigen* (*La Ronde*), at the Kleine Schauspielhaus, Berlin

1921—Feb. 1: First performance of *Reigen* in Vienna, at the Kammerspiele of the Deutsche Volkstheater

Feb. 17: After an organized agitation, the Vienna police forbade any further performances of *Reigen*, for reasons of "law and order"

Feb. 22: Organized disturbance at a performance of *Reigen* at the Kleine Schauspielhaus, Berlin

June 26: A.S. divorces his wife Olga

Sept.: The Berlin district attorney indicts the management of the Kleine Schauspielhaus, the director and the actors of *Reigen* for causing a public scandal.

Nov. 8: After five days of hearings, the 6th criminal court of Provincial Court III, Berlin, announces the acquittal of all defendants

1922—March: The ban on *Reigen*, which had been imposed on Feb. 17, 1921, is lifted

1924—Oct. 11: Première of *Komödie der Verführung* (*Comedy of Seduction*), at the Burgtheater, Vienna

Oct.: The short novel, *Fräulein Else*, appears in the *Neue Rundschau*, Vol. XXXV, no. 10

1925—1926: *Traumnovelle* (*Dream Story* or *Rhapsody*), appears in the magazine *Die Dame*, Vol. LIII, nos. 6–12, Berlin

1926—April 23: A.S. receives the Burgtheater ring from the Association of Journalists and Writers, Concordia

1926–1927—Dec. 5, 1926 to Jan. 9, 1927: The novella, *Spiel im Morgengrauen* (*A Game of Chance at Daybreak*), appears in the *Berliner Illustrierte Zeitung*, Vols. XXXV, XXXVI

1927: *Buch der Sprüche und Bedenken, Aphorismen und Fragmente,* (*Book of Maxims and Doubts, Aphorisms and Fragments*), published by Phaidon, Vienna

S. Fischer, Berlin, publishes *Der Geist im Wort und der Geist in der Tat* (*The Spirit in Word and Deed*)

1928—April 16 to May 11: Boat trip to Mallorca with his daughter Lili and his son-in-law Arnoldo Cappellini

July 26: Death of his daughter Lili in Venice by suicide; S. Fischer, Berlin, publishes *Therese, Chronik eines Frauenlebens* (*Therese, Chronicle of a Woman's Life*)

1929—Dec. 21: Première of *Im Spiel der Sommerlüfte* (*Wafted by Summer Breezes*), at the Deutsche Volkstheater, Vienna

1931—Feb. 14: Première of *Der Gang zum Weiher* (*The Walk to the Fish Pond*), at the Burgtheater, Vienna

May 13 to 30: The novel, *Flucht in die Finsternis* (*Flight into Darkness*), appears in the *Vossische Zeitung*, Berlin

Oct. 21: Death of A.S. in Vienna

Since 1931: Publication of numerous works and letters from A.S.'s estate in magazines and almanacs

1932—March 29: Première of the one-act play, *Anatols Grössenwahn* (*Anatol's Megalomania*), and also *Halbzwei* (*Half-past One*), *Die Überspannte Person* (*The Hysterical Woman*), *Die Gleitenden* (*Gliding*), and *Die Mörderin* (*The Murderess*), for the literary estate, at the Deutsche Volkstheater, Vienna

Published by S. Fischer, Berlin: *Collected Novellas:* Title: *Die kleine Komödie* (*The Little Comedy*); including: *Amerika; Er wartet auf den vazierenden Gott* (*He Is Waiting for a God Off-Duty*); *Der Witwer,* (*The Widower*); *Der Andere* (*The Other Man*); *Welch eine Melodie* (*What a Melody!*); *Der Empfindsame* (*The Sensitive Man*); *Ein Erfolg* (*Success*); *Geschichte eines Genies* (*The Story of a Genius*); *Legende,* a fragment; *Um eine Stunde* (*For One Hour*); *Wohltaten still und rein gegeben* (*Good Deeds, Done Quietly and Purely*); *Die Braut* (*The Bride*); *Die Grüne Krawatte* (*The Green Cravat*); *Exzentrik* (*Eccentric*); *Mein Freund Ypsilon* (*My Friend "Y."*); *Die Drei Elixire* (*The Three Elixirs*); *Der Fürst ist im Hause* (*The Prince Is in the House*); *Erbschaft* (*Legacy*); *Der Sohn* (*The Son*); *Komödiantinnen: Helene-Fritzi* (Comediennes: Helene-Fritzi); *Reichtum* (*Wealth*); *Die Nächste* (*The Next One*); *Die Kleine Komödie* (*The Little Comedy*)

1953: Exchange of letters between A.S. and Otto Brahm, edited by Professor Oscar Seidlin, published as Vol. 57 of the *Schriften der Gesellschaft für Theatergeschichte* (*Bulletin of the Society of Theatrical History*), Berlin

1955: Letters from Sigmund Freud to A.S., edited by Heinrich Schnitzler, appear in the *Neue Rundschau*, Vol. LXVI, no. 1

1956: Exchange of letters between A.S. and George Brandes, edited by Professor Kurt Bergel, published by Francke, Bern

1958: Exchange of letters between A.S. and Rainer Maria Rilke, edited by Heinrich Schnitzler, appear in *Wort und Wahrheit,* Vol. XVIII, no. 4., April 1958

1961–1962: S. Fischer, Frankfurt am Main, publishes the new edition of A. S.'s *Gesammelte Werke* (*Collected Works*); the *Prose Works* in two volumes; the *Plays* also in two volumes

1964: Exchange of letters between A.S. and Hugo von Hofmannsthal, edited by Theresa Nickl and Heinrich Schnitzler, published by S. Fisher, Frankfurt am Main

1967: A final volume of the *Collected Works: Aphorismen und Betrachtungen* (*Aphorisms and Reflections*), edited by Professor Robert O. Weiss, published by S. Fischer, Frankfurt am Main

II. English Translations of Schnitzler's Works

Anatol: A sequence of dialogues, paraphrased for the English stage by Granville Barker. N.Y., M. Kennerley, 1911.

——. London, Sidgwick & Jackson Ltd., 1911.

——. Little, Brown & Co., Boston, 1917.

Anatol, Living Hours, The Green Cockatoo: Translated by Grace Isabel Colbron. Introduction by Ashley Dukes, N.Y., Boni & Liverright, 1917.

Beatrice: A novel, translated by Agnes Jacques, N.Y., Simon & Schuster, 1926.

Bertha Garlen: N.Y., Boni & Liveright, 1918.

Casanova's Homecoming: Translated by Eden and Cedar Paul, N.Y., 1921. Privately printed for subscribers only.

——. London, Brentano's Ltd., 1923.

——. N.Y., T. Seltzer, 1923.

——. N.Y., Simon & Schuster, 1930.

Comedy of Words, and Other Plays: Translated and introduced by Pierre Loving. Cincinnati, Stewart & Kidd Co., 1926. Also includes: *The Hour of Recognition; The Big Scene; The Festival of Bacchus; Literature; His Helpmate* or *The Companion.*

Countess Mizzie or The Family Reunion: Translated by Edwin Björkman. In: *Twenty Non-royalty, One-act Popular Classics,* N.Y., 1946.

Daybreak: Translated by William A. Drake, N.Y., Simon & Schuster, 1927; (*Spiel im Morgengrauen*).

Dr. Graesler: Translated by E.C. Slade, N.Y., T. Seltzer, 1923.

———. N.Y., Simon & Schuster, 1930.

The Duke and the Actress: Translated by Hans Weysz. In: *Poet Lore,* Boston, 1910.

A Farewell Supper: From the *Anatol Cycle.* Paraphrased by H. Granville-Barker. In: *Fifty One-act Plays,* edited by C.M. Martin, London, 1934. In: *Five Modern Plays,* Boston, 1936.

The Festival of Bacchus: Translated by Pierre Loving. In: *Twenty-Five Short Plays,* edited by F. Shay, N.Y., 1925.

Flight into Darkness: Translated by William A. Drake, N.Y., Simon & Schuster, 1931.

Fräulein Else: A novel, translated by Robert A. Simon, N.Y., Simon & Schuster, 1925.

Gallant Cassian: (*Courageous Cassian*) A puppet play in one act, translated from the third edition by Adam L. Gowans, Gowans and Gray, Ltd., London, 1914.

———. Translated by Moritz A. Jagendorf. In: *Poet Lore,* Boston, 1922.

The Green Cockatoo and Other Plays: Translated by H.B. Samuel, Gay & Hancock Ltd., London, 1913. Also in: *The German Classics,* edited by K. Francke and W. G. Howard, N.Y., 1913–1914. And in: *Plays for the College Theatre,* translated by Ethel Van der Veer, edited by G.H. Leverton, N.Y., 1932.

The Green Cockatoo: In: *Thirty Famous One-act Plays.* Edited by Bennett Cerf and Van H. Cartnell. Modern Library, 1943.

Hands Around: (*Reigen*). A cycle of ten dialogues, N.Y. Privately printed for subscribers, 1920. Authorized translation. See also *Round Dance.*

The Hour of Recognition: Translated by Pierre Loving, International, N.Y., 1916.

Intermezzo: Translated by Edwin Björkman. In: *Plays from the Modern Theatre,* edited by H.R. Steeves, Boston, 1931.

———. English version by Alice Mattullath, N.Y., 1902.

The Lady with the Dagger: Translated by Helen Tracy Porter, Boston, 1904.

The Legacy: Translated by Mary L. Stephenson. In *Poet Lore,* Boston, 1911.

Lieutenant Gustl: see *None But the Brave.*

Liebelei: Titled: *Light-o'-love:* Translated by Bayard Quincy Morgan.

In: *Drama,* a quarterly review, Chicago, 1912. In: *Modern Continental Plays,* edited by S.M. Tucker, N.Y., 1929. In: *European Plays, Compilers of Contemporary Drama* by E.B. Watson and W.B. Pressey, N.Y., 1931. In: *Continental Plays,* edited by T.H. Dickinson, Boston, 1935. In: *Modern German Drama,* edited by Edgar Lohner, Houghton, 1966. Titled: *The Love Game,* typescript, N.Y., 1956, Titled: *Playing with Love,* Translated by P. Morton Shand, with the prologue to *Anatol* by Hugo von Hofmannsthal. Translated by Trevor Blakemore, in English verse, A.C. McClurg & Co, Chicago, 1914. Titled: *The Game of Love* in *Masterpieces of the Modern Central European Theatre,* edited by Robert Willoughby Corrigan.

Literature: Translated by A.I. du P. Coleman. In: *The German Classics,* edited by K. Francke and G. Howard. N.Y., 1913–1914. Translated by Pierre Loving, International, N.Y., 1915.

Little Novels: Translated by Eric Sutton, Simon & Schuster, N.Y., 1929. Includes: *The Fate of the Baron, The Stranger, The Greek Dancing Girl, The Prophecy, Blind Geronimo and His Brother, Andreas Thameyer's Last Letter, Redegonda's Diary, Dead Gabriel, The Murderer, The Death of a Bachelor.*

Living Hours: Translated by Grace Isabel Colbron, *Poet Lore,* Boston, 1906. In: *Chief Contemporary Dramatists,* Second Series; edited by T.H. Dickinson, Boston, 1921. In: *Ten Minute Plays;* translated by Porter Davitts; edited by Pierre Loving, N.Y., 1923.

The Lonely Way: Translated by Julian Leigh, N.Y.; acting version by Philip Moeller, N.Y. Rialto Service Bureau.

The Lonely Way, Intermezzo, Countess Mizzi: Translated by Edwin Björkman, Little, Brown, 1927; Theater Guild Inc., 1947.

None but the Brave (Lieutenant Gustl.) Translated by Richard Simon, 1926. In: *Viennese Novelettes,* illus. by Kurt Wiese. N.Y., Simon & Schuster, 1931.

Professor Bernhardi: Translated by Hetty Landstone, AMS Press, 1928. *Questioning the Irrevocable (Die Frage an das Schicksal);* Translated by W.H.H. Chambers. In: *The Drama,* edited by A. Bates, London, 1903.

Rhapsody (Traumnovelle): Translated by Otto P. Schinnerer, N.Y., Simon & Schuster, 1927.

The Way Out into the Open (Der Weg ins Freie): Translated by H. Samuel, H. Latimer Ltd., London, 1913.

Round Dance (Reigen): Ten dialogues, translated by Keen Wallis, Bloomington, Indiana Press, 1958. Modern Repertory. Series One. In: *The Modern Theatre;* edited by Eric Russell Bentley, Doubleday, 1955–1960. As *La Ronde.* In: *Masters of Modern Drama,* edited by H. M. Block, Random House, 1962. As *La Ronde.* In: *Masterpieces of the Central European Theatre,* edited by Robert Willoughby Corrigan, 1967.

Theresa, The Chronicle of a Woman's Life: Translated by William A. Drake, N.Y., Simon & Schuster, 1928.

The Vast Domain (Das Weite Land): Translated by Edw. Boticky and Alex. Caro. In *Poet Lore,* Boston, 1923.

Viennese Novelettes: Illustrated by Kurt Wiese, N.Y., Simon & Schuster, 1931. Including: Introduction by O.P. Schinnerer, *Daybreak, Fräulein Else, Rhapsody, Beatrice, None but the Brave (Lieutenant Gustl).*

Notes

1. *Vahrn:* in Italian, Varna. In A.S.'s day in South Tyrol.

    Olga: A.S.'s wife, *née* Gussmann, 1882–1970.

    Liesl: Olga Schnitzler's sister Elizabeth, 1885–1920.

    Married to the actor Albert Steinrück, 1872–1929.

    Living Hours: a one-act play. Part of a cycle of one-act plays, now in *Plays:* Vol. I.

3. *Gymnasium:* a secondary or high school, preparatory school for university, with a curriculum quite a bit stiffer than that of our high schools.

5. *Fiacre:* from the French, *fiacre*. In Austria referring to a carriage, usually for hire, drawn by two horses.

    Henry Baltazzy: correctly: Baltazzi. Of a merchant family from Smyrna. His three older brothers—Alexander, Hector and Aristides —were famous horsemen and owned their own stables. His sister Helene, Baroness Vetsera, was the mother of Baroness Mary Vetsera, who committed suicide with Crown Prince Rudolf at Mayerling, 1889.

6. *Rue Maubeuge:* where A.S. lived with Marie Reinhard during his stay in Paris, April–May, 1897.

    M.R.: Marie Reinhard. See Brief Biography, July 12, 1894.

7. *Celerina:* in the Engadine, Switzerland.

    on the Solenweg: a path from Bad Ischl to Laufen, and from there via Goisern and Steeg to Hallstatt (Austria).

Page

8. *Gross-Kanizsa:* in Hungarian, Nagykanizsa, a town in southwest Hungary.
    Lake Balaton: in German, Plattensee. A large lake in southwest Hungary.

11. *Mödling:* a small town just south of Vienna.
    Güns: in Hungarian, Köszeg.
    the youngest, Schey, Freiherr von Koromla, 1798–1880.

13. *Carltheater building:* on the Praterstrasse. Built to replace the razed Leopoldstädtertheater, 1847. Razed in 1951.
    Theater an der Wien: opened 1801. Here were presented the premières of Beethoven's *Fidelio* and his *Violin Concerto*. Kleist wrote *Käthchen von Heilbronn* for this theater. The première of Grillparzer's *The Ancestress* (*Ahnfrau*) took place here. Later it became the home of the "classical" Vienna Operetta with, among other productions, the premières of *The Merry Widow* (Lehar) and *Ein Walzertraum* (Oscar Strauss).

14. *Offenbach, Jacques:* 1819–1880. Originally Levy. Composer of operettas (*Tales of Hoffman, Orpheus in the Underworld, La Belle Hélène*).

15. *the exiled Rumanian Prince Couza:* Alexandru Ioan I, 1820–1873. The first prince to be elected by popular vote in Rumania, 1859.
    Milan Obrenovic: Milan I Obrenovic, 1854–1901. Elected supreme prince of Serbia in 1868. From 1882 to 1889, King of Serbia.

17. *The Robbers, Fiesko, The Maid of Orleans, The Bride of Messina:* classical dramas by Friedrich von Schiller, 1759–1805.
    Emilia Galotti: classical drama by Gotthold Ephraim Lessing, 1729–1781.
    the Wieden district: used to be a suburb and became the 4th Vienna district in 1861.
    Heinrich Laube: 1806–1884. Playwright. From 1849 to 1867, director of the Burgtheater, Vienna.
    Hofburg: Hofburgtheater, founded in 1741; moved to its present site in 1888. After 1918 renamed Burgtheater. Not only Vienna's most representative theater, but one of the finest institutions of its kind in the world. In the old days renowned for its extremely dramatic presentations.
    Aristocrat and Democrat: in A.S.'s literary estate.

Page

19. *Thalhof Hotel:* still open today.

Reichenau: a vacation resort approximately an hour by train from Vienna.

20. *Marguerite:* the opera is now usually known as *Faust.*

Kärntnertortheater: opened in 1763, razed in 1868.

Gustav Walter: 1834–1910. From 1856–1887, tenor at the Imperial Vienna Opera.

Dr. Schmid: Karl, 1825–1873. From 1855 to 1868, basso at the Imperial Vienna Opera.

21. *Liebelei:* play by A.S. For dates and English translations see Appendices. The title of this play is as good as untranslatable. Literally, *The Little Love* or *A Negligible Love Affair.* It has been translated and produced in English under such various titles as *Light-o'-Love, The Love Game, Playing with Love, The Game of Love, Flirtation;* none of them are satisfactory choices.

22. *by a friend:* Raoul Auernheimer, 1876–1948. Novelist, playwright, journalist, drama critic.

after getting his degree: 1860.

Bar Kochba: in Aramaic, Barcocheba, Son of the Star. Messianic name given to Simon, leader of the Jewish rebellion against Rome under Hadrian, A.D. 132–135.

Hyrtl's Anatomy: Joseph Hyrtl, 1810–1894. Anatomist.

23. *the Polyclinic:* founded in 1871, opened on January 1, 1872. Still functioning.

Concordia: founded in Vienna, 1859. An organization of journalists and writers, somewhat similar to our PEN Club of today.

Mosenthal: Solomon, 1821–1877. Pseudonym for Friedrich Lechner. Wrote *Deborah,* folk-drama, 1850 and *Lambertine von Méricourt,* tragedy, 1853.

24. *Neue Freie Presse:* the leading newspaper of the Austrian monarchy under editor-in-chief Moriz Benedikt, 1849–1920. Was forced to discontinue publication on Feb. 1, 1939, and was united with the *Neue Wiener Tagblatt,* as was the *Neue Wiener Journal.* After 1945 was re-established as the daily paper—*Die Presse.*

25. *Schönbrunn:* formerly an Imperial palace in Vienna. Begun in 1696 by Fischer von Erlach; completed by Empress Maria Theresa, 1744–50. In 1805 and again in 1809 Napoleon's headquarters.

Page

Hietzing: a residential section of Vienna, 13th district.

Charlotte Wolters: 1834–1897. Actress at the Burgtheater.

Pötzleinsdorf: 18th district of Vienna.

Mariahilf: 6th district of Vienna.

26. *the Rote Stadl:* popular inn near Rodaun, south of Vienna.
    the Brühl: summer resort, south of Vienna.

    Vöslau: Bad Vöslau, a spa, approximately three-quarters of an hour by train from Vienna.

    Alt-Aussee: a summer resort in the Styrian section of the Salzkammergut.

27. *Moser's farce, Founder's Day:* a comedy in 3 acts, 1873. Gustav von Moser, 1825–1903. Playwright.

    Munich Residenztheater: built by François de Cuvillies, 1751–1753. Destroyed by bombs, 1944. Rebuilt near the original site, 1949–1951. Reopened, Jan. 28, 1951.

    Kaisergarten: today the Burggarten. Was partly destroyed in 1894 to make way for a new wing of the Neue Hofburg. The remaining park was reopened in 1919.

    Akademische Gymnasium: founded in 1553 as the first Jesuit *Gymnasium* on Austrian soil. Became the state *Gymnasium* in 1852. Moved in 1866 into a new building on the Beethovenplatz, which stands, unchanged, to the present day. Besides A.S., Peter Altenberg, Richard Beer-Hofmann and Hugo von Hofmannsthal were pupils here.

28. *a romantic tragedy:* Aegidius.
    in the Ibsen manner: from *Poems*—A Verse. *To live* implies—the struggle/Within oneself against dark powers./*To be a poet* is to pass judgment on oneself.

29. *the intimate "Du";* or "thou," used in German speaking countries to indicate a more intimate relationship.

30. *Monk and Soldier:* drama, 1850, by Friedrich Kaiser, 1814–1874. Kaiser was playwright and actor. His plays were folk-dramas. He founded the first "Concordia," 1840, to take the place of the "Ludlamshöhle," which had been disbanded. Franz Grillparzer, 1791–1872, playwright; Nicolaus Lenau, 1802–1850, poet; and other famous *literati* had been members of the latter.

Page

for personal reasons: the actress Marie Glümer, 1873–1925, with whom A.S. was later to have a passionate love affair, was engaged as actress in Salzburg for some years.

31. *Sardanapalus:* King of Assyria, 669–626 B.C. Sometimes identified with Ashurbanipal.

a little book of Egyptian dream interpretations: with superstitious connotations.

a manual of geomancy: divination by figures or lines. Originally from natural configurations of the earth (topography, crevices, etc.), or by markings in the sand or handfuls of earth thrown on the ground.

33. *Hofrat:* a complimentary title equivalent to the English "privy councillor," but including no function whatsoever.

34. *Scheffel:* Joseph Victor von, poet, 1826–1886. *The Trumpeter of Säckingen*, 1854, an epic in verse.

Der Weg ins Freie: a novel by A.S. Appeared first, serialized, in the *Neue Rundschau*, Vienna, 1908. Later included in the S. Fischer *Complete Works.* Translated into English as *The Way Out into the Open*, London, 1913.

36. *Heiligenblut:* in Carinthia, at the foot of the Grossglockner Pass.

Kaiser Joseph: Joseph II, 1741–1790. Holy Roman Emperor, eldest son of Empress Maria Theresa. A champion of the Era of Enlightenment with relatively liberal and democratic ideas. He was renowned for his conviviality and liked to mingle with the "simple folk," which was unusual for the absolute monarch of his day and an image he was anxious to avoid.

39. *Black Friday:* May 9, 1873.

Zschokke: Heinrich, 1771–1848, Swiss writer, mainly historical novels.

Hackländer: Friedrich Wilhelm, 1816–1877. Writer, mainly travelogues.

son of the famous etcher: Karl Radintzsky, 1818–1901. Sculptor, famous for his medallions.

41. *Debreczin:* in Hungarian—Debrecen.

42. *the operetta composer:* Franz von Suppé, 1819–1895.

until his early death: 1894.

fates of the other three: it should be "four." Melanie married later;

Page

there were no children. Elsa and Clara were divorced. Anna committed suicide in 1923.

43. *My mother's oldest brother:* Edmund Markbreiter, lawyer, died in
New York, 1909.
Raoul: law candidate. Was forced to leave Austria because of a
charge of embezzlement. Emigrated to America. Became hotel
manager in Chicago. Died in 1933.

44. *Schachendorf:* in A.S.'s day—Hungary. Today part of Austria.
Pressburg: in Czech—Bratislava. In A.S.'s day it belonged to the
Kingdom of Hungary.

47. *Hans Makart:* 1840–1884. Popular and fashionable Viennese painter
of mainly historical and allegorical themes.
Maecenas: a patron, especially one generous to artists.

48. *Barmizvah:* from the Aramaic "bar" for son, and the Hebrew
"mitzwah" for command. Religious ceremony when a boy of Jewish faith comes of age at thirteen.

51. *Fännchen:* Franziska Reich, 1862–1930.

52. *Kotzebue:* August von, 1761–1819. Was one of the most successful
playwrights of his day, not only in his own country (Germany), but
also in England.

54. *Maximilian Harden:* pseudonym for Wilkowski, 1861–1927. German
publisher, critic and essayist. Founded the weekly, *Die Zukunft.*

55. *Faust:* Tragedy in two parts by Johann Wolfgang von Goethe,
1749–1832, on which he worked more or less all his life.
Uriel Acosta: a tragedy, 1847, by Karl Gutzkow, playwright and
critic, 1811–1878.
the Prater amusement area: a part of the Prater, a six-square-mile
park in Vienna. Once a hunting ground for the Emperor; opened
to the public in the second half of the eighteenth century. Has a
large and world-renowned amusement area, with the largest ferris
wheel in the world.
Götz: Götz von Berlichingen, play by Johann Wolfgang von
Goethe, 1773.

56. *E.T.A. Hoffmann:* 1776–1822. German writer, composer, artist.
Tieck: Ludwig, 1773–1853. German novelist of the Romantic

Page

School. *Franz Sternbalds Wanderungen,* 1798; *William Lovell,* 1795–96.

Immermann: Karl, 1796–1840. German novelist of the Romantic School. *Münchhausen,* 1838–39, a period novel; *Die Epigonen,* 1836, a novel.

Kater Murr, 1820–22.

57. *Jean Paul:* pseudonym for Johann Paul Friedrich Richter, 1763–1825. German novelist. *Quintus Fixlein,* 1796; *Katzenbergers Badereise,* 1809.

58. *Hellmesberger Quartet:* Joseph Hellmesberger, 1828–1893. Conductor and violinist from a famous family of Austrian musicians.

Moritz Rosenthal: pianist, 1862–1946. A pupil of Franz Liszt.

60. *Salonblatt: Wiener Salonblatt.* A journal, founded by Otto von Hentl and Victor Silberer; 1870–1938.

opposite the old church which was to assume such importance to me in later years: in a diary entry, Feb. 4, 1895, A.S. mentions "the old church in the Lerchenfelderstrasse" in connection with a walk with Marie Reinhard, who played such a decisive role in his life from 1894 until her death in 1899.

62. *The Fourth Commandment:* 1877. Folk-drama by Ludwig Anzengruber, 1839–1899. Writer of realistic peasant dramas and comedies.

64. *two Viennese writers:* Egon Friedell, 1878–1938; suicide. Writer, actor, drama critic, cultural historian. Alfred Polgar: 1875–1955. Writer, drama critic. Emigrated to the United States in 1940. The piece in question: *Goethe,* 1908.

Grillparzer: Franz, 1791–1872. Austrian playwright.

65. *Weidlingau:* small town near Vienna.

Richard Tausenau: 1861–1893; suicide.

66. *the Book of Job:* chapter 3, verses 1–6.

71. *Kaposi atlases:* Moritz Kaposi, 1837–1902. Founder of modern dermatology. *Pathology and Therapy of Diseases of the Skin,* 1860; *Pathology and Therapy of Syphilis,* 1891.

75. *Conservatory of Music:* "Konservatorium für Musik." Founded in 1817 as "Konservatorium der Gesellschaft der Musikfreunde in Wien." Became, in 1909, the "Staatsakademie für Musik und darstellende Kunst," (State Academy for Music and the Performing

Page

Arts, and exists as such today. Professor Johann Schnitzler, the author's father, lectured here on "Physiology and Pathology of the Voice" from 1874 to 1877.

76. *Couleurs:* dueling corps or associations at the German and Austrian universities. The "colors" were worn on the individual caps and cross-bands.

78. *Renan:* Ernst Renan, 1823–1892. French philologist and historian.

81. *Egmont:* drama by Johann Wolfgang von Goethe, 1775–88. Concerns Count Egmont, leader of the Netherlands revolt against Spanish tyranny.

Ernst Hartmann: 1844–1911. From 1864 until his death, actor and producer at the Burgtheater.

Alexander Girardi: 1850–1918. Famous actor of character roles. Was engaged at the Burgtheater just two months before his death. His last role was that of Hans Weiring in A.S.'s *Liebelei.*

82. *the Central:* famous café in Vienna's 1st district, frequented by *literati.* Ceased to exist after World War II.

Olmütz: in Czech: Olomonc. In A.S.'s day in the Austrian Crownland of Moravia.

84. *The Lady of the Camellias:* novel, 1848, and in this case drama, 1852, by Alexander Dumas the Younger.

Marie-Anne, a Woman of the People: a pageant-play in 5 acts, 1845, by Adolphe Philippe Dennery, 1811–1890, and Julien de Mallian 1805–1851.

86. *Goethe aphorism:* Goethe sometimes wrote prologues and epilogues for plays, in this case "Epilogue for the Tragedy, Essex," an old English play by Banks, adapted for the Weimar stage in 1813. Later included in *Proverbialisms* (Sprichwörtlich): A man experiences,/Be he whoe'er he may,/A final joy, also/A final day.

89. *the famous German opera singer, Marchesi:* Mathilde Marchesi de Castrone, 1821–1913.

90. *the banker, Jacob Lawner:* however, Franziska Reich married Simon Lawner, a general representative of the French life insurance company, "Le Phénix," in 1888.

91. *Purkersdorf:* a small town near Vienna.

92. *Czernowitz:* formerly the capital of the Austrian Crownland of Bukovina, today Cernauti, in the U.S.S.R., Ukraine.

Page

95. *a paper on the theory of cognition:* in all probability "The Basis of Psycho-Mechanics, Part One: The Autonomy of the Soul." Published by George Szelinski, Vienna, 1912.

the poet Lorm: Hieronimus Lorm, pseudonym for Heinrich Landesmann, 1821–1902. Austrian lyricist, writer, essayist.

97. *Dioscuren:* literary annual of the First General Civil Servant Association of the Austro-Hungarian monarchy. 1872–1896.

The Flea: satirical journal, 1869–1920; published by Joseph Frisch and Moritz Deutsch, Jr.

Bisamberg: northwest of Vienna.

99. *the new literary current from North Germany:* naturalism, a movement which produced writers such as Gerhart Hauptmann and his contemporaries. It exerted considerable influence in the literary generation of the last decades of the nineteenth century in Austria.

100. *Baron Berger:* Alfred Freiherr von Berger, 1853–1912. From 1887 to 1890, cultural secretary of the Burgtheater. 1894, Professor of Esthetics at the University of Vienna. 1900, became director of the newly founded Deutsche Schauspielhaus in Hamburg. From 1910–1912, director at the Burgtheater.

101. *in the Baumbach style:* Rudolf Baumbach, pseudonym for Paul Bach, 1840–1905. German lyricist and writer.

the illustrated magazine Heimat: Published by Carl von Vincenti, Vienna, 1876–1889.

102. *The Diary of an Idler:* sub-title of the novella *On Unsteady Ground*, by Maximilian Bern, 1849–1923.

105. *Spring Night in the Dissecting Room:* a fantasy, 1880, published in the Fischer Almanac, "The 76th Year," 1962. In A.S.'s literary estate we find a poem with the same title, dated "18.VII. 1880."

106. *Max Waldau:* pseudonym for Richard Georg Spiller von Hauenschild, 1825–1855.

According to Nature, a novel, 1850.

107. *Kneipe:* a simple tavern or inn.

110. *Max Kalbeck:* pseudonym for Jeremias Deutlich, 1850–1921. Music and art critic.

Anton Bruckner: 1824–1896. Austrian composer.

111. *Zell am See:* resort in the province of Salzburg.

Page

Raff: Joachim, 1822–1882. Composer of light music for orchestra and choir, also chamber music.

112. *the greatest German theater:* meaning the Vienna Burgtheater as the greatest of all theaters where plays were presented in German.

113. *Anatol:* protagonist of the *Anatol Cycle* which evolved from a series of one-act plays.

the so-called "armory": a section of the medical faculty was established at the time in a building of the former state armory.

115. *Garnisonsspital:* military hospital.

119. *Dr. Lueger:* Karl, 1844–1910. Lawyer. 1897–1910, mayor of Vienna.

120. *tarot:* a game played with a special deck of cards, introduced in Italy in the fourteenth century.

121. *as if I had never kissed your throat:* last line of the poem, "As we sat so quietly at the same table," dated April 1883, in the literary estate.

"I countered with a poem. . . : "Else," dated April 1883, in the literary estate.

125. *a native . . . of Tharau:* Ännchen von Tharau, poem, 1637, by Simon Dach translated into High German by Herder in 1778. Melody, 1825, by Friedrich Silcher. Has become a folk song. The refrain: "Ännchen von Tharau, my wealth and my treasure; Thou, my soul, my flesh and my blood."

"Love requires endless study . . .": "*Die Lieb' erfordert Studium, und wer nur einmal liebt bleibt dumm, dumm, dumm.*"

in one of those Heine style poems: In the literary estate there are two poems, "To Therese," dated 14.4.83, and "Therese," dated April 1883.

127. *the Riedhof:* a popular small inn and restaurant, named after the builder, Joseph Ried, taken over by the restaurateur Benedikter in 1850 and transformed into an elegant restaurant.

128. *the priceless Waidhofen manifesto:* the final version of the manifesto of the *"Waidhofener Verband der Wehrhaften Vereine Deutscher Studenten in der Ostmark,"* (The Waidhofen Association of Militant German Student Organizations in the Ostmark), March 11, 1896, went as follows: "With all due respect to the fact that such a profound moral and psychic difference prevails be-

Page

tween Gentiles and Jews, and that our racial character has already suffered so much from Jewish abuse, and in view of the vast amount of proof that the Jewish student has given us of his dishonorableness and character deficiency, and since he is totally lacking in honor, according to our German understanding of the word, the German militant student organization meeting today has come to the conclusion: *henceforth not to give a Jew satisfaction, with any type of weapon whatsoever, since he is not worthy of same.*"

It is interesting to note that under Hitler, the German and the Austrian National-Socialists liked to refer to Austria as "the Ostmark," which is originally a designation of the Middle Ages. The Bavarian Ostmark is now Lower Austria; the Saxon Ostmark was later Mark Lausitz.

129. *Theodore Herzl:* 1860–1934. Austrian. Founder of Zionism. Born in Budapest, educated in Vienna. Journalist and dramatist.

135. *Hermann Bahr:* 1863–1934. Austrian dramatist and writer.
my first novel: probably *Anatol.*

the 1848 days: the revolutions of 1848. Uprisings against the monarchy under Emperor Ferdinand I, in Hungary, Bohemia, Lower Austria.

136. *Vienna Hausregiment:* a regiment with its base in Vienna.

141. *Aspern:* northeast of Vienna. Here, in 1809, Napoleon lost his first battle.

143. *Maria Elend:* site of a shrine.
gehorsamst: literally "most obedient"; indicatively the American soldier says, "Yes Sir."

148. *Leoben:* a small town in Styria.

151. *Sofie- or Blumensaal:* the *Sophiensäle* still exist in Vienna's 3rd district. The *Blumensäle* on the Parkring were razed in 1959.
Ambition in the Kitchen: comedy by Auyustin Eugène Scribe, French dramatist, 1791–1861.

Hans Sachs: 1494–1576. Poet and dramatist from Nürnberg.

152. *A Cup of Tea:* a one-act comedy by Charles Nuitter, pseudonym for Truinet, and Joseph Derley.
Two Deaf Men: or *He must be deaf!* adapted from the one-act play, *Les Deux Sourds,* by Jules Moinaux, 1815–1895.

Page

153. *Arco:* at the time South Tyrol, now in Italy.

158. *the magazine, Fliegende Blätter:* illustrated humorous weekly, founded in 1844 by Caspar Braun and Friedrich Schneider. Wilhelm Busch was a collaborator. In A.S.'s diary, under Sept. 17, 1883, the following entry: "Just got back from *Fliegende Blätter* five poems I had sent them, with thanks: "Sweet child, you don't love me." "As we sat so quietly at the same table." "The Orchestra of Life." "Ännchen." "Liaison."

159. *Temesvar:* today Timisoara, town in the Banat (Danube Basin), Rumania.

165. *the so-called game of kalakaux:* possibly "kalakaua." A game of billiards that may have been named after the King of the Sandwich Islands, David Kalakaua, 1836–1891, who visited Vienna in August, 1881.

166. *Archduke Rainer:* 1827–1913. Grandson of Kaiser Leopold II.

Professor Monti: Alois, 1839–1909. After the death of Professor Johann Schnitzler, Monti became director of the Vienna Polyclinic, 1893.

167. *Rokitansky:* Karl Freiherr von Rokitansky, 1804–1878. Austrian pathologist and pioneer in the science of pathological anatomy. President of the Vienna Academy of Sciences in 1869. Favored the liberal party and became speaker of the house.

171. *Baden:* a spa, a half-hour by train from Vienna.

in a humorous poem: "Elephant," 1884, in the literary estate.

175. *Spagnuoli:* Spanish and Polish Jews, expelled from Spain in 1492, now scattered in the Balkan states. They speak old Castilian, intermingled with Arabic and Hebrew.

at Sacher's: famous Vienna hotel.

Lodz: in A.S.'s days in Russian Poland, today in Poland.

178. *Peter Altenberg:* pseudonym for Richard Engländer, 1859–1919. Wrote impressionistic prose. Liked to sign his letters: P.A.

179. *A novella . . . : Die Belasteten (The Burdened.)*

181. *Prince Ferdinand von Koburg:* 1861–1948. In 1908 became Ferdinand I, King of Bulgaria.

Mensdorf: Count Albert Mensdorf-Pouilly-Dietrichstein, 1861–1945. 1904 to 1914 was Austro-Hungarian ambassador in London.

Page

Cathedral Provost Marschall: Dr. Gottfried, 1840–1911. Later suffragan bishop of Vienna.

Princess Metternich: Pauline, *née* Countess Sandor, 1836–1921.

182. *Emil Brüll:* pseudonym, Emil Limé, 1861–1930. Banker, librettist.

185. *Conductor Robert Fuchs:* Austrian composer, 1847–1927.

Bozen: belonged to Austrian South Tyrol until 1918. Now Bolzano, Italy. Situated at the junction of the Brenner route from Germany to Italy.

186. *Meran:* resort formerly famous for treatment of consumptives. Was part of Austrian South Tyrol until 1918, when it became Merano, Italy.

190. *with her younger sister, Gabrielle:* Gabrielle Schneider, 1865–1939. Married Count George Haugwitz. Her youngest son, Kurt, married Princess Barbara Mdivani, *née* Hutton, in 1935. In 1947 he married Margaret Astor Drayton.

191. *in the blasé poems of my earlier days:* an untitled poem with six verses, dated "January 1884" is in the literary estate. The last verse read as follows:

"It seems to me almost as if my feelings
  Liked to dally; surely I could have felt true bliss.
Now they would like to burn belatedly in ashes;
  The hour of happiness was missed."

199. *The Way Out into the Open: Der Weg ins Freie,* a novel, appeared first in the *Neue Rundschau,* Vienna, Vol. 19, Nos. 1–6, Jan. to June, 1908.

200. *my soul was "a vast land:"* a reference to A.S.'s tragi-comedy, *A Vast Land,* Act III, where the hotel director Dr. von Aigner says, "Don't tell me you haven't noticed what complicated creatures we human beings really are? So much has room inside us at the same time—love and deceit, faithfulness and unfaithfulness, adoration for one woman and the desire for another, perhaps for more than one. I suppose we do our best to keep our house in order, but in the last analysis this order is superficial. The natural thing is chaos. Yes, my dear Hofreiter, the soul is a vast land, as the poet once said . . . or perhaps it was a hotel director. . . ."

202. *Wolfgang:* St. Wolfgang in the Salzkammergut.

Page

Somlauer: from a wine district in Hungary—the Somlauer Berg.

203. *Kammer:* resort on the Attersee, Salzkammergut.

Emperor's birthday: Emperor Franz Joseph I's birthday, August 18.

204. *Schneedörfl:* a village near Reichenau.

205. *Payerbach:* a village near Reichenau, with the railway station for that resort.

206. *Junker:* corruption of "junger Herr" or "young gentleman," but colloquially a slightly derogatory designation for an aristocratic East Prussian landowner.

207. *Charles' taciturn father, old Waissnix: Kaiserlicher Rat* or Imperial Councillor, Alois Waissnix, 1818–1913. An honorary title with no function whatsoever.

213. *Virginia straw:* the straw that pulled out of the long, thin Virginia cigar, so popular in A.S.'s day, and often, in a sporting gesture, stuck behind the ear.

214. *Gloggnitz:* town in Lower Austria, at the northeast foot of the Semmering Pass.

Meidling: district of Vienna with the Meidlinger South Station.

220. *Gödöllö:* a spa and artist's colony north of Budapest.

225. *For an atlas:* "Clinical Atlas of Laryngology and Rhinology, with Instruction for Diagnosis and Therapy of Diseases of the Larynx and Trachea." (*"Klinischer Atlas der Laryngology und Rhinology, nebst Anleitungen zur Diagnose und Therapie der Krankheiten des Kehlkopfes und der Luftröhre."* Published by Dr. Johann Schnitzler in collaboration with Dr. M. Hayek and Dr. A. Schnitzler, Vienna and Leipzig, Wilhelm Braumüller, published 1891–1895.

226. *Urban and Schwarzenberg:* publishers and book sellers of works of medical and natural science, Munich, Berlin, Vienna. Ernst Urban, 1838–1923, and his brother-in-law, Eugene Schwarzenberg, died in 1908.

227. *Deutsche Wochenschrift:* a weekly journal with the byline, "Mouthpiece for the mutual interests of Austria and Germany," 1883–1886. Published by Heinrich Friedjung. After that, and until its final edition in 1888, published by Joseph Eugene Russell. One of the many precursors of the all-German sentiments pro-

Page

claimed later by Hitler and National Socialism as an excuse for uniting Austria and Germany.

He Is Waiting for a God Off-Duty (*Er wartet auf den vazierenden Gott*)*:* in *Prose Works:* Vol. I of the S. Fischer *Complete Works of Arthur Schnitzler.*

228. *Rohrerhütte:* popular inn in the Wienerwald. Still in existence.

233. *Judith:* in *Comedy of Seduction,* 1923. In *Plays:* Vol. II of S. Fischer's *Complete Works of Arthur Schnitzler.*

236. *a pretty young lady:* Jeanette Heger.

a Makart bouquet: of dried flowers, grasses and sometimes feathers, named after the popular painter, Hans Makart.

237. *this endearing appellation, "sweet girl":* "*Das süsse Mädel*" became a classic appellation for a certain type of Viennese girl, after being used in the title of two scenes of *Reigen.* 1896–1897. But already in 1891, in *Christmas Shopping* (*Weihnachtskäufe*), A.S. uses the now famous designation.

Rüdesheim: a town on the Rhine.

239. *Rudolf Spitzer:* pseudonym Rudolf Lothar, 1865–1933; died in exile.

Fuchs-Talab: Otto Fuchs, pseudonym Talab, 1852–1930.

Writer. *J. J. David:* Jacob Julius, 1859–1906. Writer.

240. *Human Love: Menschenliebe,* later called *Belastet* (*Burdened*) in the sense of hereditarily tainted. In the literary estate.

Heritage: Erbschaft. Now in the *Prose Works:* Vol. I.

The Madness of My Friend Y, novella: (*Mein Freund Ypsilon. Aus den Papieren eines Arztes.*) Now in *Prose Works:* Vol. I.

The Adventure of His Life: (*Das Abenteuer Seines Lebens*), a comedy in one act. First printing by O. F. Eirich, Vienna, 1888. Now in *Anatol.* Published by Ernest L. Offermanns in the series *Komedia,* Vol. 6, Walter de Gruyter & Co., Berlin, 1964.

241. *How this actually did come about a few years later:* in February 1891, Professor Friedrich, director of a school for actors, produced the one-act play, *The Adventure of His Life,* at the Rudolfsheimer Theater, together with two one-act plays by different authors. He had accepted the former because he thought it had been written by Professor Johann Schnitzler, A.S.'s father, and according to

Page

later notes by A.S. on the story of *Anatol Cycle,* Professor Friedrich was "somewhat disappointed" when, instead of the famous doctor, his son turned up at the rehearsal. This was the first performance of a play by A.S.

244. *Josef Kainz:* 1858–1910. Famous Austrian actor, born in Hungary.

Agnes Sorma: 1865–1927. Actress. Sometimes called "the German Duse."

Julius Rodenberg: born Levy, 1831–1914. Writer. Founded the *Deutsche Rundschau* in 1874.

Karl Emil Franzos: 1848–1904. Writer.

Kaiser Friedrich: Friedrich III, 1831–1888.

MacKenzie: Sir Morell, 1837–1892. English laryngologist.

247. *rastacouère:* a foreigner whose claim to rank or wealth is suspect.

249. *Brühl Terrace:* famous promenade along a bend in the Elbe River, with a magnificent view of the city. Today called the Elbe Terrace.

Blasewitz: a suburb of Dresden. Residence of Friedrich von Schiller, 1786–87.

250. *that I was to have so much more time for it all a few years hence:* April 12 to May 24, 1897.

Crystal Palace: famous exhibition hall just outside London. Built in 1851, destroyed by fire in 1936.

253. *Alma-Tadema:* Sir Lawrence, 1836–1912. British painter of Dutch extraction. Historic genre paintings. Famous for his scenes from Greek and Roman life.

254. *Monsieur et Madame Cardinal:* novellas in dialogue by Ludovic Halévy, 1834–1908.

with Woods conducting: Sir Henry Joseph Wood, 1869–1944. Promenade concerts.

Hans Richter concert: 1843–1916. From 1875 to 1900, conductor in Vienna, gave Wagner concerts in London, 1877, with Richard Wagner.

260. *Prossnitz:* today Protejov in Czechoslovakia. In A.S.'s day in Southern Moravia.

261. *Baden-Baden:* German spa in the Black Forest.

262. *Beatrice:* from the drama, *The Veil of Beatrice,* Act I.

Page

263. S. *Fischer:* Samuel, 1859–1934. Founded the publishing house: S. Fischer Verlag in Berlin. Practically all A.S.'s works were published by him.

the Schöne blaue Donau: literal translation: the Beautiful Blue Danube.

Fedor Mamroth: 1851–1907. Critic and journalist. Founded the magazine, *An der schönen blauen Donau* (*On the Beautiful Blue Danube*), Vienna, 1886. Later became the literary supplement of the *Neue Freie Presse.*

267. *I would probably have lost my commission a few years before it was my fate to do so:* as a result of the publication of *Lieutenant Gustl,* December 1900, A.S. was ordered to appear before a military Court of Honor to justify his writing of the novella. He refused to appear because he felt that such a military Court of Honor was not to be considered an authority on literary matters. On June 14, 1901, he received the following notice: "The K.K. (meaning *kaiserlich königlich,* or Imperial Royal) Reserve Command in Vienna, in accordance with a decree of June 1 of last year (file 646,) and as a result of the decision arrived at by this Court of Honor on April 4, 1901, according to which you were declared guilty of violating professional honor, and in accordance with pps. 30 and 33 of the provisions for procedure of such a Court of Honor of the K.K. Reserve Forces, has stripped you of your commission as a reserve officer." (Das k.k. Landwehroberkommando in Wien hat Sie mit dem Erlasse vom 1. Juni l. J. Präs. 646 auf Grund des vom hiesigen Ehrenrate am 26.4.1901 gefassten Beschlusses, mit welchem Sie der Verletzung der Standesehre schuldig erkannt wurden, Sie gemäss den ʃʃ 30 und 33 der Vorschrift für das ehrenrechtliche Verfahren in der k.k. Landwehr ihres Offizierscharakters für verlustig erklärt.)

Put briefly—he lost his commission as army doctor in the reserves.

269. *Catulle Mendès:* 1841–1909. French writer.

270. *and had published some case histories:* "On functional ephonia and the treatment of same by hypnosis and the power of suggestion," in the *Internationale Klinische Rundschau,* Vol. III,

Page

Nos. 10, 11, 12, 14. March 10–April 7, 1889. Special edition printed by Wilhelm Braumüller, Vienna, 1889.

271. *Dr. Paul Goldmann:* 1865–1935. Journalist and critic. Berlin and Paris correspondent for the *Neue Freie Presse.* Editor of *An der schönen blauen Donau,* in which magazine A.S.'s earliest works appeared under the pseudonym of "Anatol."
America: 1887. Now included in *Prose Works,* Vol. I.

From the Brief Biography and Main Works:

276. *Bauernfeld Prize:* Eduard von, 1802–1890. Austrian writer and playwright. Light comedy.

279. *Raimund Prize:* Ferdinand, 1790–1836. Wrote comedies and fantasies for the theater.